IMAGES
of America

CALABASAS

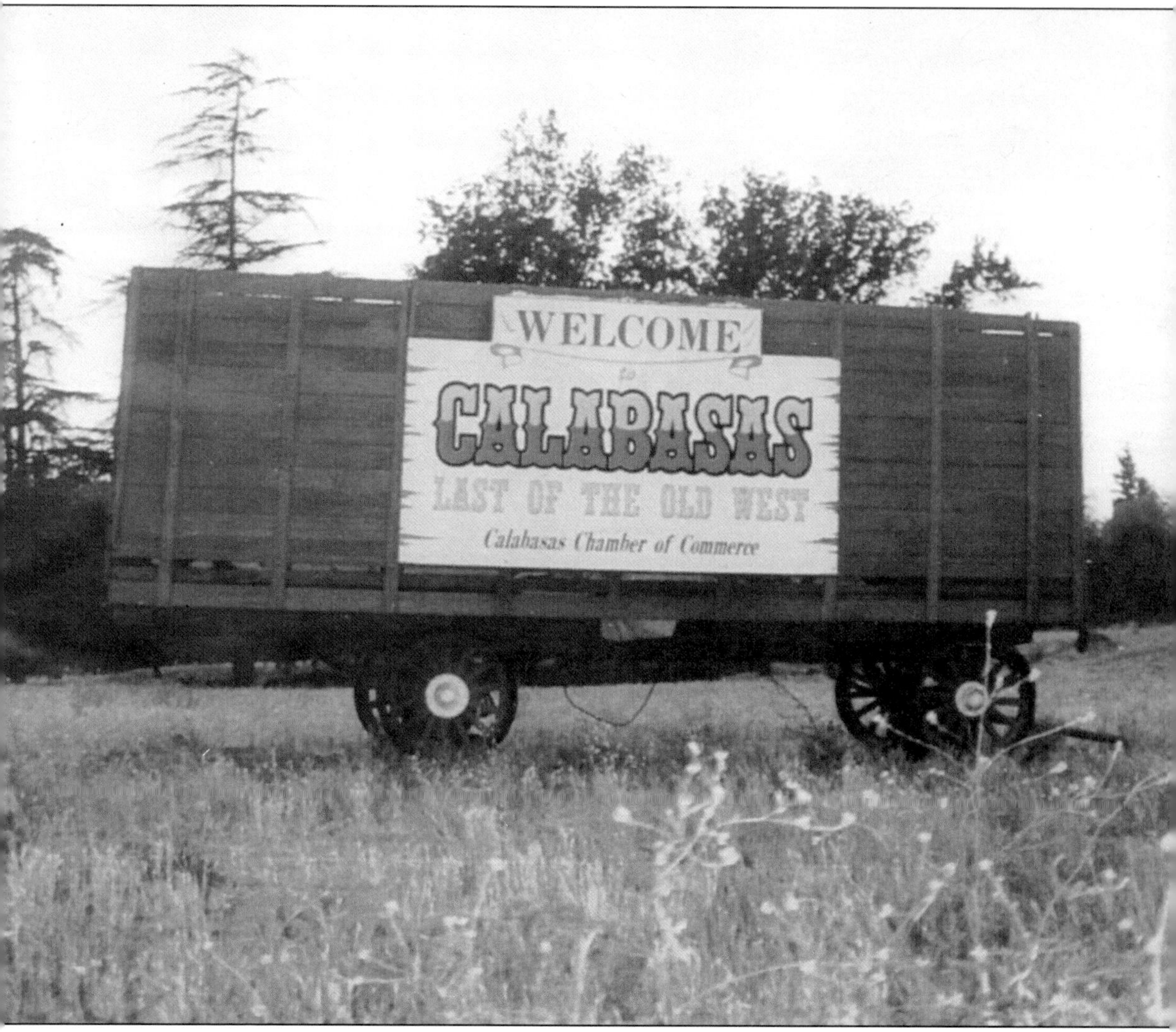

This welcoming wagon was located at the southeast corner of Old Town Calabasas and greeted everyone to the "Last of the Old West." The wagon was installed by the Calabasas Chamber of Commerce. (Courtesy of the Calabasas-Las Virgenes Historical Society.)

On the Cover: The Kramer Store, a simple Craftsman-style structure built by Charles Cooper, was brought on wagon-wheel rollers from Mulholland Highway to its present location in Old Town Calabasas in 1905. The building was originally owned by Charles and Alice Cooper and called Hunter's Inn, providing rooms and a store for hunters and travelers. After Charles died, Alice married Lawrence Kramer and for 50 years ran the store, until 1968. Between 1969 and 1978, the building was leased by Helen Woodward as the Sundance Saloon. (Courtesy of Bison Archives.)

IMAGES
of America

CALABASAS

Cimberly Castellon and the
Calabasas-Las Virgenes Historical Society
Foreword by Mayor James R. Bozajian

ARCADIA
PUBLISHING

ISBN 978-1-4671-3415-6

Published by Arcadia Publishing
Charleston, South Carolina

Printed in the United States of America

Library of Congress Control Number: 2015943287

For all general information, please contact Arcadia Publishing:
Telephone 843-853-2070
Fax 843-853-0044
E-mail sales@arcadiapublishing.com
For customer service and orders:
Toll-Free 1-888-313-2665

Visit us on the Internet at www.arcadiapublishing.com

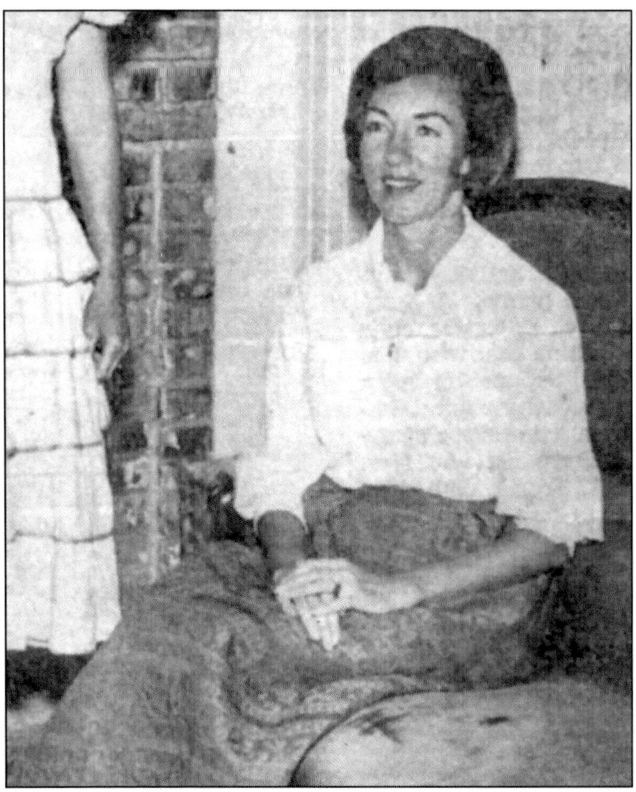

This publication is dedicated to Kathleen G. "Cathy" Brown, who is seated on the velvet settee in the living room of the historic Leonis Adobe. Brown is pictured here after accepting the dedication of the El Camino Real Bell on behalf of the Leonis Adobe as first president of the Friends of the Leonis Adobe from the Native Daughters of the Golden Valley in 1967. We miss you Mom. (Courtesy of the Calabasas-Las Virgenes Historical Society.)

Contents

FOREWORD

Centuries ago, the Chumash Indians led a peaceful existence amidst the rolling hills of Calabasas. Spanish explorers were the first Europeans to arrive in the area. In 1770, an expedition headed by Gaspar de Portola crossed through Calabasas on its return southward to Mexico after venturing into Northern California. In 1776, another party of explorers led by Juan Bautista de Anza camped in Calabasas on its way northward from Mexico.

The earliest surviving written reference to Calabasas in a geographical context appears in a document found at the San Fernando Mission dated August 18, 1795. Some legends suggest that the name Calabasas is derived from *calabazas*, the Spanish word for pumpkins or gourds—a tribute to the pumpkin patches that reputedly dotted the area long ago. Other sources contend that Calabasas comes from a Native American term meaning "where the wild geese fly."

Present-day Calabasas Road was once part of the historic El Camino Real (The King's Highway), a pathway dating back to 1769 that linked Spanish settlements and missions up and down California. Bisecting Old Town Calabasas, this thoroughfare runs through the heart of the city today. Old Town has some of the region's longest-surviving structures, the most prominent of which is the Leonis Adobe.

The Leonis Adobe stands frozen in time, a rustic reminder of a bygone era. It once served as the seat of a much larger parcel, Rancho El Escorpión, which covered around 1,100 acres of land in the southwest San Fernando Valley. The adobe was originally built c. 1844 and after passing through a series of owners was ultimately saved from demolition in the 1960s. It was then renovated, dedicated to the public, and designated as a historic cultural monument. The adobe's most notorious occupant was Miguel Leonis, a Basque immigrant who became a local land baron in the latter part of the 19th century after acquiring Rancho El Escorpión via marriage into a Native American family.

Control of California shifted from Spain to Mexico and from Mexico to the United States. As the world around it changed dramatically, the passage of time left Calabasas largely untouched. Families of early settlers struggled against the rough-and-tumble character of frontier life.

Calabasas remained a rural enclave well into the 20th century, with a small population and limited interaction with outsiders. Tales both true and tall portray Calabasas as a rugged outpost of the American West, complete with an ominous hanging tree in the middle of town. All of this was to change as California entered a period of explosive growth.

The first planned housing subdivision in Calabasas was Park Moderne, originally settled by artists, craftsmen, and writers. Dating from the 1920s, many of its original units are still intact and reflect some of the most intriguing residential architecture in California. The topography in and around Calabasas is breathtaking; as testament to this fact, it has been a favorite location for filming motion pictures since the early 20th century.

The rapid growth of the area's population brought an accompanying need to provide higher levels of service to the community. The Calabasas Chamber of Commerce was founded in 1955, the Las Virgenes Municipal Water District was created in 1958, and the Las Virgenes Unified School District was established in 1962. The Calabasas branch of the US Post Office opened in 1971.

But the most significant landmark in Calabasas history was unquestionably the formal incorporation of the City of Calabasas. An ever-increasing desire to exercise local control over land use decisions fueled the drive for cityhood. The two neighboring cities to its east—Los Angeles (1850) and Hidden Hills (1961)—had already incorporated. Calabasas's own road to cityhood was strewn with many obstacles, primarily because of resistance from Los Angeles County officials and developers who had by this time recognized the area's enormous potential.

The first incorporation drive began in the 1970s as a broader effort to create one sprawling regional city. The city's borders were to stretch east to west from the Los Angeles city line to the Ventura County border and north to south from Ventura County to what would later become the city of Malibu (itself eventually incorporated just eight days before Calabasas). Weighing in at roughly 44 square miles, the would-be city of Rancho Las Virgenes was contemplated to include what is now Calabasas, Agoura Hills, Westlake Village, and a large swath of unincorporated territory surrounding those cities. Los Angeles County quashed this proposal in 1981.

Shortly thereafter, residents moved successfully to incorporate separately the cities of Westlake Village (1981) and Agoura Hills (1982). A similar attempt to incorporate Calabasas fizzled in 1988 after being rejected by Los Angeles County. Discouraged but not defeated, advocates for Calabasas cityhood redoubled their efforts, and a couple of years later, county officials gave final approval for a vote to be taken to incorporate an 11.3 square mile area as the new City of Calabasas.

On March 5, 1991, local voters flocked to the polls and approved incorporation by an overwhelming margin of 91 to 9 percent. The investment of many years of hard work by cityhood proponents had finally been rewarded. The first Calabasas City Council was sworn into office on April 5, 1991. Calabasas was at long last free to chart its own destiny.

By all measures, Calabasas has thrived in the quarter-century since incorporation. Several annexations have raised the city's total land mass to 13.6 square miles. The city is now home to approximately 25,000 residents. Calabasas prides itself on remaining one of the most sparsely populated municipalities in Southern California.

Meanwhile, Calabasas's infrastructure has grown exponentially. The first annual city budget was $5.5 million; today the yearly budget is $22.5 million. Having weathered no less than three national recessions, the city has nonetheless consistently maintained a healthy general reserve fund.

In 1991, Calabasas had but one municipal property. Today, the city owns and operates a diverse array of 12, including several attractive parks and recreational facilities. The beautiful Calabasas Civic Center, site of city hall and the municipal library (and future home for its senior enrichment center), was completed and opened in 2008. The city has restored Old Town Calabasas to its original appearance. The city sponsors hundreds of educational and recreational programs, including the Calabasas Pumpkin Festival, a premier annual event celebrating its heritage.

Calabasas is comprised of more than 50 different homeowners associations and residential subdivisions. They range in size from less than 10 homes to nearly 3,000 and in flavor from rural to urban. To meet the needs of its residents, the city has worked cooperatively with the private sector to bring many new commercial and retail enterprises to the community.

City incorporation did not bring an end to the pitched battles over land use, and struggles concerning development both within city limits and in adjacent unincorporated territory continued to be highly contentious. Many of these conflicts raged on for years, but in the end those promoting slower growth usually prevailed.

Fully 43 percent of the land within Calabasas is protected open space, a figure that dwarfs most other cities in the area. Perpetual preservation of open space and resources, along with severe restrictions on future development, are specifically enshrined in the Calabasas Municipal Code. The city's official logo, a red-tailed hawk flying over the Santa Monica Mountains, symbolizes an unwavering commitment to maintaining the community's natural beauty and semirural quality of life.

The material contained within this book has been compiled from many sources and offers a survey of the rich history of Calabasas. Poring over its contents, you will journey through the past and gain a better understanding of what makes Calabasas such a wonderful place to live.

—James R. Bozajian
Mayor of Calabasas

Acknowledgments

Calabasas is dedicated to the many active community leaders, individuals, and volunteers of various preservation efforts. It is because of the tirelessness of similarly invested historical enthusiasts whose countless hours of volunteer work searching out long-term residents; recording oral histories, composition articles, and books; and documenting photographs and news clippings that the heart and soul has been kept alive for future generations. The Calabasas-Las Virgenes Historical Society continues to preserve the archival efforts of philanthropist Kay Beachy and historian Ruth Loring since 1979 and proudly shares the collection with you.

The charter board members and the first officers of the Kay Beachy Library, then located at Pierce College, included Catherine Mulholland, Arliss Wilhelm, Ruth Loring, Mary Ann Hart, Juliana Gensley, Dolores Belling, Inger Hansen, Dottie Heitz, Marie Wood, Mona Neels, Micky Metschan, and Geraldine Benedict.

Creating this book was a walk through the past. As a resident since 1964, I experienced many firsthand accounts of the area's growth and was exposed to a great deal of local history as the daughter, one of two siblings, of actively involved parents. Our family home was in Hidden Hills, and both my brother, Charley Brown, and I attended Round Meadow Elementary and A.E. Wright Middle School. I graduated from Agoura High School in 1974, while Charley was in the first graduating class from Calabasas High School in 1979. Our parents were founding members of the Hidden Hills Players theater group and were active in early community rallies for preservation and restoration. After college, I moved back to Hidden Hills where my husband, Eddie Castellon, and I purchased a home and raised three outstanding boys—Wesley, Teagan, and Quintin. Life can throw some curves; Eddie passed away suddenly, and the kids and I moved to Calabasas Hills, where they also attended the Las Virgenes Unified School District. Our roots are deep, and we have great appreciation for a community lifestyle that is family-oriented and has been so instrumental in providing a quality existence.

Unless otherwise noted, all images are courtesy of the Calabasas-Las Virgenes Historical Society.

INTRODUCTION

Calabasas is a city in Los Angeles County, California, located in the hills west of the San Fernando Valley and the northwest Santa Monica Mountains between Woodland Hills, Agoura Hills, West Hills, Hidden Hills, and Malibu.

It is widely believed that the name Calabasas is derived from the Spanish word *calabaza*, meaning "pumpkin or gourd." The story goes that a farmer on his way to market lost a wagon wheel, turned over, and scattered gourds, whose seeds eventually grew throughout the area. Others hold that the name possibly descended from the Chumash Indian word for "where the wild geese fly." The fact that geese still fly in the area today lends this theory support. Though no one knows for sure where the name originated, we do know Calabasas was named before August 18, 1795, when Padre Santa Maria slept there that night and evidently thought the occasion worth recording.

Later, homesteaders staked their claim to land and were said to have squabbled over boundaries. As the area expanded, amenities became necessary, and the pioneers carved needed commerce along the Old Road. As the community grew, land was purchased, and the entrepreneurial spirit prevailed, as land was allocated to housing and filming ventures. Once the need for precious water was resolved, Calabasas boomed. Planned housing developments, schools, shopping centers, recreation, and a safe haven for artists arose with the overarching dynamic and driving force sought after by locals to provide future generations with a continued sense of community.

Calabasas was incorporated on April 5, 1991, becoming California's 88th city in Los Angeles County. Now, it is noted for its wealthy residents and gated neighborhoods, the result of the many forward-minded activists who insisted that the bar be high and the investor's creativity top notch. It is not surprising then that the E! television show, *Keeping Up with the Kardashians*, which began airing in October 2007, spotlighted the city—a well-kept secret for years.

There should be no argument that Calabasas is unique. The city's diverse history of the Wild West cowboys, Indians, explorers, squatters, bandits, buried treasure, homesteaders and pioneers, film studios, and celebrities mixed with the scenic beauty featuring majestic oak trees, mountains, wildlife, scenic corridors, and a rural setting conveniently located next door to Los Angeles make this city one of a kind.

One

The Wild, Wild West

The Chumash Indians were the first early Californians to have contact with European explorers when Juan Cabrillo, a Portuguese explorer, sailed north along the coast from Mexico in 1542. Cabrillo left a record of the Chumash people and their villages, as did Spanish explorer Sebastián Vizcaíno in 1602.

The Portola Expedition (1769–1770) was the first recorded Spanish entry and exploration of the present-day state of California. The route was integral to the settlement of Alta California by the Spanish Empire and made it possible for the Franciscan friars to found a string of 21 missions. The missions were the first foreign settlements in California; they established a cattle-ranching economy and converted thousands of Native Americans to Christianity.

The first quarter of the 19th century saw the colonization of the southern and central California coast by Spanish missionaries, ranchers, and troops. By 1820, Spanish influence was marked by the chain of missions reaching from Loreto, north to San Diego, to just north of today's San Francisco Bay Area and extending inland approximately 25 to 50 miles. Outside of this zone, perhaps 200,000 to 250,000 Native Americans continued to lead traditional lives.

The California missions were secularized in 1834; this made land that was previously mission property available for settlement. The discovery of gold in California created an enormous surge in population throughout the state. By the turn of the 20th century, Calabasas had developed a reputation as a rough-and-tumble stagecoach stop frequented by outlaws and apprehensive travelers. Life was plenty wild for the handful of families who settled in the area, scraping together a living by farming or ranching and protecting their homestead boundaries.

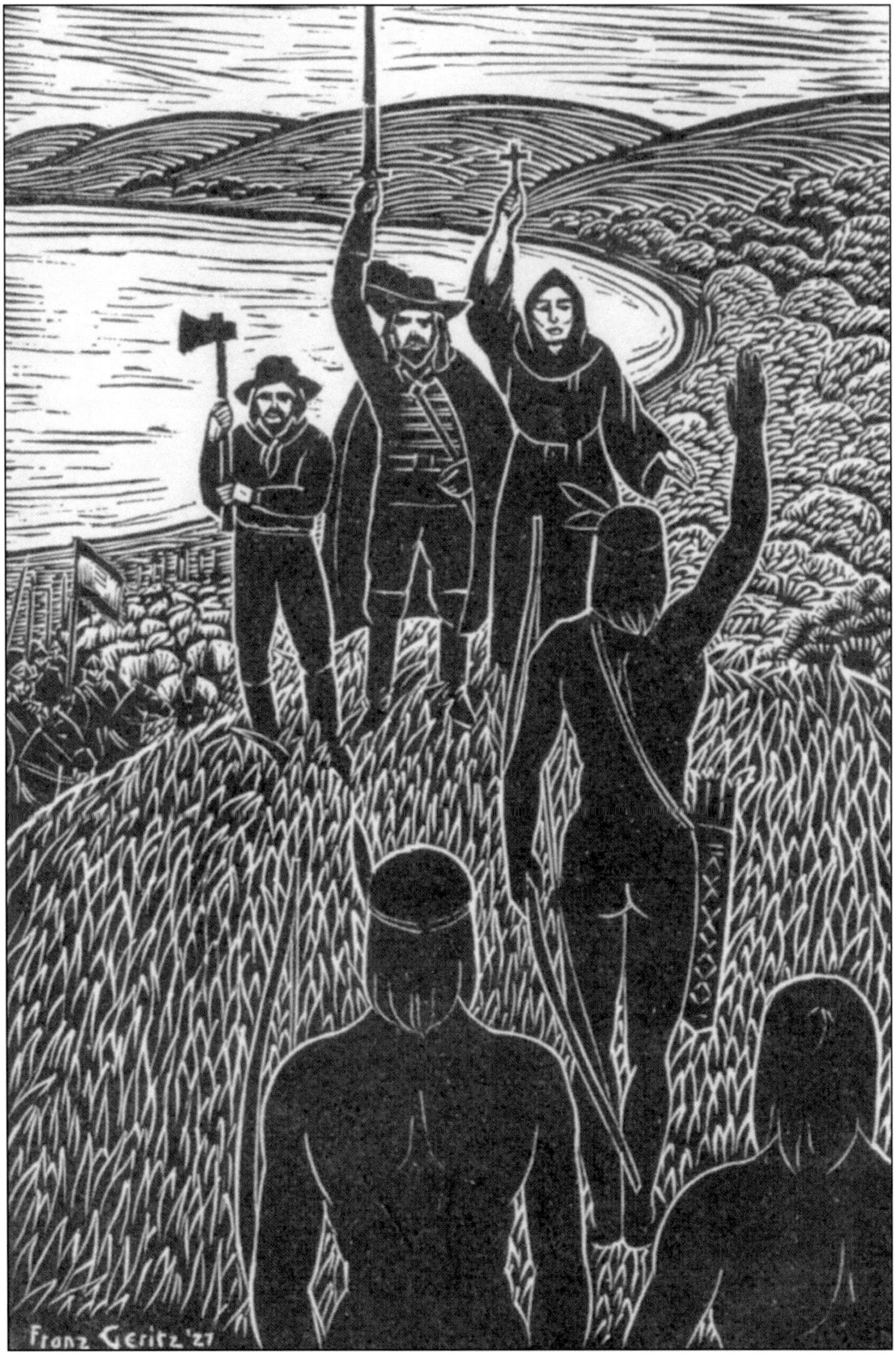

The Chumash were displaced in the 1770s, as Spanish explorers moved into the region. This is a block print of the Portola Expedition, in which Gaspar de Portola and Fr. Juan Crespi made their 1769 journey through the area. The expedition took four months from San Diego to Monterey, carving the El Camino Real route into the California landscape. Among the 64 Spanish Portola soldiers on the expedition were explorers whose names have dotted California history: Ortega, Alvarado, Amador, Carrillo, and Yorba.

The map shows land expeditions led by commander Juan Bautista de Anza between 1775 and 1776 from the Sonora y Sinaloa Province of New Spain in Colonial Mexico through to the Las Californias Province. On the second exploration, de Anza took 240 men, women, and children and 1,000 cattle to establish a colony in San Francisco. On February 22, 1776, the colonists made camp in the Las Virgenes area. Their exact campsite is unknown, but it is referred to in historical documents as Agua Escondida, or Hidden Water. This could possibly be a destroyed spring in the Deer Springs tract off Lost Hills Road in Calabasas. Today, this trail is over 1,200 drivable miles connecting Mexico to San Francisco. The photograph shows a portion of the trail at the 101 Freeway and Las Virgenes Road. (Below, photograph by Karlo Gorgin; courtesy of the Calabasas Media Department.)

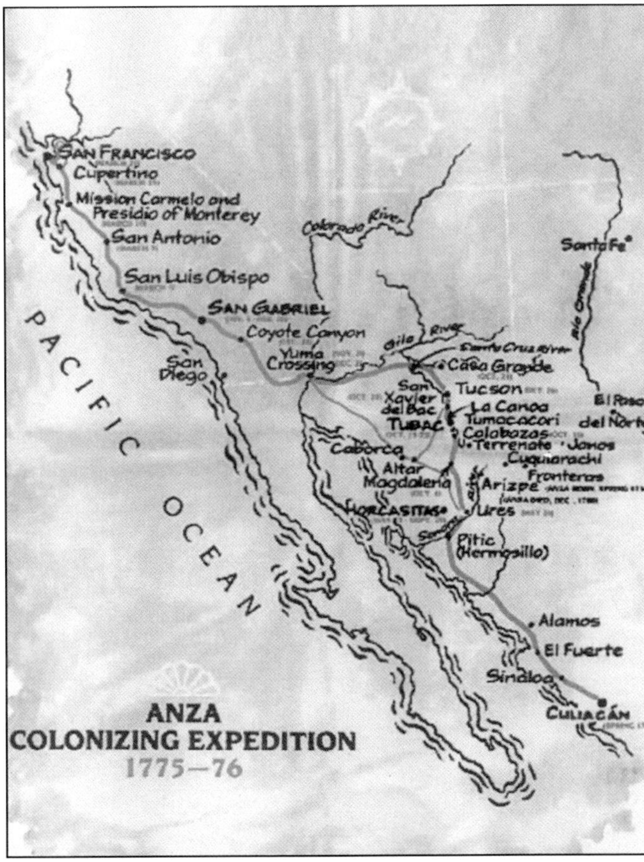

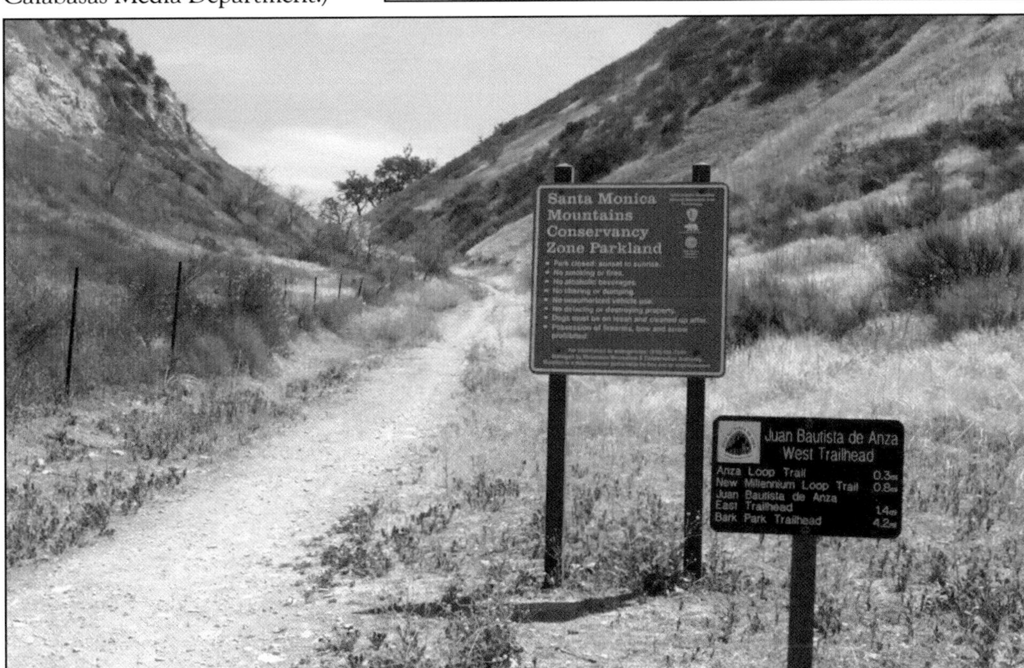

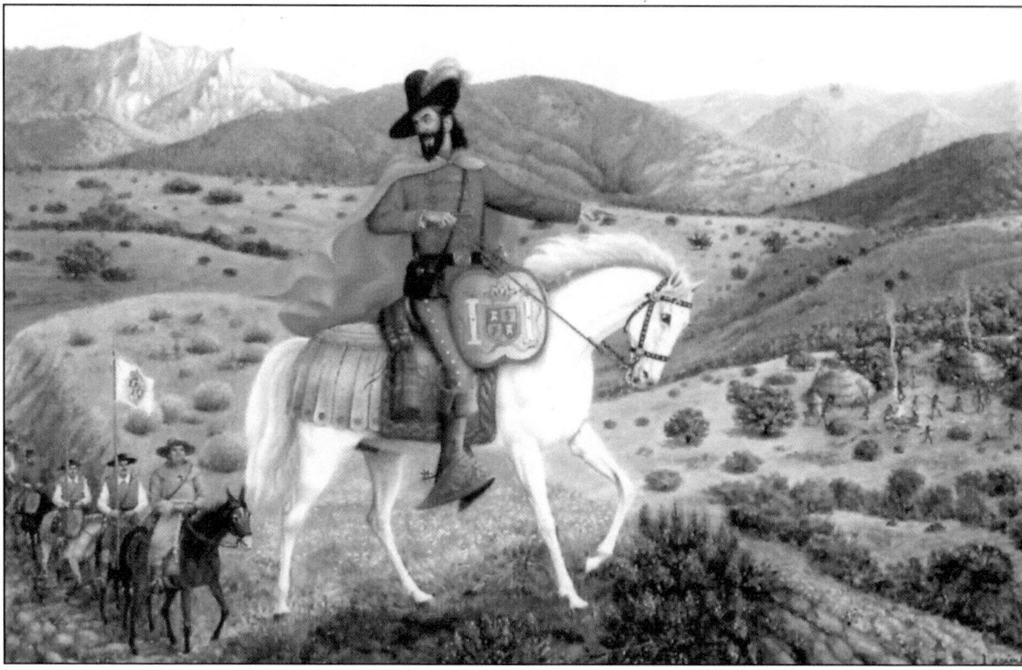

On February 22, 1776, the same year as the Declaration of Independence was written, the Chumash lifestyle changed forever, as the Juan Bautista de Anza Expedition camped in the Las Virgenes Valley with 240 colonists, 500 head of cattle, and 400 beasts of burden, all on their way to the Bay Area with a charter for a Spanish pueblo, now San Francisco. This portrait of Juan Bautista de Anza was painted by Carlos Lacamara, a Cuban American artist and longtime Calabasas resident, and presented during the dedication of Juan Bautista de Anza Park in Calabasas. The painting above hangs in the Calabasas Municipal Library. Pictured below are, from left to right, artist Carlos Lacamara, National Parks cultural anthropologist Phil Holmes, historian Juliana Gensley, and Councilmember Dennis Washburn at the Juan Bautista de Anza Park dedication in 1996. (Both, courtesy of George French.)

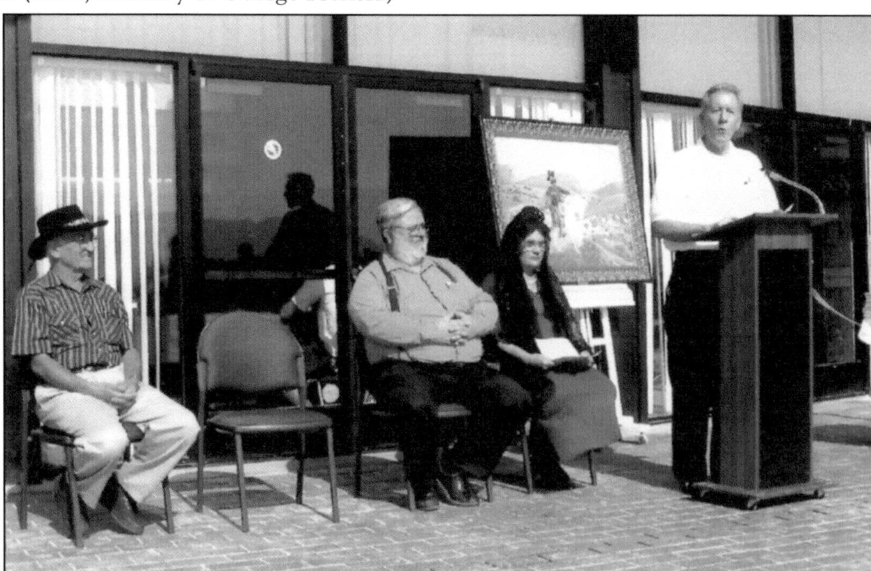

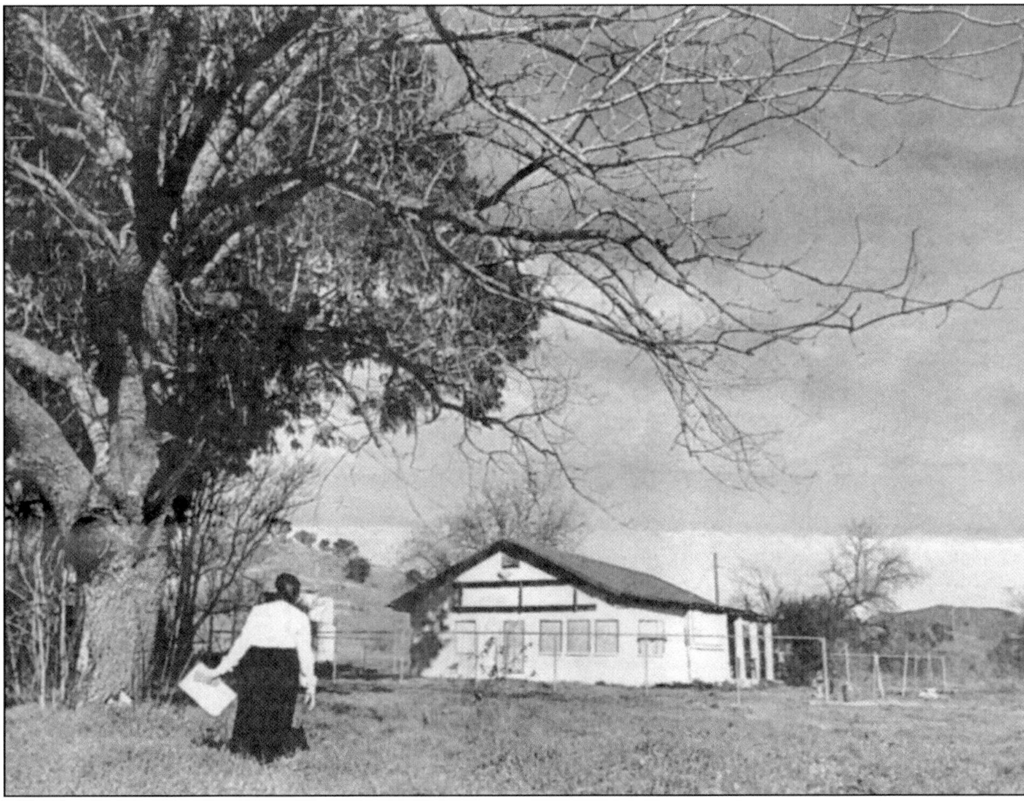

A young adolescent on the Juan Bautista de Anza Expedition, Jose Bartolome Tapia, returned to the Las Virgenes Valley after receiving a grant from the king of Spain. Today, this area is known as Tapia Park. In 1863, the grandson of Jose Bartolome Tapia, Pedro Alcantara Sepulveda, built an adobe there for his wife, Maria Magdalena Soledad Dominguez. Prof. Juliana Gensley is seen in the field in front of the Sepulveda Adobe home.

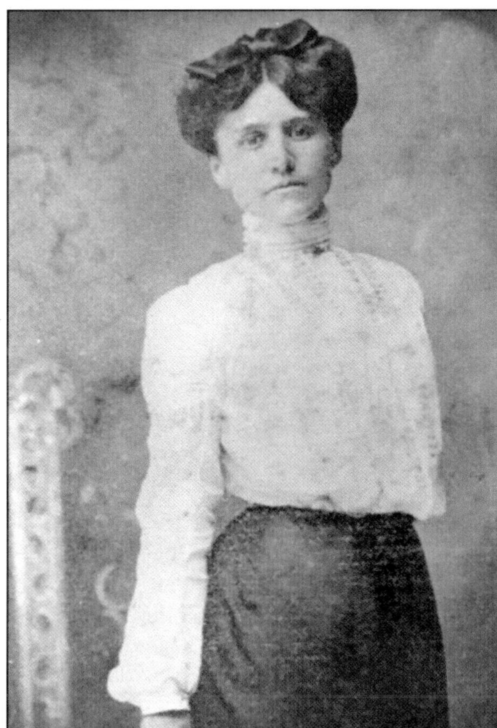

Pictured here is Sally Sepulveda, nicknamed Chula, the 12th child of Soledad and Pedro Alcantara Sepulveda, who built the adobe home. Sally married Joseph Hunter, who purchased the adobe in 1898. Their marriage did not last, and the adobe, through inheritance, remained in the Hunter family's possession until 1946, when it was sold to 20th Century Fox. The silent movie *Amateur Daddy* was filmed here and released in 1932.

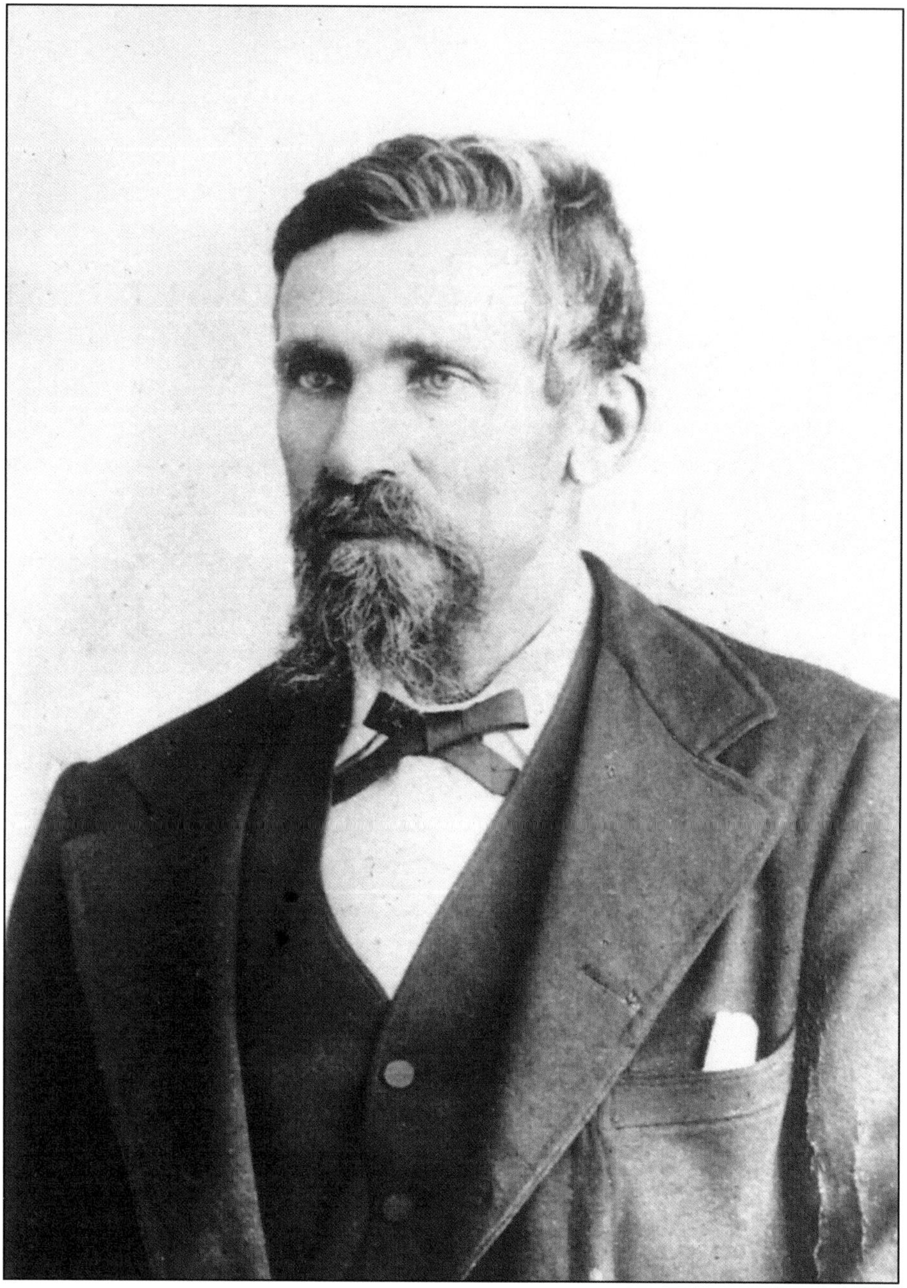

Miguel Leonis was one of several Basque settlers in the Calabasas area around 1870. He was born on February 15, 1822, in the small village of Cambo-les Baines, France. Leonis arrived in Los Angeles in 1854 and was hired as a foreman for Joaquín Romero, who owned a portion of Rancho El Escorpión. Shortly after he was employed, Leonis was promoted to ranch manager. Romero was reputedly a heavy drinker and allowed his rancho to deteriorate. When Romero's condition worsened, Leonis persuaded him to sell his interest in the ranch in 1861 for $100. Under Leonis's ownership, the rancho prospered and his livestock increased in number. Leonis felt the need to expand and set his sights on the other half of El Escorpión, which was then owned by Espiritú del Santo. (Courtesy of the Leonis Adobe.)

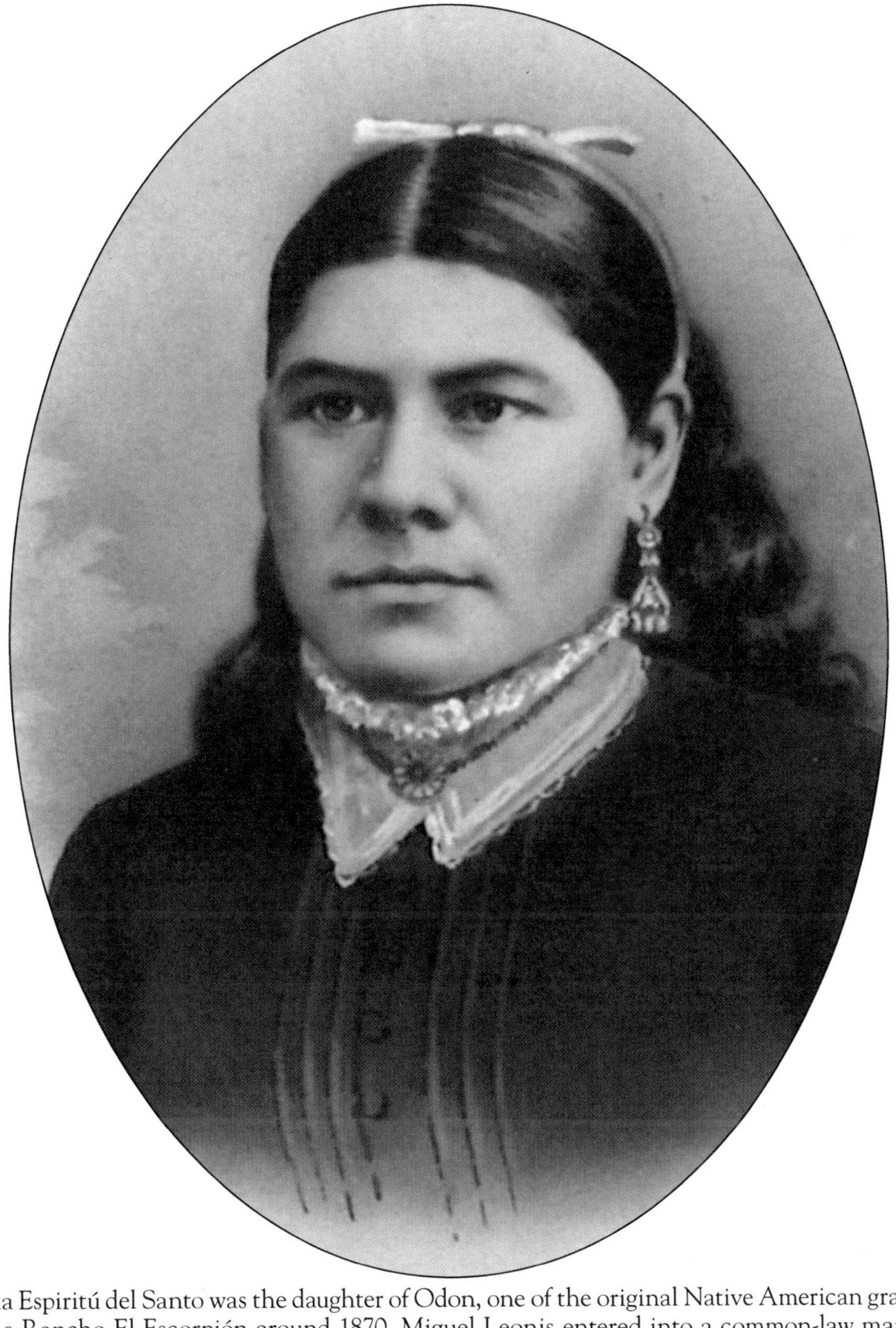

Maria Espiritú del Santo was the daughter of Odon, one of the original Native American grantees of the Rancho El Escorpión around 1870. Miguel Leonis entered into a common-law marriage with Espiritú in 1859; in 1860 they had a daughter they named Juana Marcelina Leonis. Espiritú had a son, Juan, from an earlier relationship with a Spaniard named Jose Antonio Menendez. The homestead claim for the Leonis Adobe property states that Miguel, Espiritú, Juan, and Marcelina moved into the adobe in Calabasas in 1869. Oral history indicates that the adobe was built in 1844 by persons unidentified and abandoned until the Leonis family moved to the property. (Courtesy of the Leonis Adobe.)

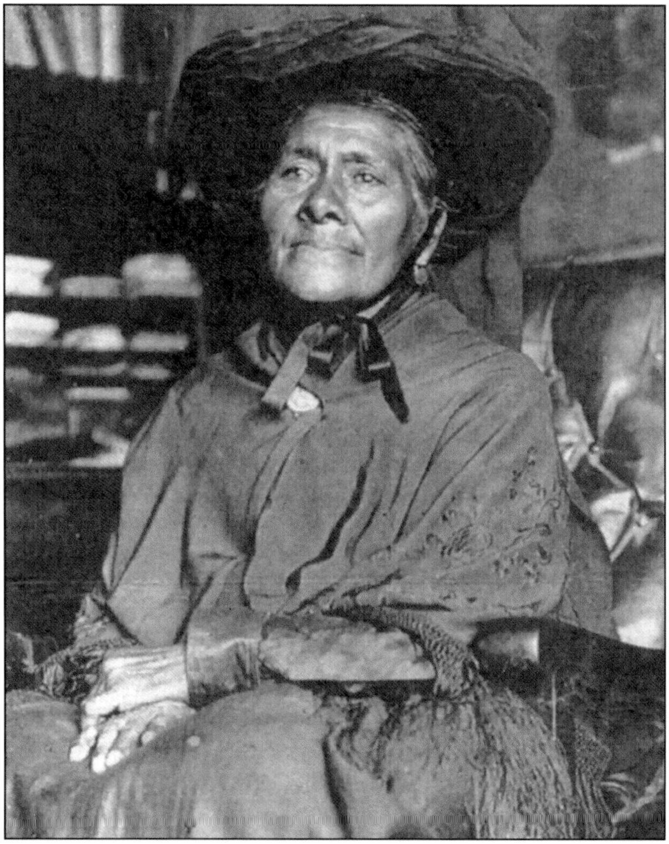

Miguel Leonis died after a wagon accident in 1889; his death set off a 16-year legal struggle for Espiritú to receive a widow's share of his estate. Although they were not legally married, Espiritú won the right to call herself Leonis's widow and received a portion of his estate. Espiritú lived in the adobe until her death in 1906. Her son Juan and his wife continued to live in the adobe until 1922, when it was sold to Lester and Frances Agoure. Michelle Covello, the adobe's curator, speculated that the photograph at left was taken of Espiritú in her attorney's office after winning her court case in 1891. The Leonis Adobe is pictured below around 1905. Espiritú is standing at the fence, and Juan is standing with Nellie (the mare) in the vineyard area. (Both, courtesy of the Leonis Adobe.)

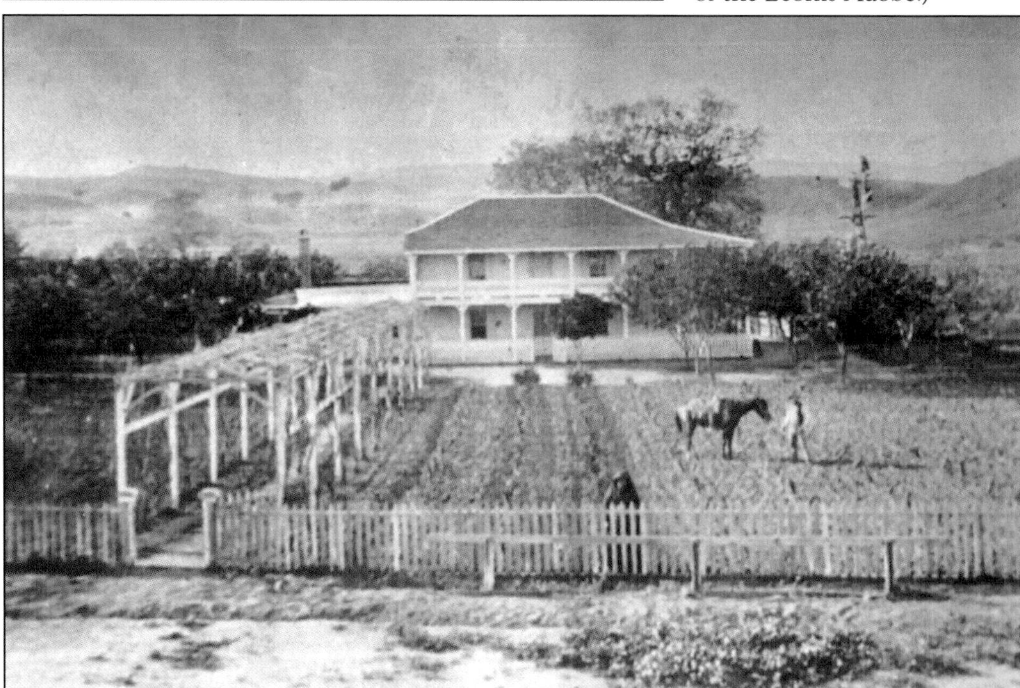

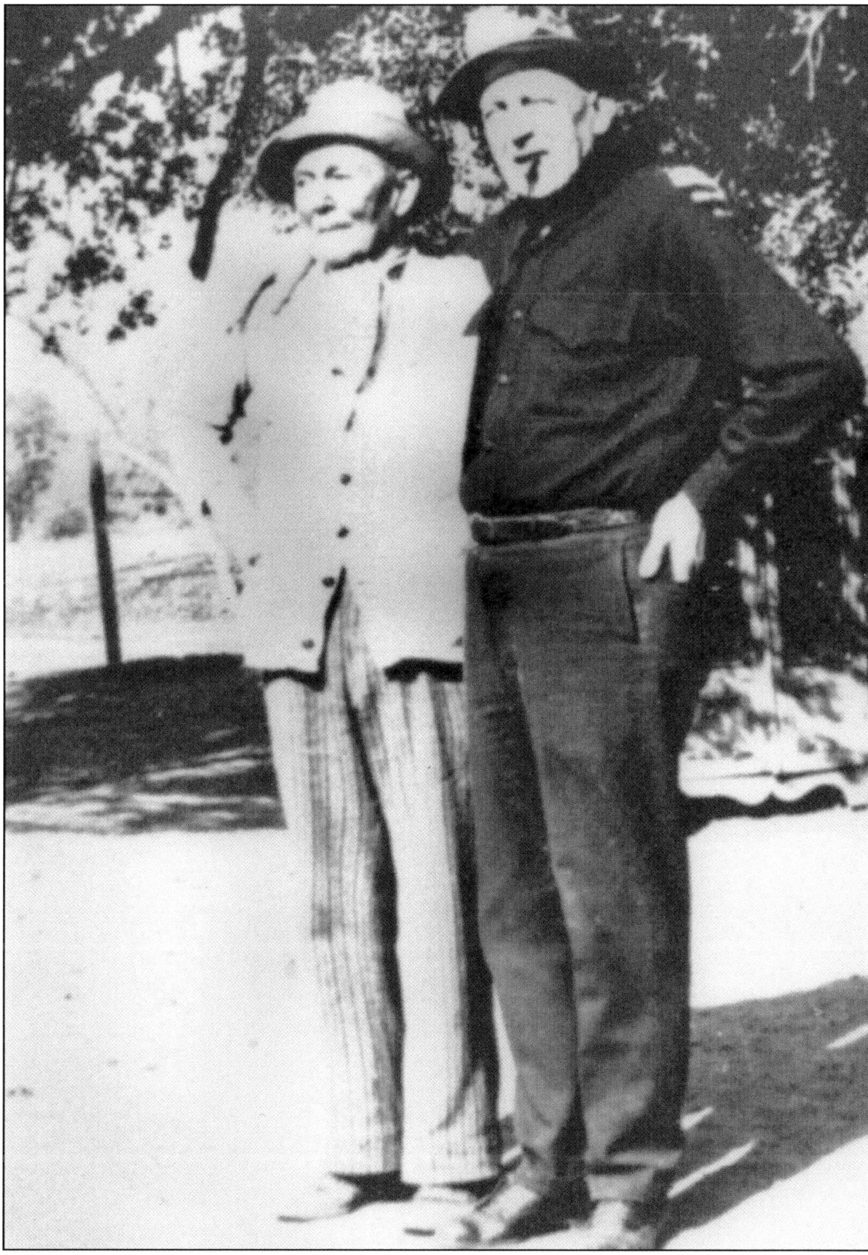

In 1931, the Agoures lost the adobe ranch through foreclosure to Spinks Realty Company; while Spinks owned the adobe, it was rented out to a succession of tenants until 1950, when the Hidden Hills Corporation purchased the property. Archie Hanson Jr., developer of Hidden Hills, renovated the adobe and lived there with his family for several years. Other adobe tenants included the acting Carradine family, singer-dancer Anna Leffinwell, artist Olinka Hardy, and Robert Witt Ames. Shown are Francisco Leivis, nicknamed "Pancho" (left), and Lester Agoure (right). The city of Agoura Hills was named after the Agoure family. Pancho lived in a shack on land owned by Agoure. Supposedly, Pancho had a reputation as being the "King of Love," welcoming visitors to his love nest. After his death in 1932, the property was found with holes throughout the yard, dug by people who thought Pancho had buried gold somewhere on his property.

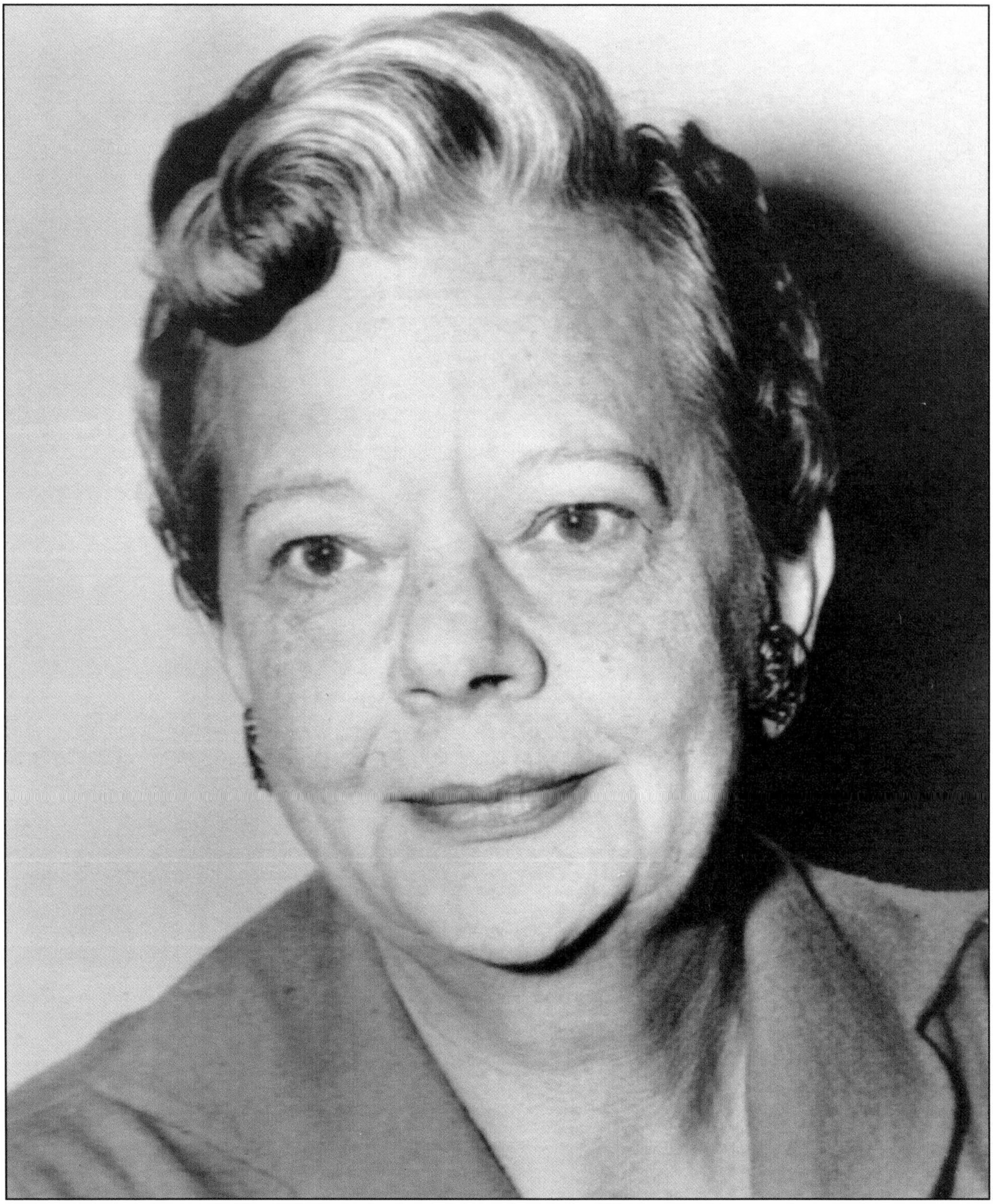

Hanson sold the adobe in 1957. When a developer wanted to demolish the adobe and build a shopping center on the property, philanthropist Kay Beachy, with the help of Carl Dentzel, director of the Southwest Museum, formed the Charter Los Angeles Cultural Heritage Board. The board's first meeting was on August 6, 1962. During this landmark event, five initial sites that were all considered to be threatened were declared historic cultural monuments. Within three hours, the Leonis Adobe in Calabasas was designated as one of the City of Los Angeles's first historic cultural monument in the area. Kay Beachy of Woodland Hills, seen above, founded the nonprofit Leonis Adobe Association. On March 28, 1963, she bought the adobe, and restoration began. The Leonis Adobe opened as a museum in 1966 and is one of the oldest surviving buildings in the San Fernando Valley.

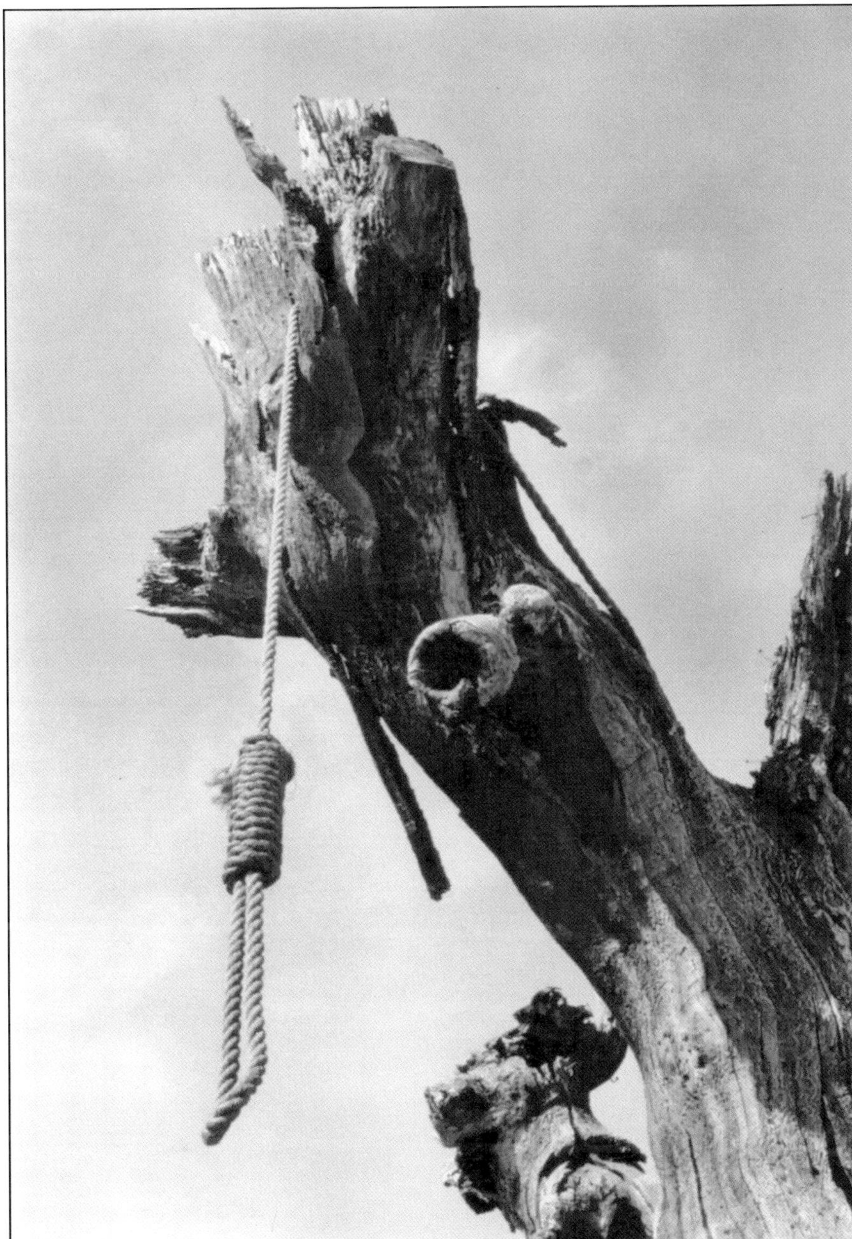

The legend of the hangman's tree implied that just outside the jail was a white oak tree used for hangings. Although no one was recorded as being hanged, the tree was an icon, even when the gas company came to Calabasas and ran its pipeline through the roots and killed it. Later, Calabasas was part of the route to truck a Rocketdyne rocket engine overland to its test site. The large engine could not fit between the gas station pumps and hangman's tree on Calabasas Road, so the dead tree was removed. The remaining portion of the dead tree was installed in concrete outside the Sagebrush Cantina, where it eventually rotted. The tree was then removed and relocated nearby and lies there today. The Calabasas Chamber of Commerce incorporated the hangman's tree as an icon for their newsletter publication, *Noose Notes*. Local complaints about the title reference resulted in a name change.

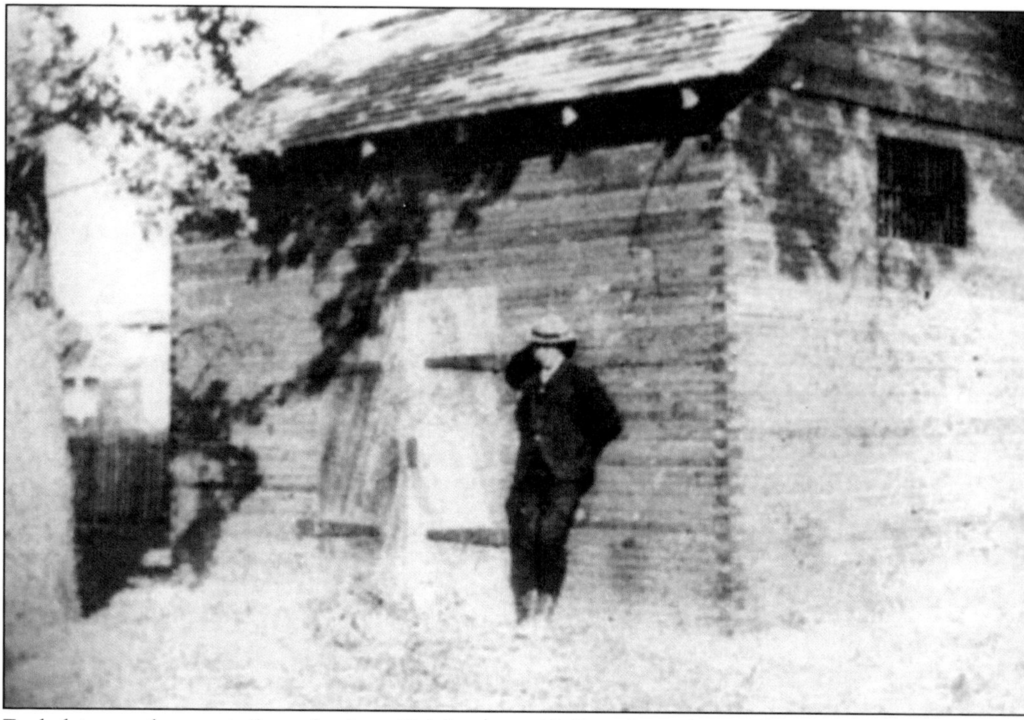

Early history shows a jail was built in Calabasas in 1869 and was later relocated to Chatsworth to manage unrest during the building of the railroad tunnel through the Simi Hills. Legend claims that offenders were supposedly locked up or run out of town with gunfire.

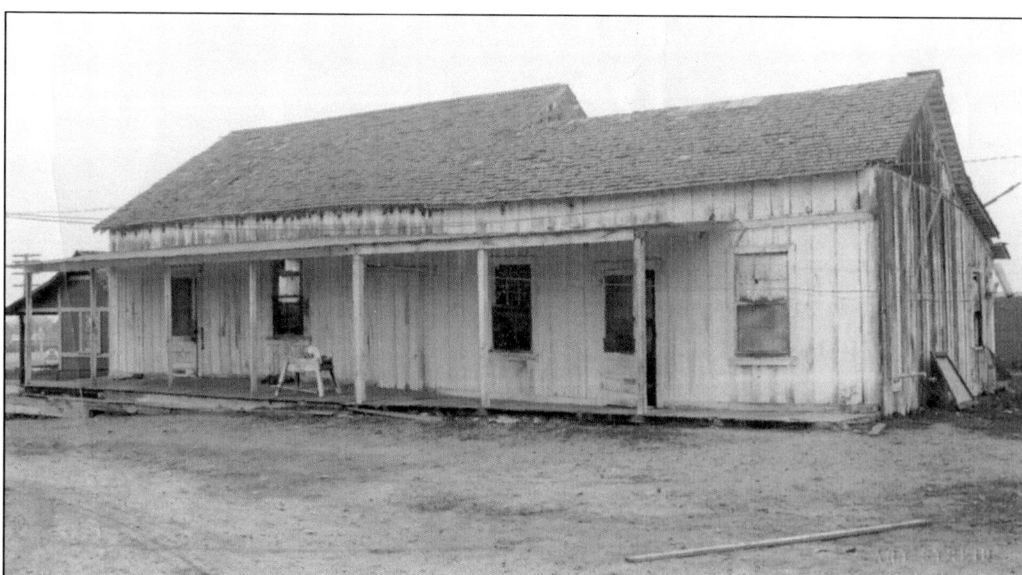

Shown is the Calabasas Butterfield Stage Coach corner stop around 1910. The building is in some disrepair. The sign seen to the far left reads, "Union Gasoline." The location was estimated to be at the east end of Old Town Calabasas.

Two

Early Years Survive in the Memory of its Founders

The Calabasas-Las Virgenes Historical Society archival collection of oral history tapes, letters, and books written by local historians documents the early days of Calabasas. Many of the interviews speak about the "kind goodness" of neighbors juxtaposed with descriptions of Calabasas as a "rough and tumble town." Accounts also cite a devastating drought during the 1890s and a squatters' war in the 1870s, with settlers being harassed first by Miguel Leonis, the "King of Calabasas," and then Harvey A. Branscomb, constable of Calabasas.

There were no cemeteries close to Calabasas in those days, so the general practice for residents was to bury the dead in a secluded spot on their own ranches. Lawrence Kramer, an early Calabasas resident, remembers helping bury a number of people "right in the back of the store close to the Calabasas wash," including an unidentified traveler who died behind the Kramer Store. Kramer and others buried him in a hole that was too small, leaving one leg sticking out in the open air. Eventually, the stench from the decaying limb was so bad that a Los Angeles undertaker was summoned to remove the body.

Catherine Mulholland writes about one of the first Calabasas homesteader families, Isaac and Edith Ijams and children, who were passing through Calabasas one stormy night "bedraggled, sodden, and unprotected" when they were taken in and provided shelter and food by the Palma y Mesa family. Soon after this generous act of hospitality, Isaac claimed 160 acres of land stating, "The land spoke, and I ceased to care to wander on . . . exchanging the gold of nuggets and pay dust for the riches of golden grain."

When one reads about the early years, it is surprising what the settlers endured just to survive. Even facing adversity, early Calabasans had an appreciation for the area's scenic beauty, the land they homesteaded to raise cattle, grow crops, and live alongside their similarly minded neighbors. Their pioneer spirit resolved conflict, initiated programs when they saw a need for education and a better way of life, and built the initial framework of Calabasas.

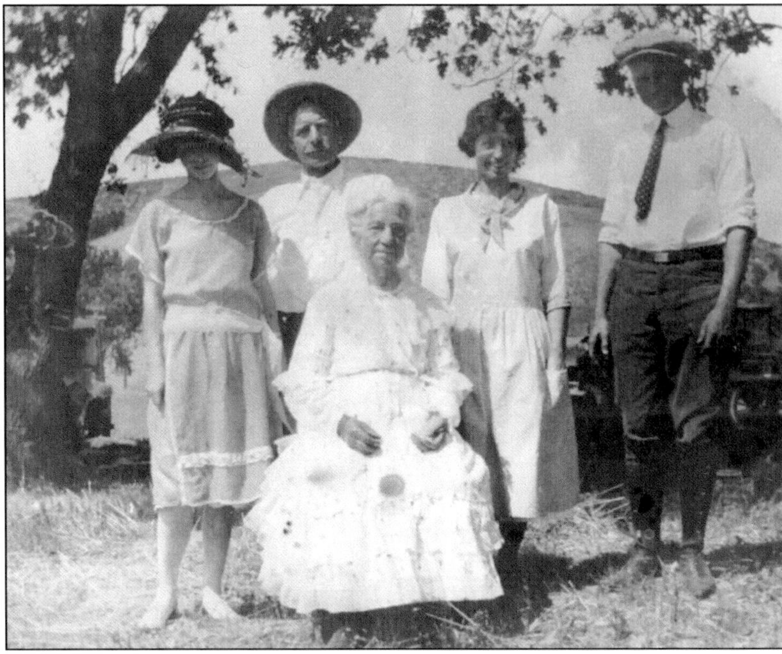

Pictured here are the Perrets, a Calabasas homesteading family, around 1900. From left to right are (seated) Mary Perret; (standing) Minnie, Frank, Ollie, and Roy Case. Minnie Perret and Roy Case were married on September 26, 1917. (Courtesy of the Calabasas Municipal Library.)

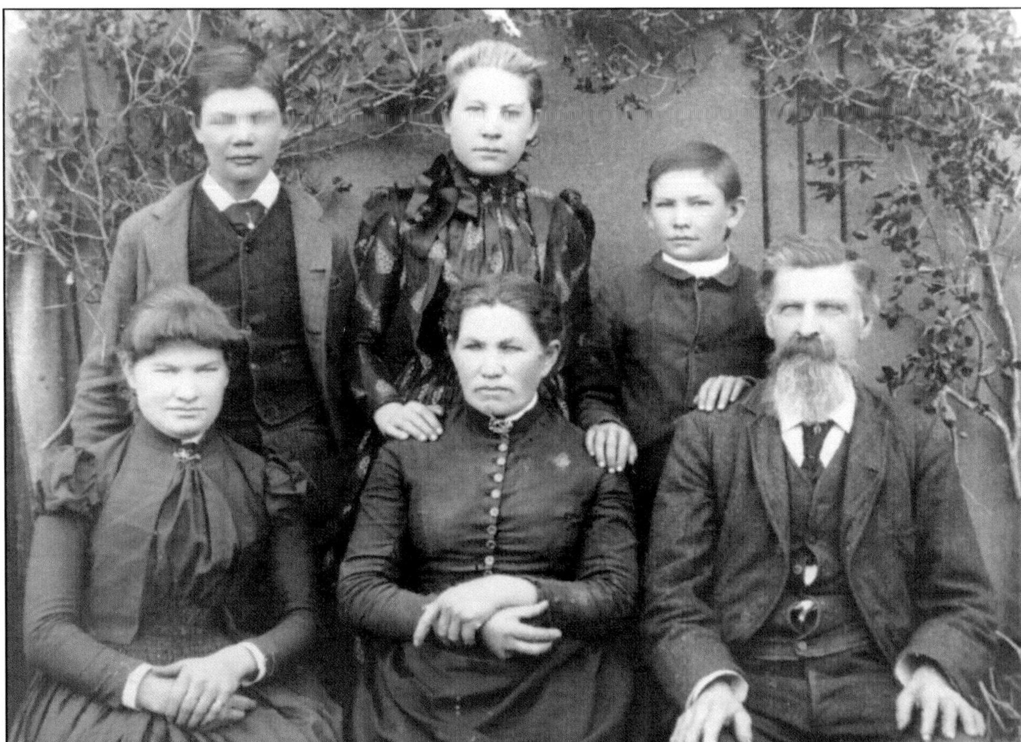

Pictured here around 1880 are members of the Ijams family, early homesteaders and Calabasas settlers. From left to right are (first row) Nettie, Edith, and Isaac Clay Ijams; (second row) Isaac Edward, Katie, and Willie Ijams. (Courtesy of the Calabasas Municipal Library.)

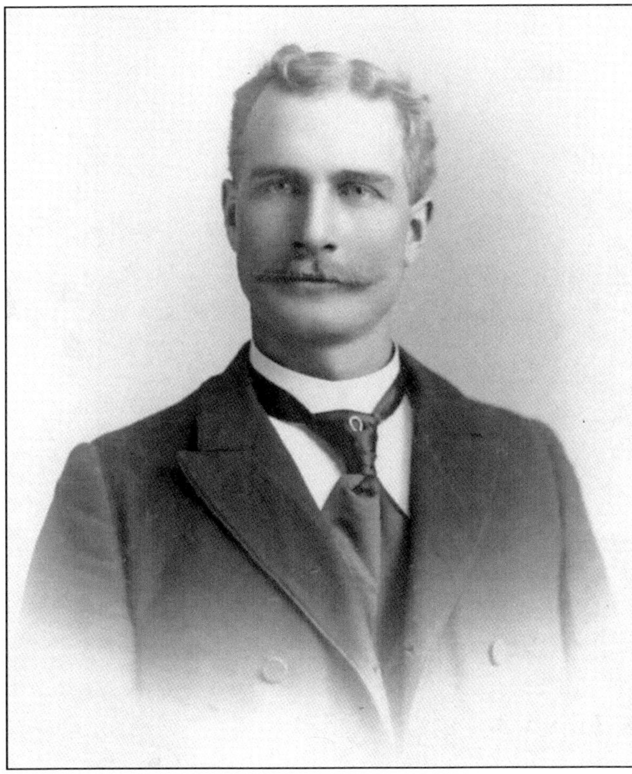

Calabasas homesteader Valentin Haas lost his sweetheart and bride, Mary Maddie Hattie Dora Canesse Haas, when she ran off to Australia with John Perret from Alsace Lorraine, France. Mary Maddie left behind a five-year-old son named John, who became the husband of Katie Ijams. Seen are sweethearts John Haas and Katie Ijams, whose respective fathers were Calabasas pioneer settlers Valentin Haas and Issac Ijams. (Both, courtesy of the Calabasas Municipal Library.)

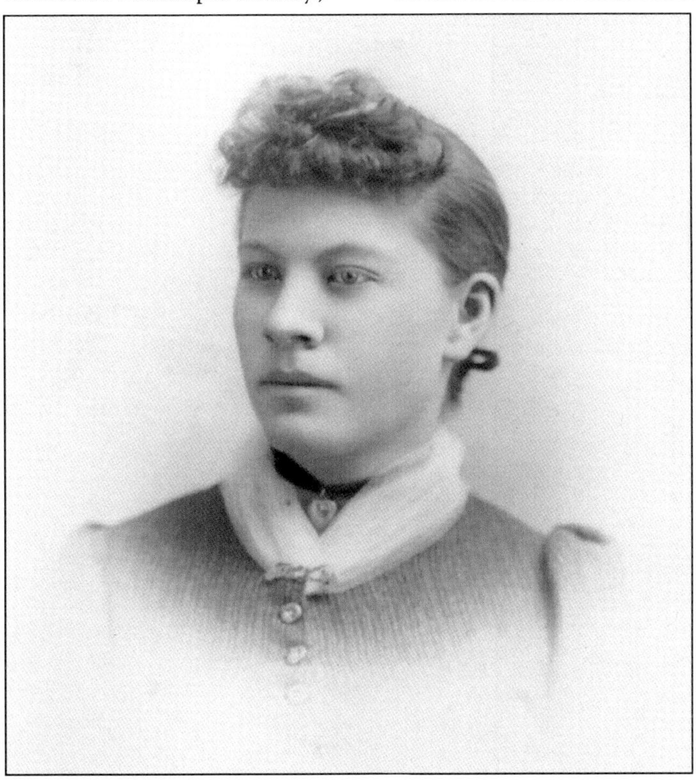

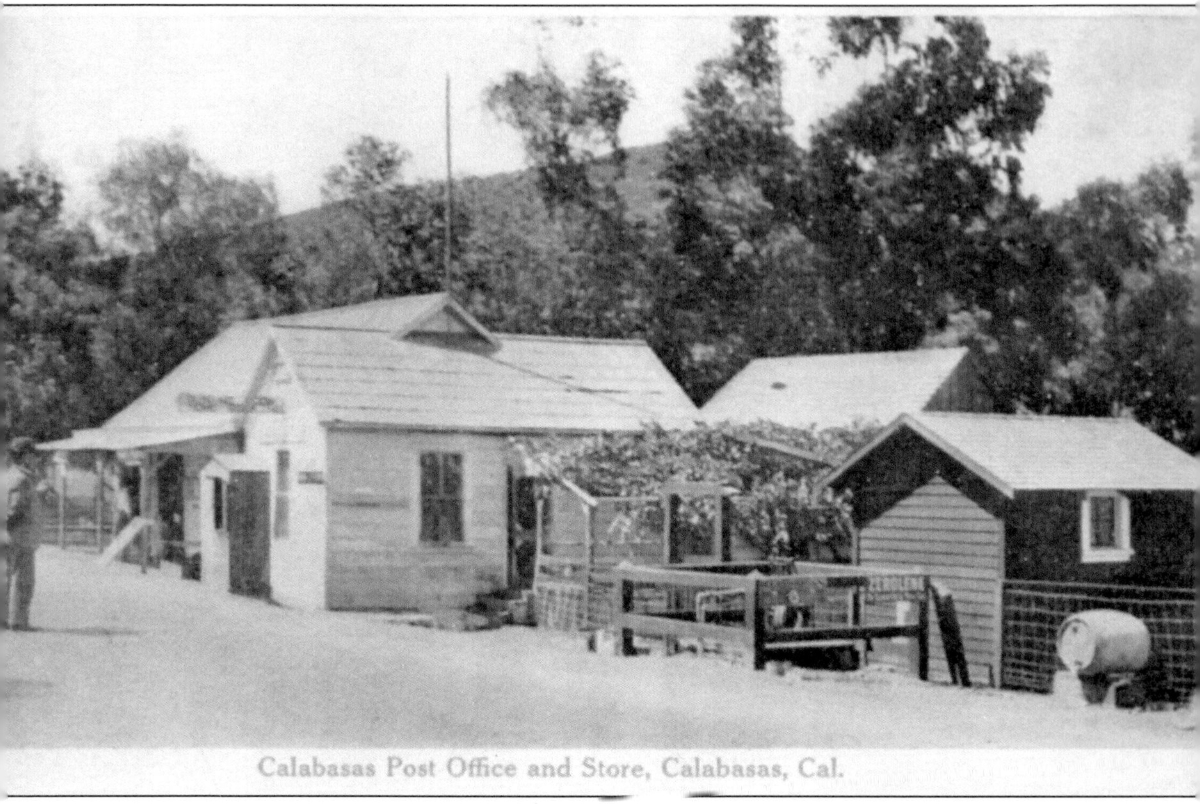

Judge Isaac Ijams and family came to Calabasas by wagon in 1887, becoming one of the first families to homestead in the area. The Ijams property was located on what is now upper Calabasas Road, adjacent to the Perrets' land. Ijams opened the first Calabasas School in a small granary and established the first post office in 1888, which he operated out of the family home. His teenage daughter Nettie Ijams was the first postmaster. Nettie's sister Katie married John Haas, who was a county road foreman in Calabasas. Their daughters became schoolteachers and returned to teach in the Calabasas School. Above is the original post office site, built by bachelor Mike Lordon, who was later shot. Mary Perret purchased the building at the turn of the 20th century.

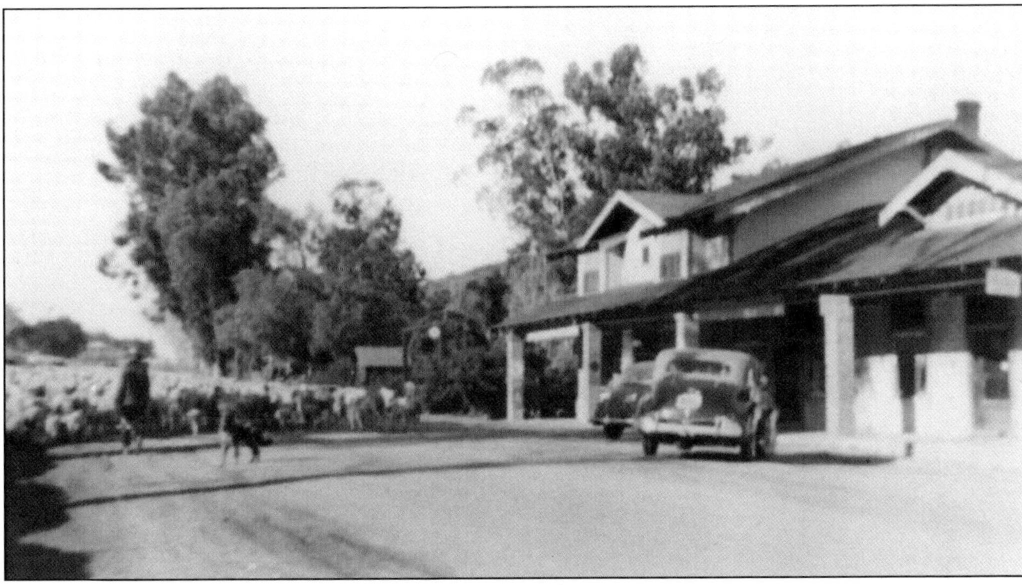

Around 1910, Anton Weber, a barber by profession, and his wife purchased the post office from Mary Perret and later rebuilt the structure, adding a restaurant, barbershop, and inn, making it the largest building in Calabasas. Around 1924, a portion of the Webers' building was rented to the county to house the Calabasas Courthouse. The courtroom was initially used as a dance hall, but later the stage served as the judge's podium and the side door of the courtroom led directly into the Webers' living quarters, which doubled as the jury room. The photograph above shows a view looking north; note the sheepherder making his way south on Calabasas Road. The postcard below is dated on the back, January 27, 1917, but it was never sent.

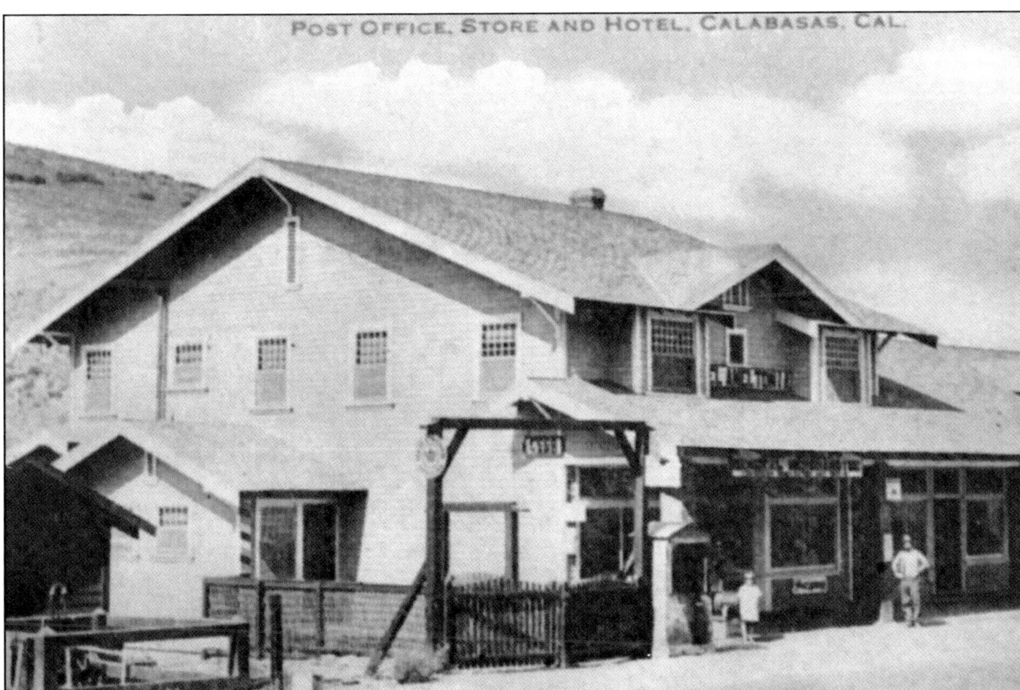

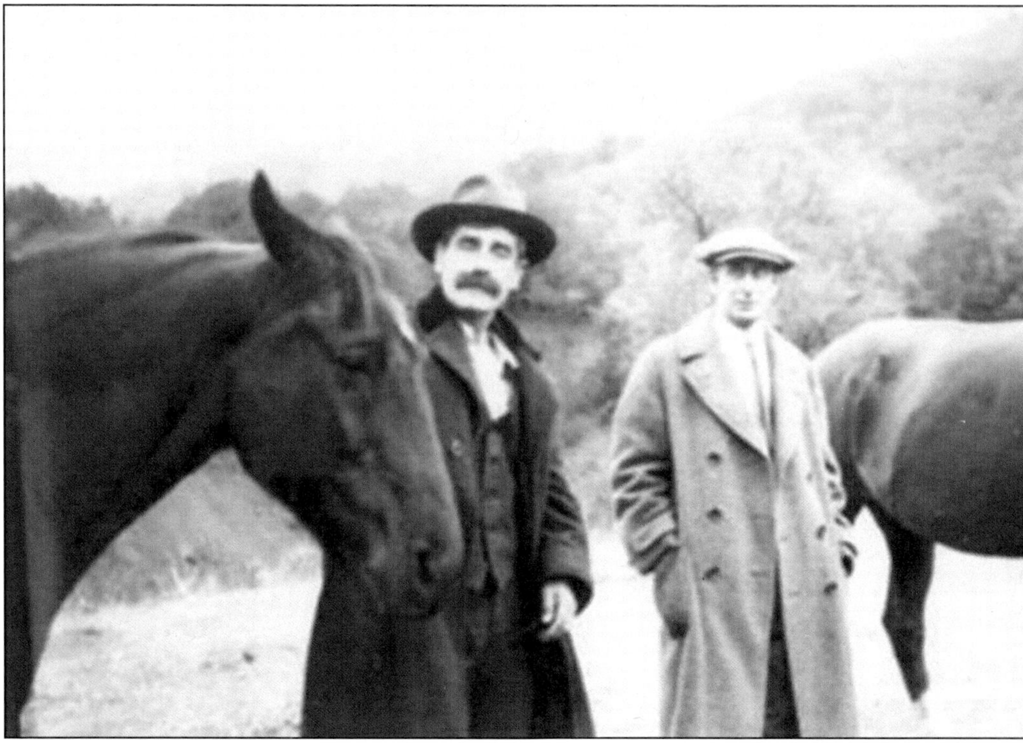

The Stunt brothers, Harry, Walter and Ernest, developed a homestead on the north slope of Saddle Peak in the late 1800s. In 1919, they built a larger cabin on the property, after their first one was destroyed by fire. The Stunt brothers lived and worked in Hollywood during the week and used the ranch on weekends. Walter died in 1928; Harry and his sister Ethel moved to the ranch in 1937. Harry and Ethel Stunt became well known in the area for their hospitality. Seen below is a local philanthropic group that led a fundraiser to restore the Stunt Ranch in the 1970s. Pictured outside the Stunt home are, from left to right, Juliana Gensley, Calista Thomas, Fausto Velarde, Winn Velarde, and Brenda Thomas.

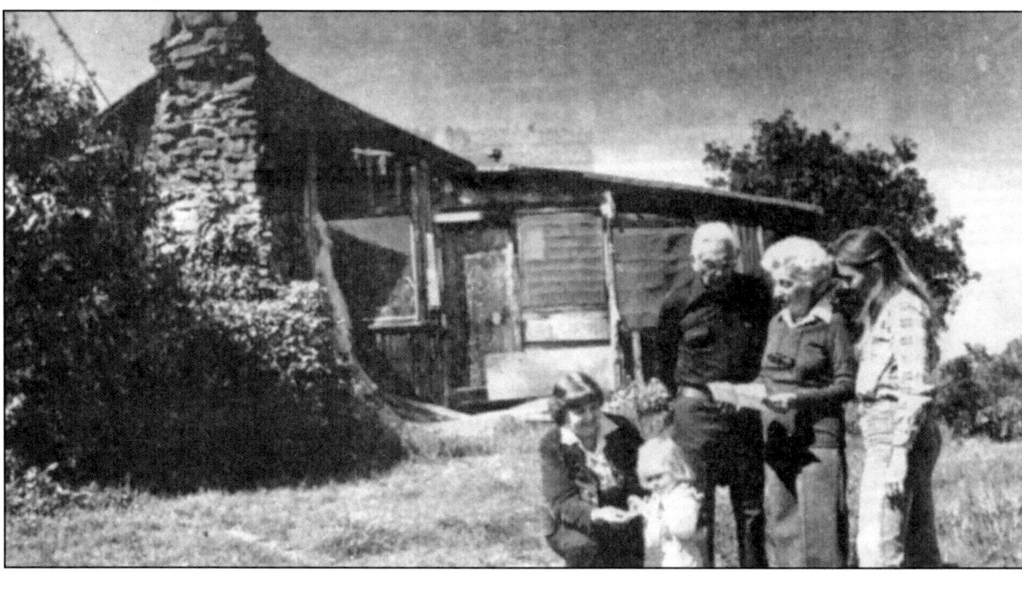

Pictured here are Robert and Bertha Straubinger with their daughter, one of three children. They homesteaded 450 acres; today the location includes part of Old Town Calabasas and Hidden Hills. The Straubingers' grandson Frank Hill cites a story in which his grandfather and Miguel Leonis squared off over a land squabble with their gun barrels pointed directly at each other's midsections.

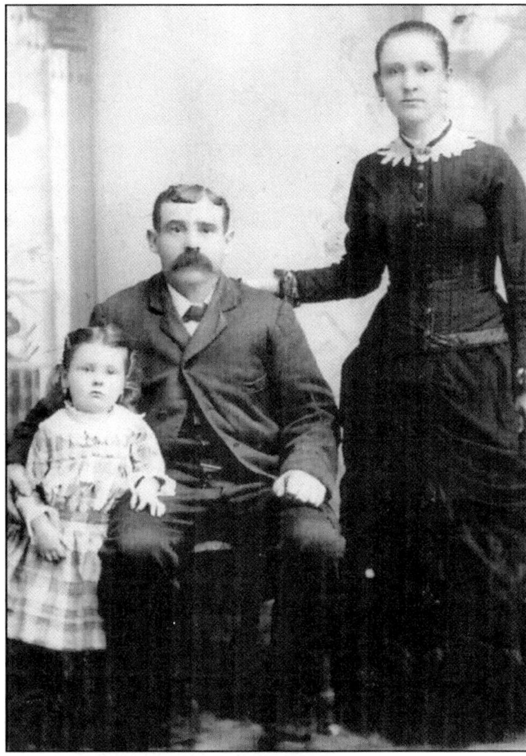

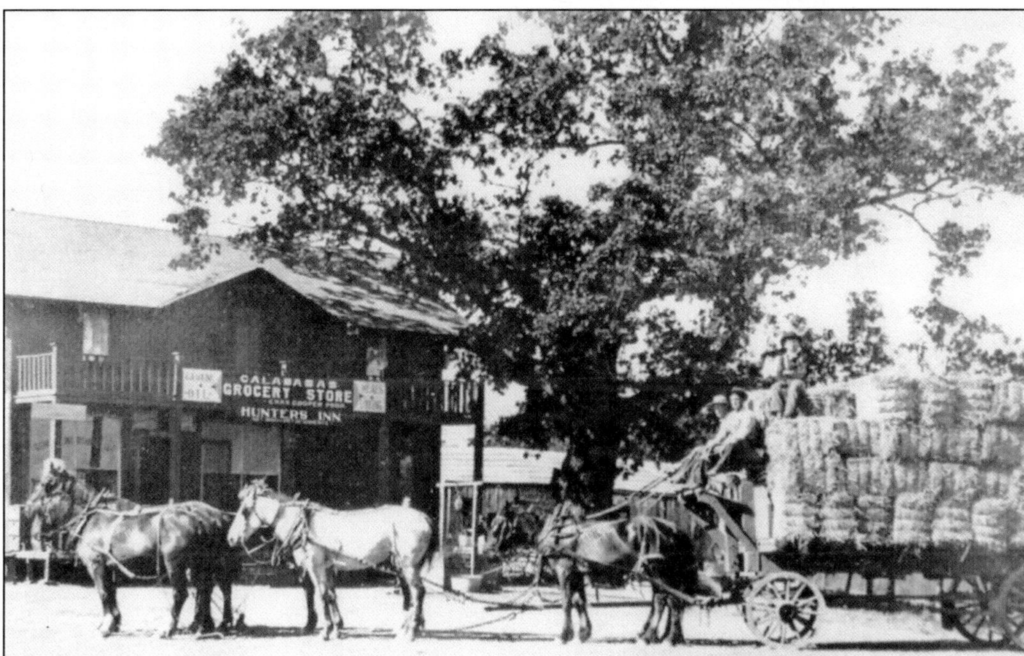

The Straubinger family raised alfalfa, wheat, and other crops along with horses and mules. Father Robert Straubinger died of a heart attack while hauling hay in 1919. His son Frank, who continued to farm using mules in the Calabasas area, was known as the "Mule Man" by the movie industry because his mules pulled wagons for the movie teams.

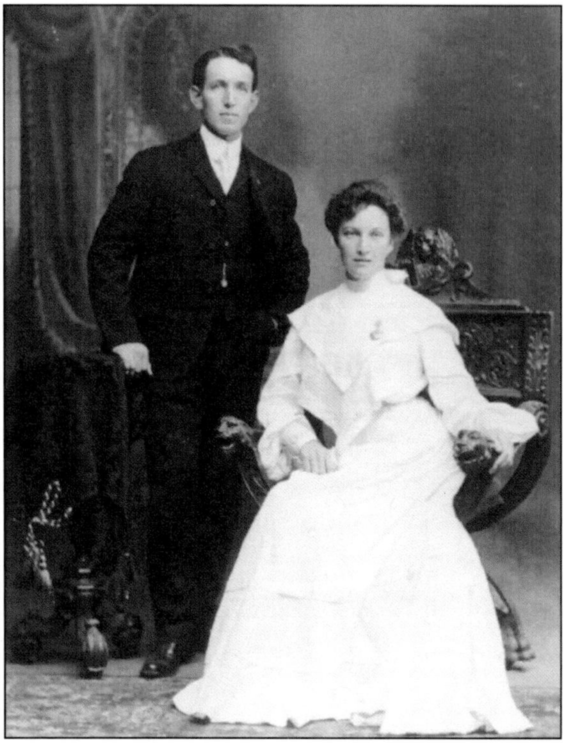

Samuel Cooper and his wife, Mary, claimed 160 acres in Calabasas. English-born Mary Cooper would serve tea in dainty china cups while chickens strutted about the kitchen table. Their son Charles Cooper married Alice Kimball and ran the Hunter's Inn at Calabasas Junction until his death in 1914, providing rooms for hunters and travelers while raising their eight children. According to historians, Cooper's other sons, Samuel and Mathew, were good cooks and opened the first pie factory in Los Angeles. Pictured at left around 1910 are Charles and Alice Cooper. Below is the inn as it appeared around 1950, when it was owned by Lawrence Kramer, who married Alice Kimball after Charles Cooper passed away. This structure still stands in Old Town Calabasas, housing boutique shops. (Below, courtesy of Bison Archives.)

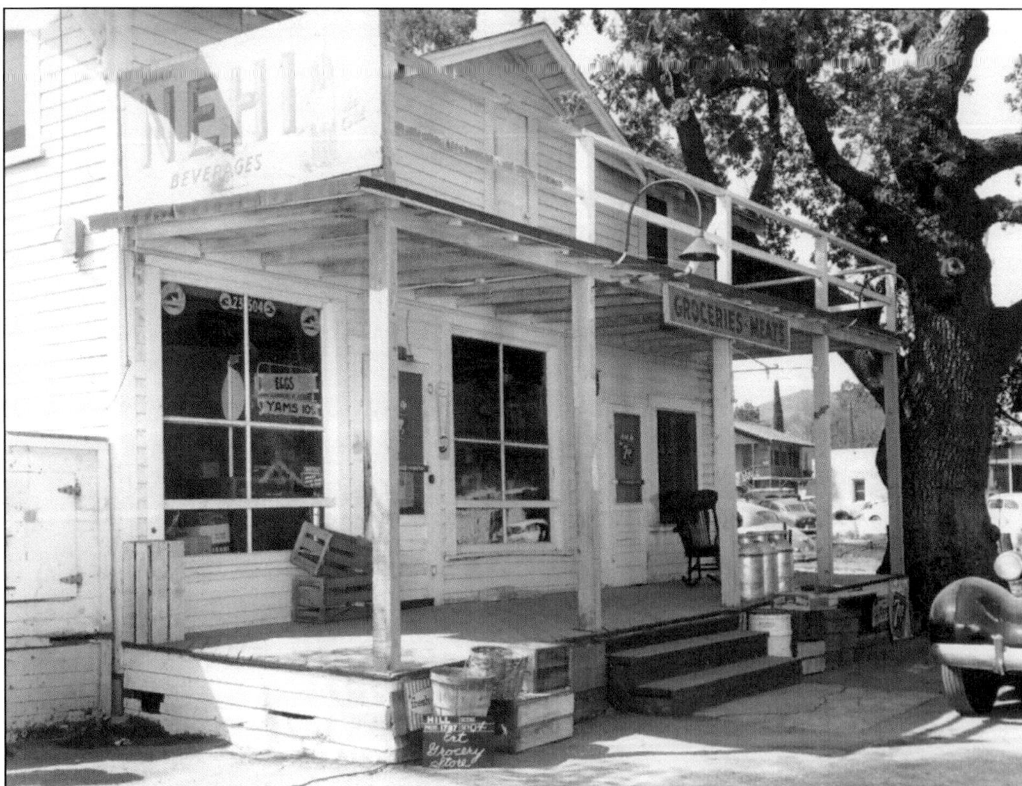

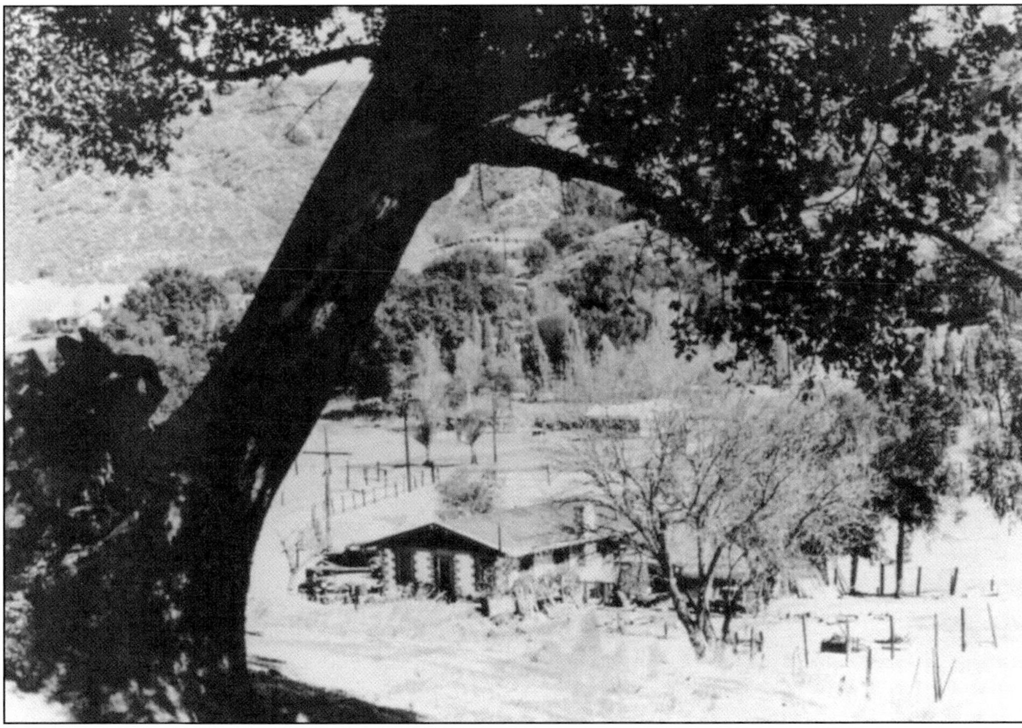

Pictured here around 1920 is the Samuel John Cooper ranch home located off Old Topanga Canyon Road. One of the largest walnut groves in the state was adjacent to the Cooper ranch.

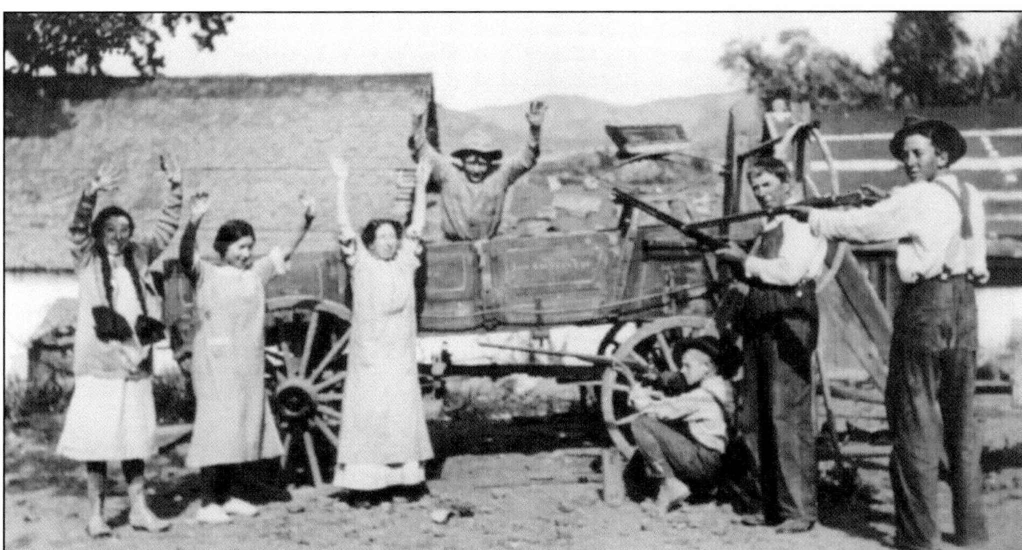

Shown here are the members of the Samuel John Cooper family joking around for the camera on their ranch in Calabasas in 1915. From left to right are Rosie, Dollie Farnum, Rose, unidentified (in the wagon), Stanley Masson, Samuel John, and son Samuel Cooper.

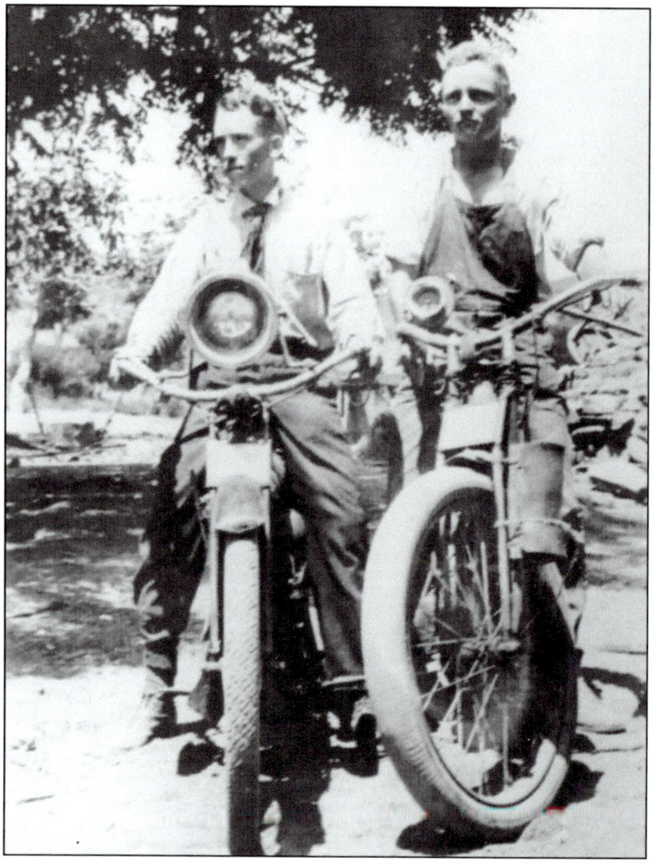

Samuel Cooper, son of Samuel John Cooper (left), is with one of the Masson boys in Calabasas on their motorcycles about 1918.

The Masson House, built between 1890 and 1900, is registered as Calabasas Historical Landmark No. 1 and was strategically placed on the only route to Santa Monica, where the 1910s Port of Los Angeles Long Wharf was built. The Masson House is one of the only remaining homesteads in the city and one of few in Southern California. Today, the house is part of Headwaters Corner, the headquarters for the Mountain Restoration Trust on present-day Mulholland Highway. (Photograph by Karlo Gorgin; courtesy of the Calabasas Media Department.)

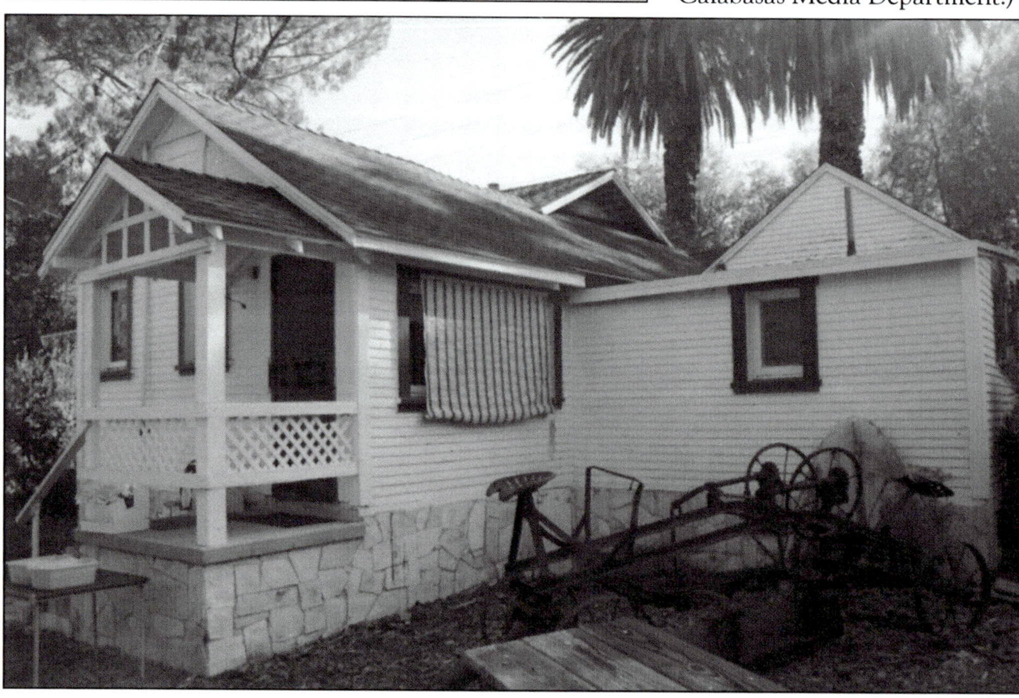

Charles Cooper (left) stands outside the Oak Garage around 1910. Cooper was killed in a hunting accident two weeks after this photograph was taken. His widow, Mary Cooper, then married Lawrence Kramer and renamed the store Kramer's. The old El Camino Real Bell is seen just over Charles Cooper's head.

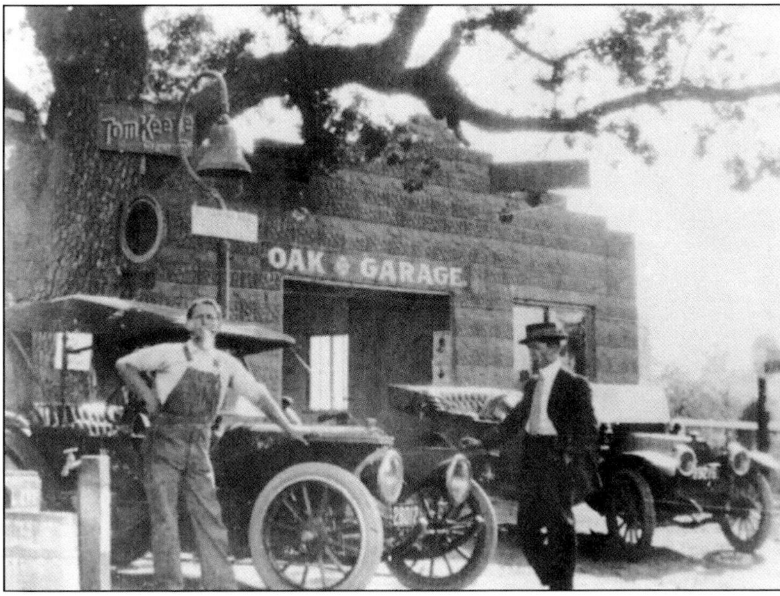

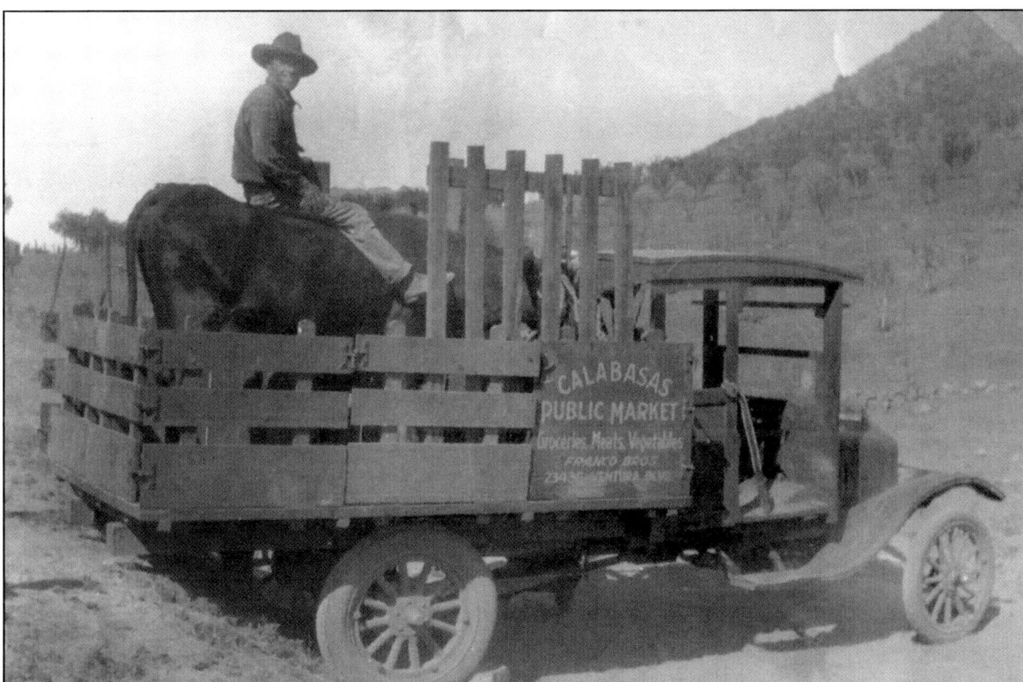

Manuel Correia is pictured here driving the Calabasas Public Market truck, a 1922 Ford. The Franco brothers owned the market in 1923. Correia lived on Peeler Ranch off Cornell Road. The Peeler Ranch later became Yearling Ranch, owned by future president Ronald Reagan. It is now known as Reagan Ranch.

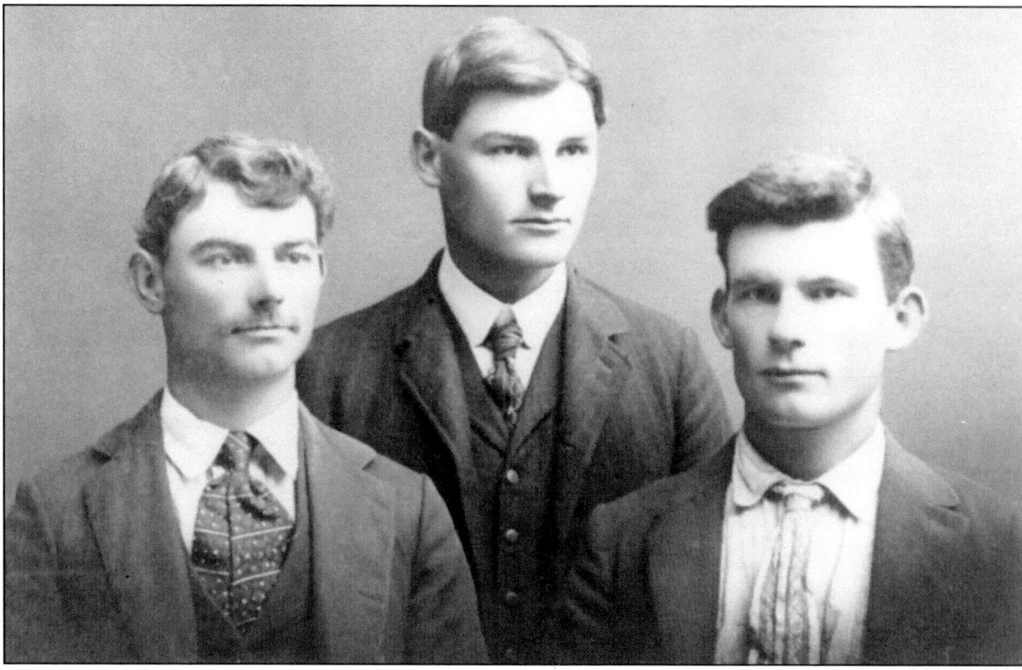

Pictured here are the Daic brothers, Joseph, Charles, and Al, all descendants of homesteaders in the area. Joseph Daic was born in 1893 and attended the Liberty School and Hollywood High School. He learned to be a mechanic in a machine shop in Los Angeles. In 1915, Joe purchased property in Calabasas from Juan Menendez (Espiritú's son) and built his garage across from the Leonis Adobe. Two of his mechanics were Max Cooper and Jimmy Gleason.

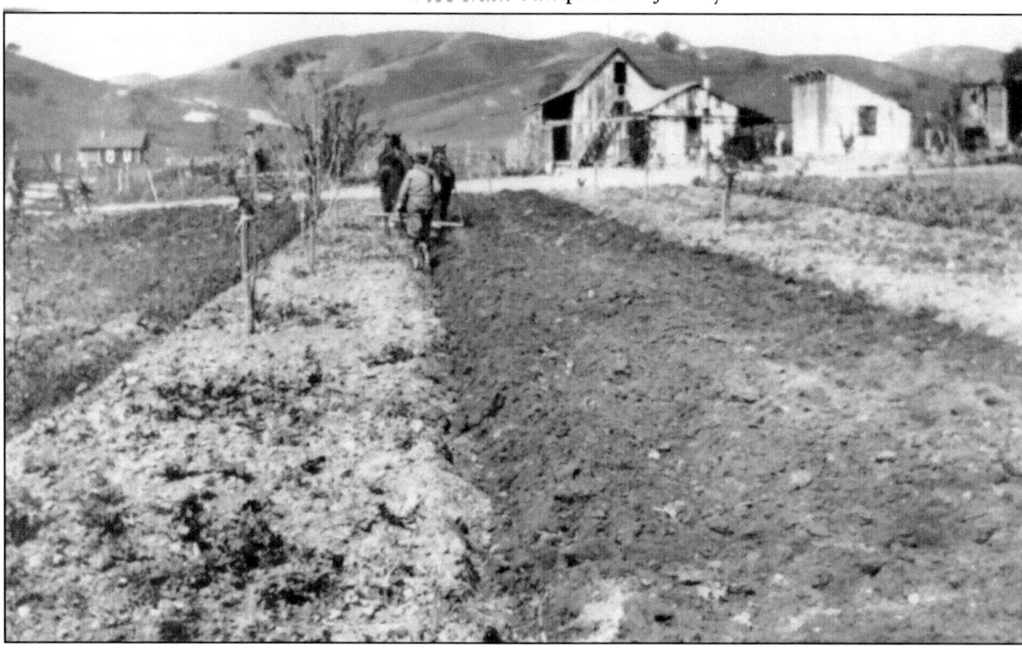

Here is the Daic Ranch as it appeared around 1908. The ranch was located at the west edge of Calabasas near what is now the Lost Hills Road exit off the Ventura Freeway. The Liberty School, one of the first one-room schoolhouses in the area, is shown in the distance on the left.

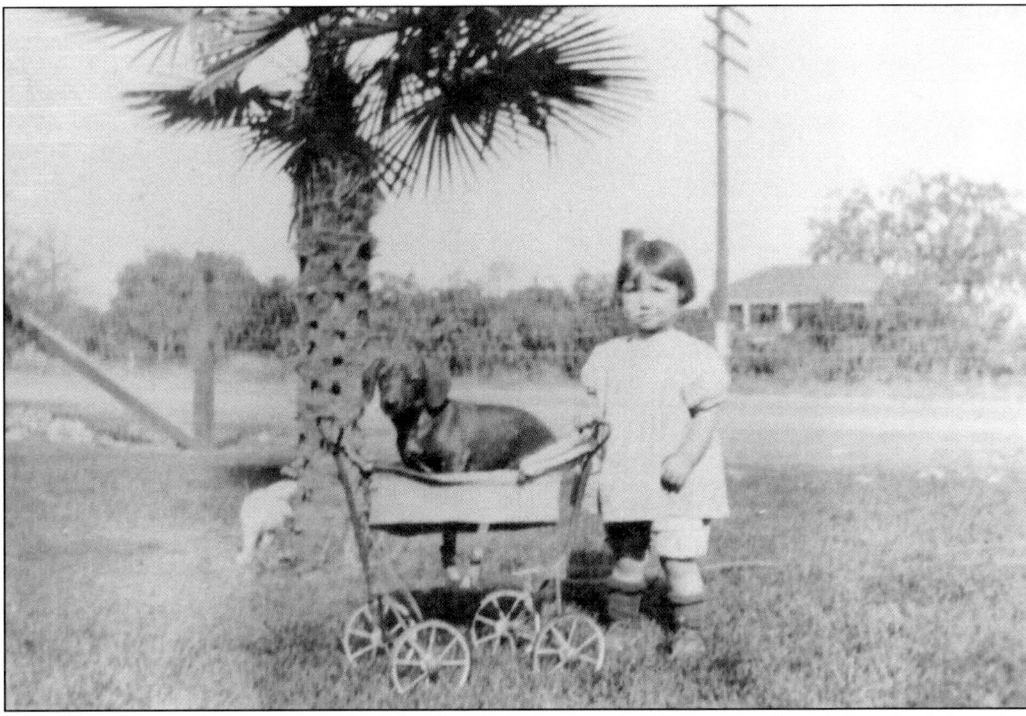

Beverly Daic is in the front yard of the family home on Calabasas Road with her dachshund in the doll pram around 1920. The Leonis Adobe is seen in the background.

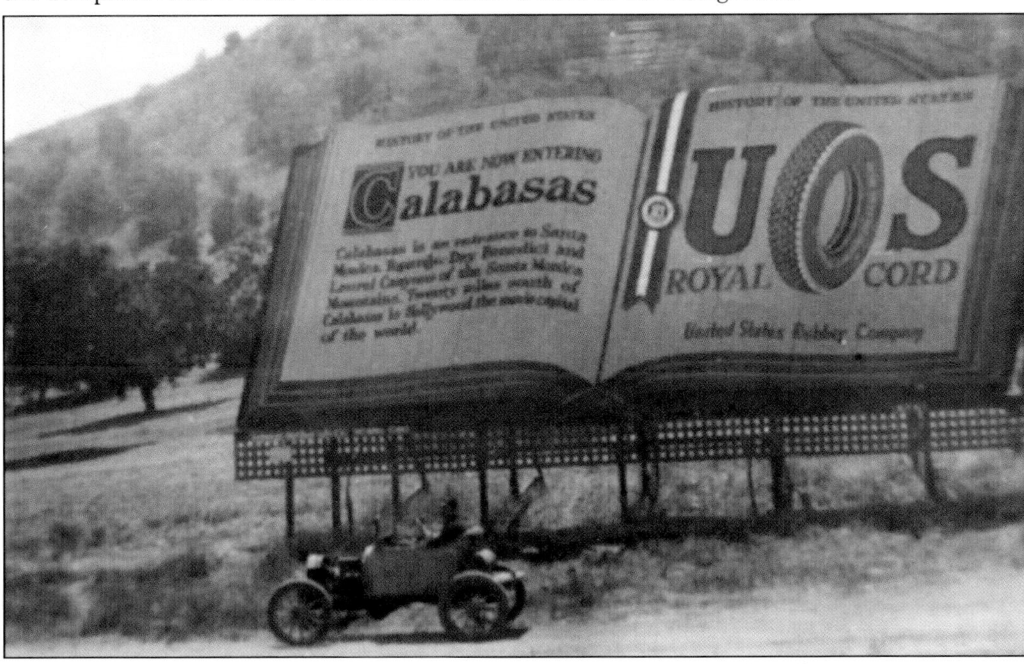

Pictured here is a billboard on Ventura Boulevard telling drivers that they are now entering Calabasas, "an entrance to Santa Monica, Topanga, Dry Benedict and Laurel Mountains . . . 20 miles south of Calabasas is Hollywood, the movie capital of the world." The billboard was sponsored by US Royal Cord Tires around 1917.

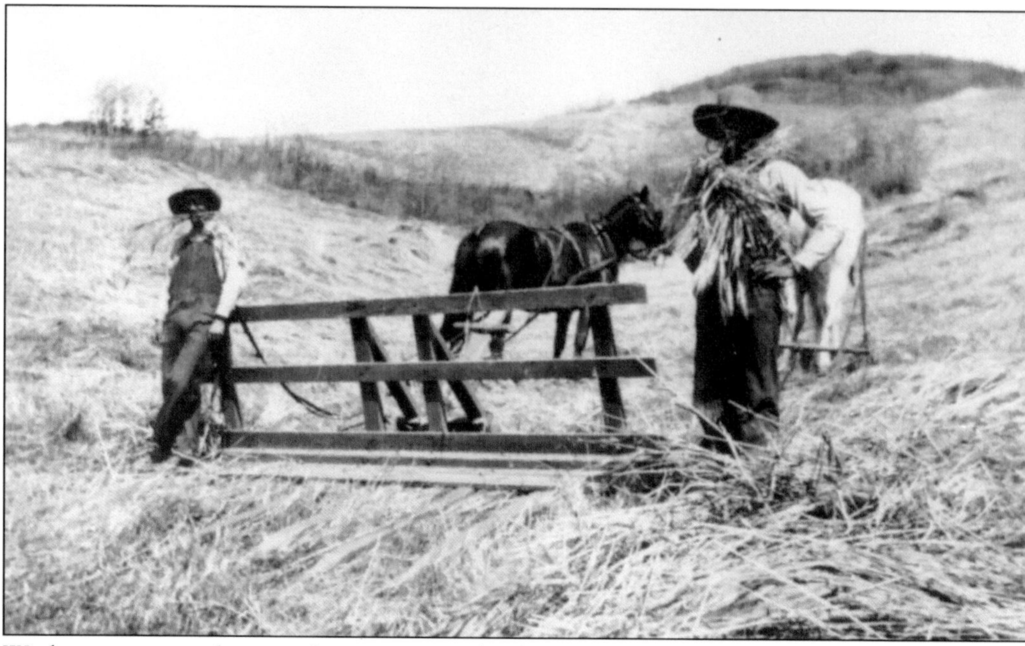

Workers are seen cultivating hay using a go-devil on the Daic Ranch around 1900. The go-devil is another name for a sled lister cultivator.

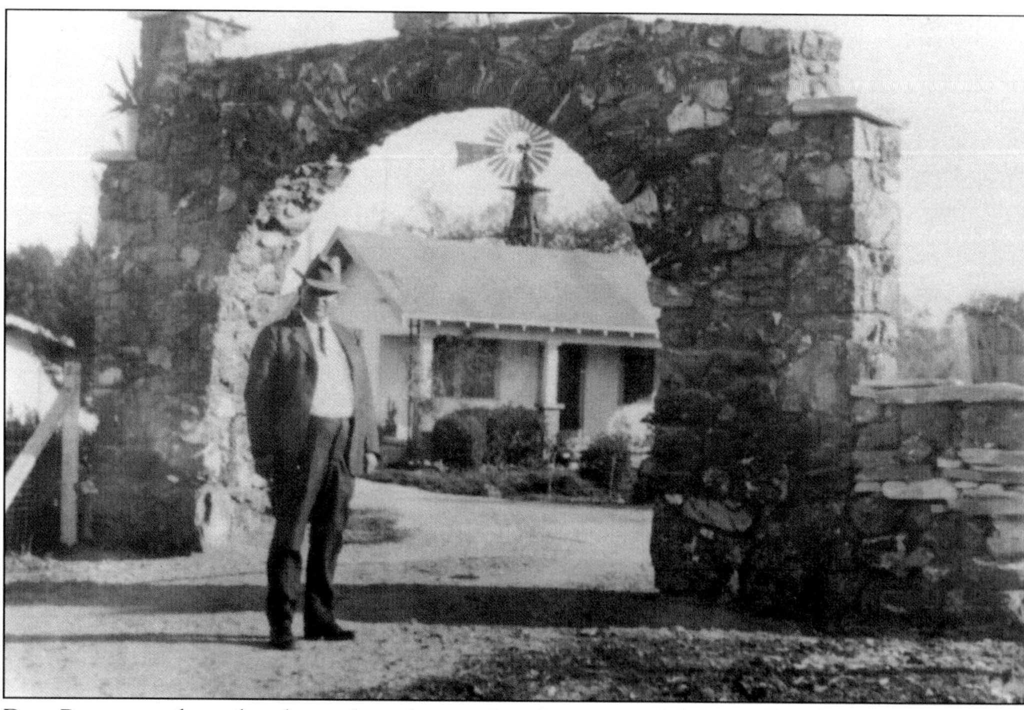

Don Poyer stands under the rock arch outside a home on Calabasas Road around 1920. The legend is that Poyer found buried treasure near the property because when he originally arrived in Calabasas he was a man of modest means. He became suddenly wealthy and "wanted for nothing the rest of his life," according to the book *Land of the West Valley* by Laura B. Gayle.

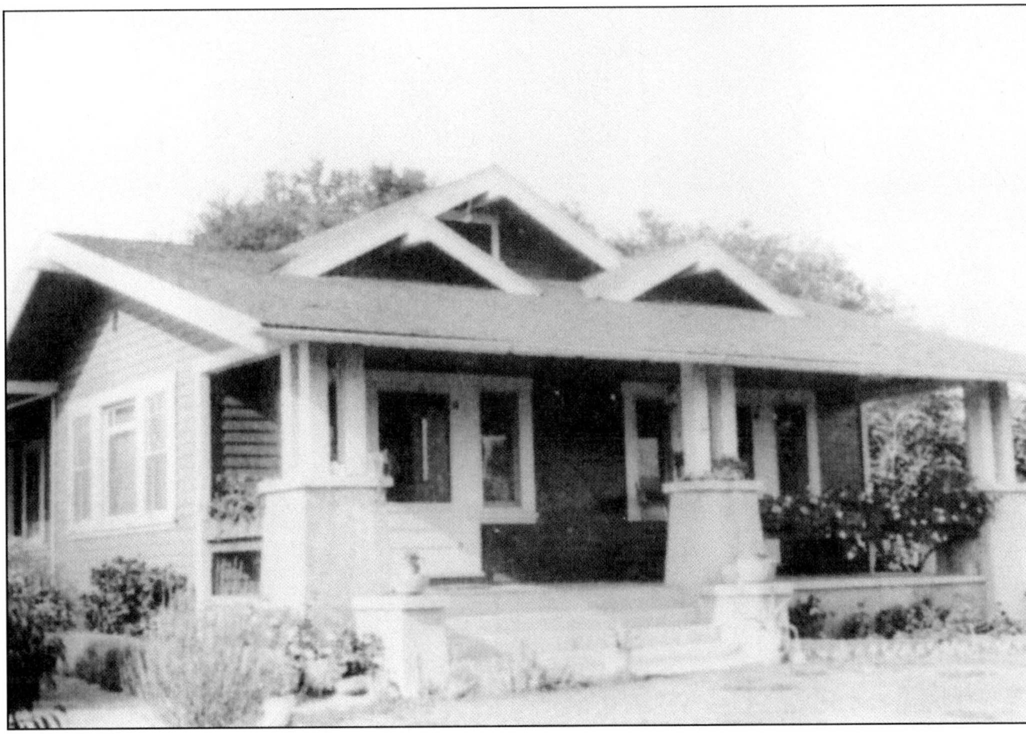

Pictured here is the Coig Ranch house, built in 1906.

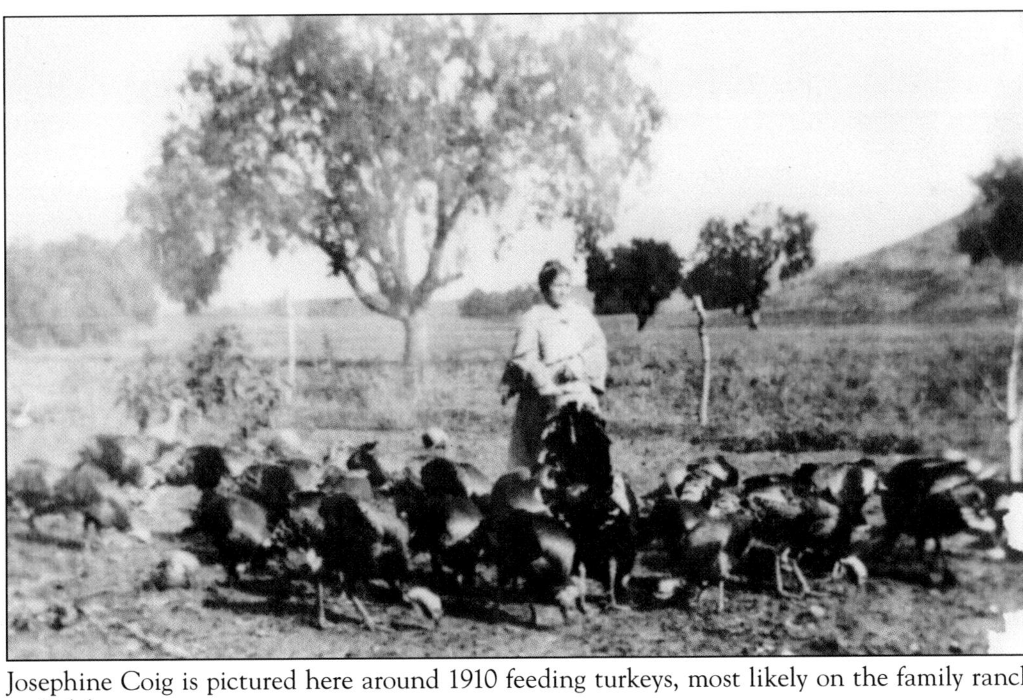

Josephine Coig is pictured here around 1910 feeding turkeys, most likely on the family ranch in Calabasas.

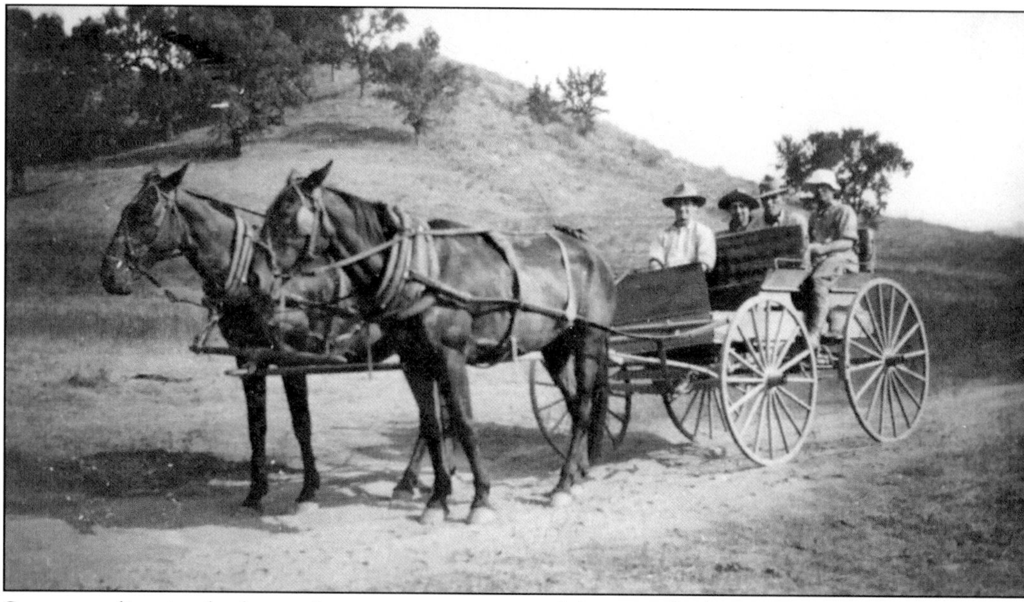

Seen traveling in the horse-drawn wagon is part of the state highway survey party about 1912 in the vicinity of Las Virgenes on the Calabasas route. The third man from the left is J.B. Watson, who married Lottie Lewis, from an early family in Agoura Hills. (Courtesy of Eileen Watson-Carter.)

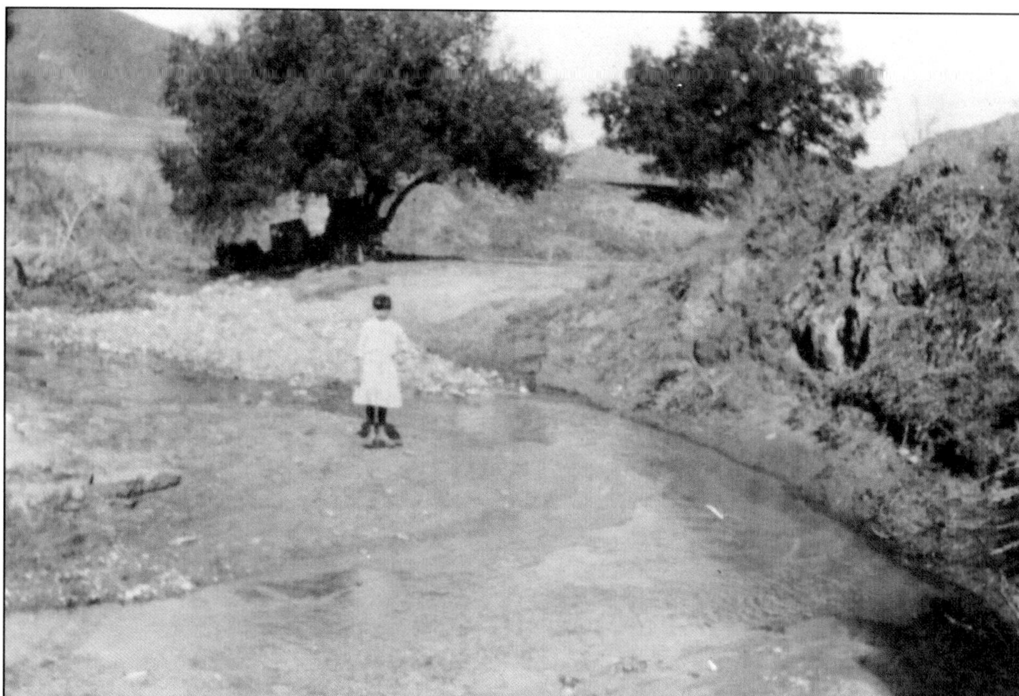

Juanita Domingues is standing next to the Calabasas Creek around 1910. The creek was formed by natural springs in the hills; Calabasas Creek joins Bell Creek to begin the Los Angeles River. Miguel Leonis used a windmill to supply water from the creek to the adobe ranch house.

Three

A Focus on Education

The first school in the Las Virgenes area was established in 1888 by a judge, Isaac C. Ijams, who started the school for his own four children and other area youngsters in an empty granary near present-day Calabasas High School.

In 1890, Los Angeles County took over and built the new Victorian-style Calabasas School, which consisted of one room.

In addition to the Calabasas School, three other grammar schools were established in the area in the late 1800s and early 1900s. The Las Virgenes School began in 1884. In 1896, the Liberty School was created from territory taken from the Las Virgenes and Calabasas Districts. Finally, in 1913, the Cornell School District was established from the southwest portion of the Liberty District. Each area school was contained in a one-room schoolhouse and had its own board until 1948.

In 1957, the Las Virgenes Union School District was formed and located on the present site of A.E. Wright Middle School, with an enrollment of 400 students. During that period, seventh and eighth grade students had the option of attending either the Las Virgenes Elementary School or Sutter Junior High in Canoga Park. Local high school students attended Canoga Park High.

By the middle of 1959, many Las Virgenes residents were determined to make their district complete from kindergarten through high school. On July 1, 1962, Las Virgenes was unified and became the Las Virgenes Unified School District but faced challenges in building a high school. By 1965, Agoura High School was able to accept all high school grades; the completed four-year high school graduated its first class in June 1968.

The increase in population in the 1960s required that additional schools be built. Present-day Calabasas area schools include Calabasas High School, A.E. Wright Middle School, Alice C. Stelle Middle School, Bay Laurel Elementary School, Chaparral Elementary School, Lupin Hill Elementary School, and Round Meadow Elementary School.

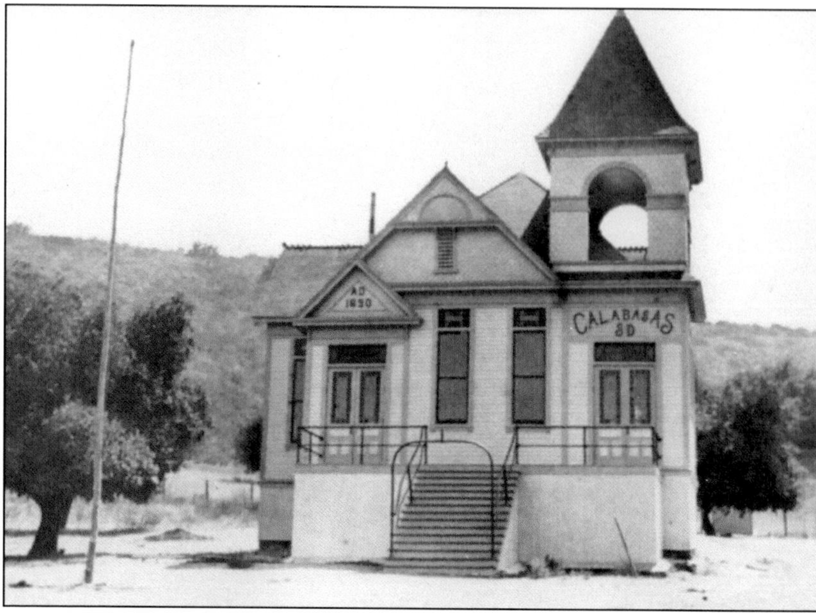

Pictured here is the Calabasas School in 1890. After Judge Ijams established a school in the area, he taught classes himself in the absence of a schoolteacher. About 17 students attended this school, but by the 1930s enrollment had grown to 50 students.

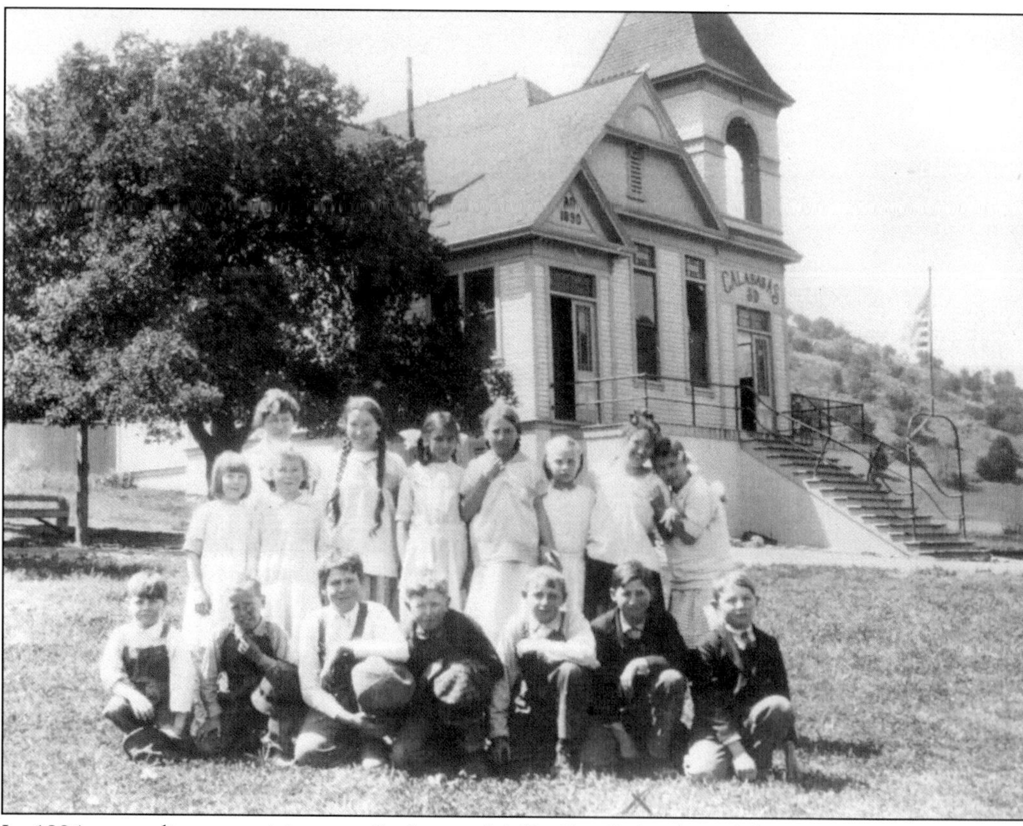

In 1894, according to writings in Catherine Mulholland's book *Calabasas Girls*, student Katie Ijams described school sessions as being unruly: "Tis the toughest school here you ever saw or heard of. They do just as they please—talk and laugh and fight, make fun of the teacher, holler at people, in and out of school alike."

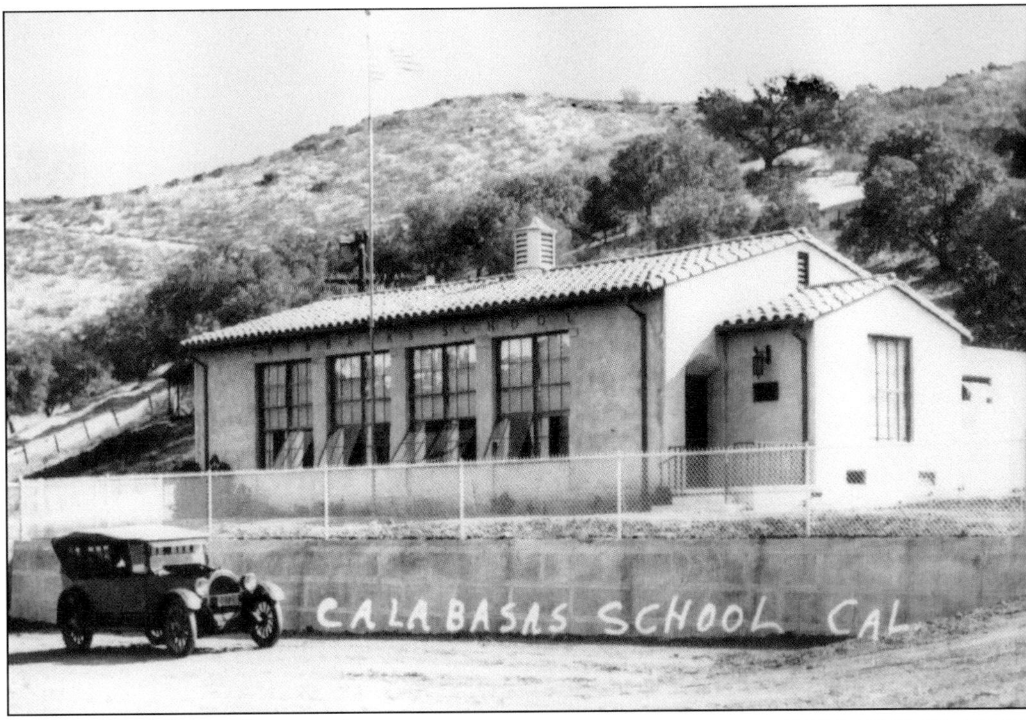

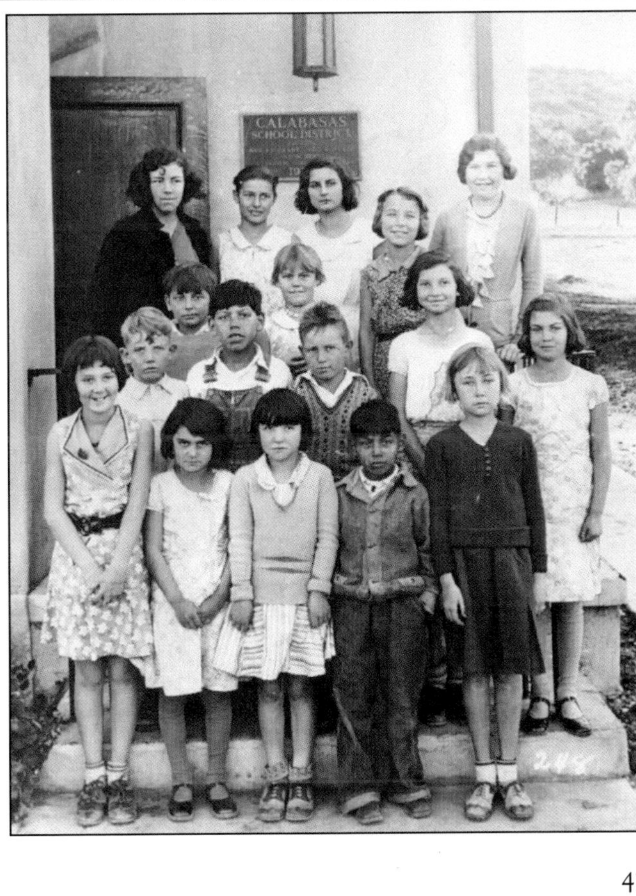

This postcard shows the second Calabasas School on the property in the 24400 block of Calabasas Road, sometime in the late 1920s. Built in the 1924–1925 fiscal school year, it was a one-teacher one-classroom school. In 1947, the Calabasas School joined Liberty, Cornell, and Las Virgenes to form the Las Virgenes Union Elementary Unified School District. Charles Mureau, a local investor, purchased the school and three acres in 1952. During Mureau's ownership, the property was rented and modified for a succession of tenants, including Country Manor, the Mine Shaft, and Pelican's Retreat, only preserving the school building's original front wall, the retaining wall, and the steps up from the road. Pictured here are some Calabasas students in 1933. Frank Farmer, an early Calabasas settler, is standing in the middle of the second row.

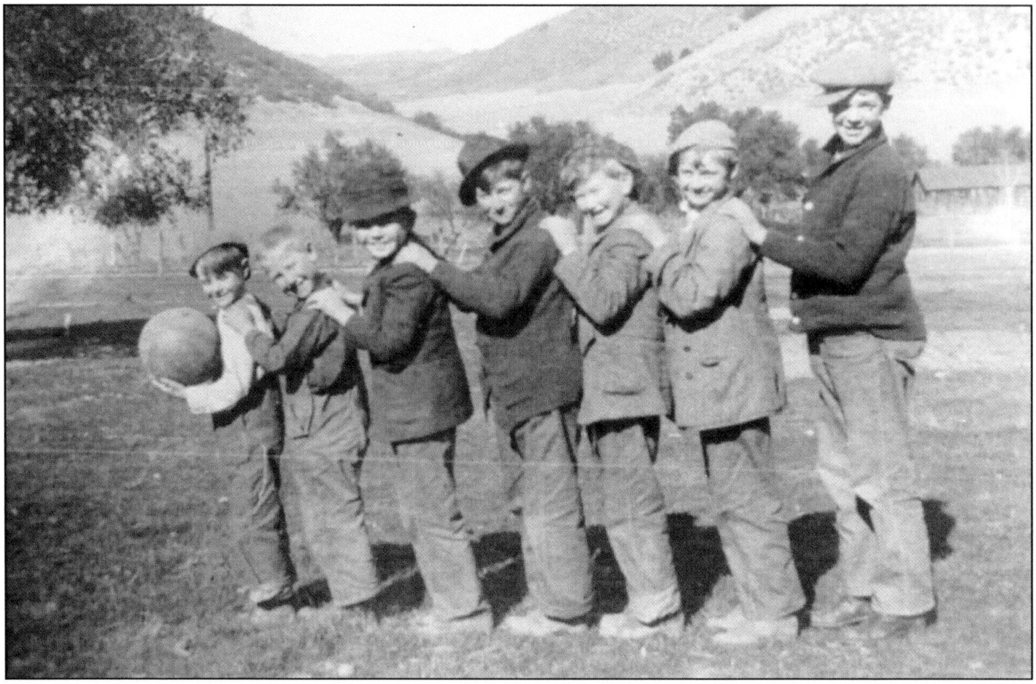

Here are some of those mischievous Calabasas School boys posing in a lineup about 1920. Included in the lineup are, from left to right, Percy Masson, Fred Tucker, Frank Cooper, Walt Penland, Joe Lee, Stanley Masson, and Jerry Grant.

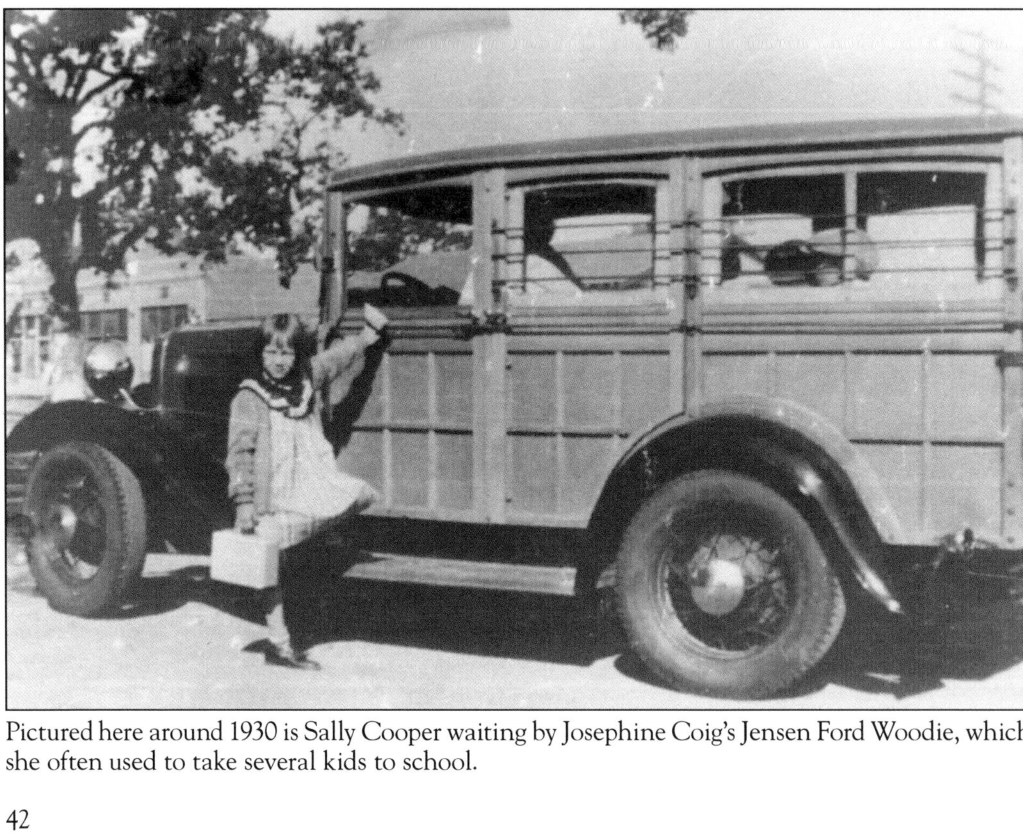

Pictured here around 1930 is Sally Cooper waiting by Josephine Coig's Jensen Ford Woodie, which she often used to take several kids to school.

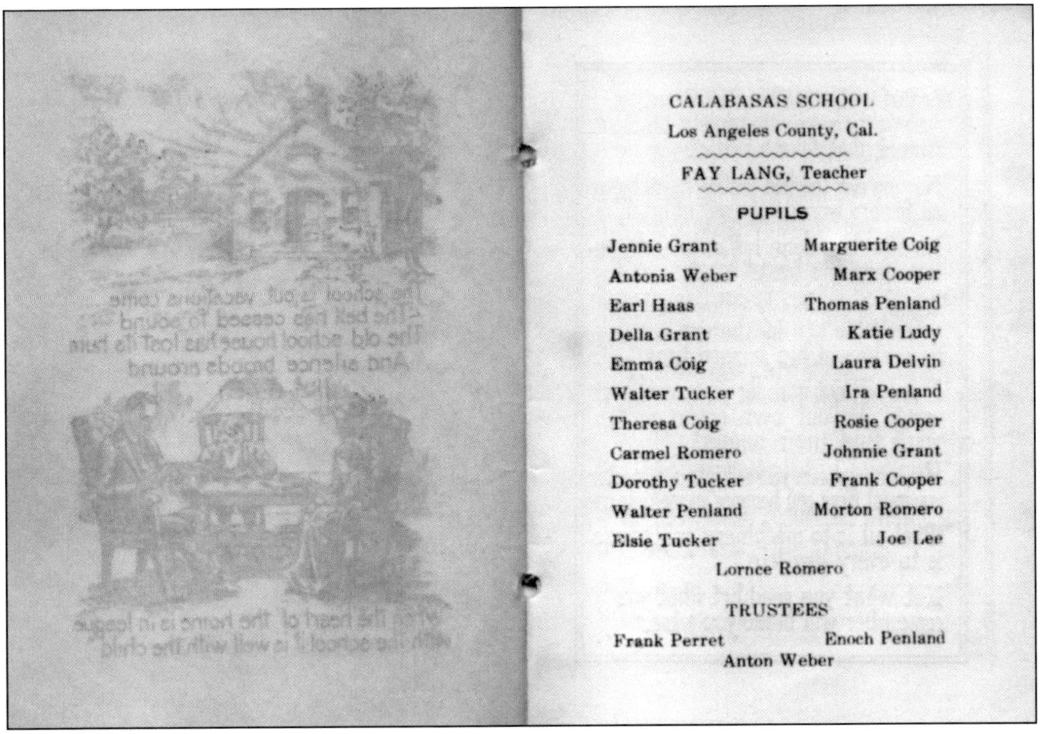

CALABASAS SCHOOL

Los Angeles County, Cal.

FAY LANG, Teacher

PUPILS

Jennie Grant	Marguerite Coig
Antonia Weber	Marx Cooper
Earl Haas	Thomas Penland
Della Grant	Katie Ludy
Emma Coig	Laura Delvin
Walter Tucker	Ira Penland
Theresa Coig	Rosie Cooper
Carmel Romero	Johnnie Grant
Dorothy Tucker	Frank Cooper
Walter Penland	Morton Romero
Elsie Tucker	Joe Lee

Lornce Romero

TRUSTEES

Frank Perret　Enoch Penland

Anton Weber

This memory book is from 1913 and acknowledges the class that studied in the original Calabasas School that year. The names of the children listed belong to early Calabasas pioneers whose respective fathers acted as the school's trustees. The little booklet is pocket size, and the cover is a heavy stock paper with Victorian embossed details tied together with string. (Courtesy of Mayor James Bozajian.)

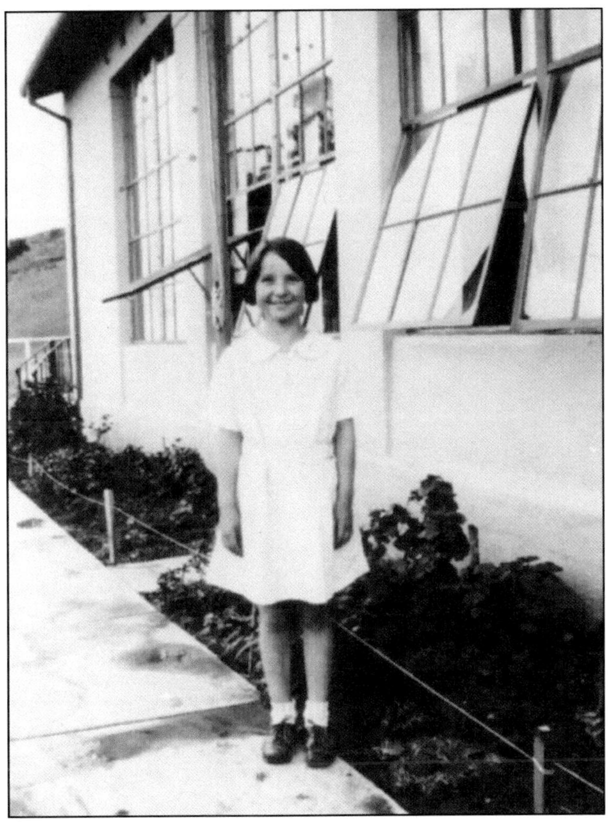

Beverly Daic stands outside the second Calabasas School in 1925. In the *Los Angeles Times*, Daic shared, "We were like family here at the school. The teacher would teach the older children and the older children would help the younger ones. The little ones would draw and the older ones would watch after them." Beverly Daic's parents became concerned about her reading progression and later sent her to Canoga Park School.

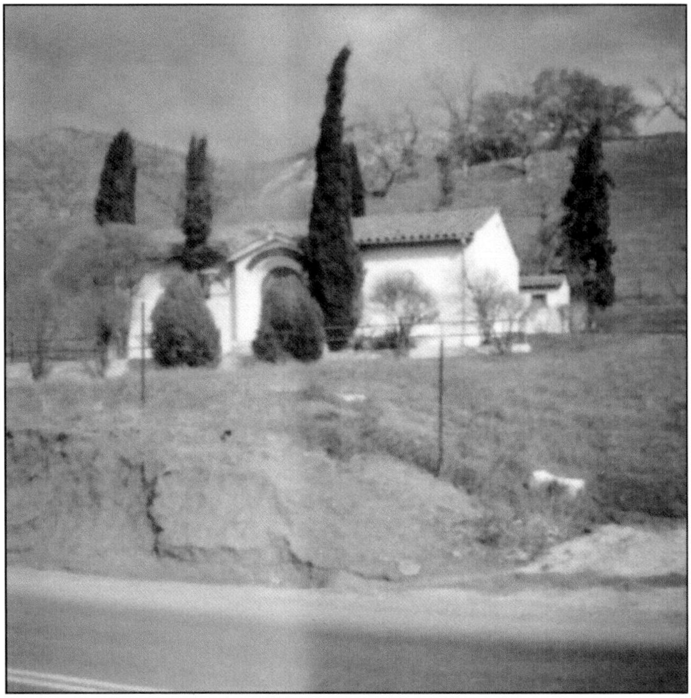

The Las Virgenes School was originally built in 1884 on the east side of the present-day Las Virgenes Road south of A.E. Wright Middle School. This was the only school of four that did not have an on-site water well. In the early days, a student named Mae Smith rode her mare and was paid for hauling five gallons of water to school each day.

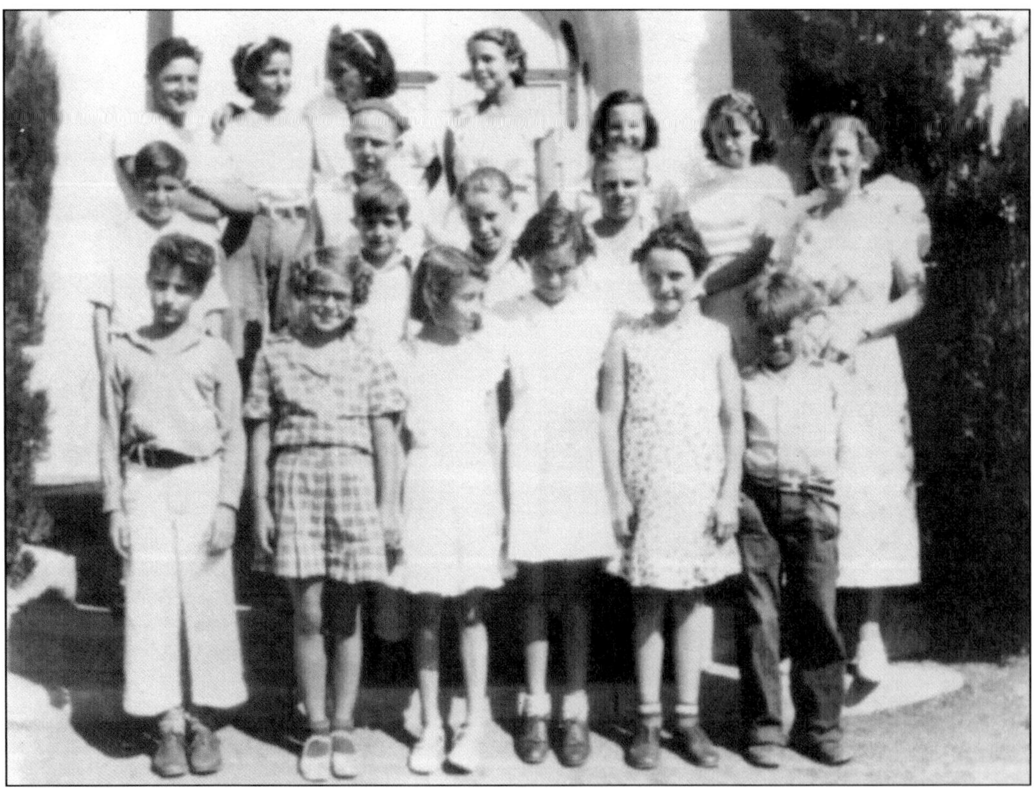

Although a well was eventually built, this school did not have an inside toilet until the late 1930s. In 1934, the Las Virgenes School had enrolled 12 students. Pictured here is the May 1935 class.

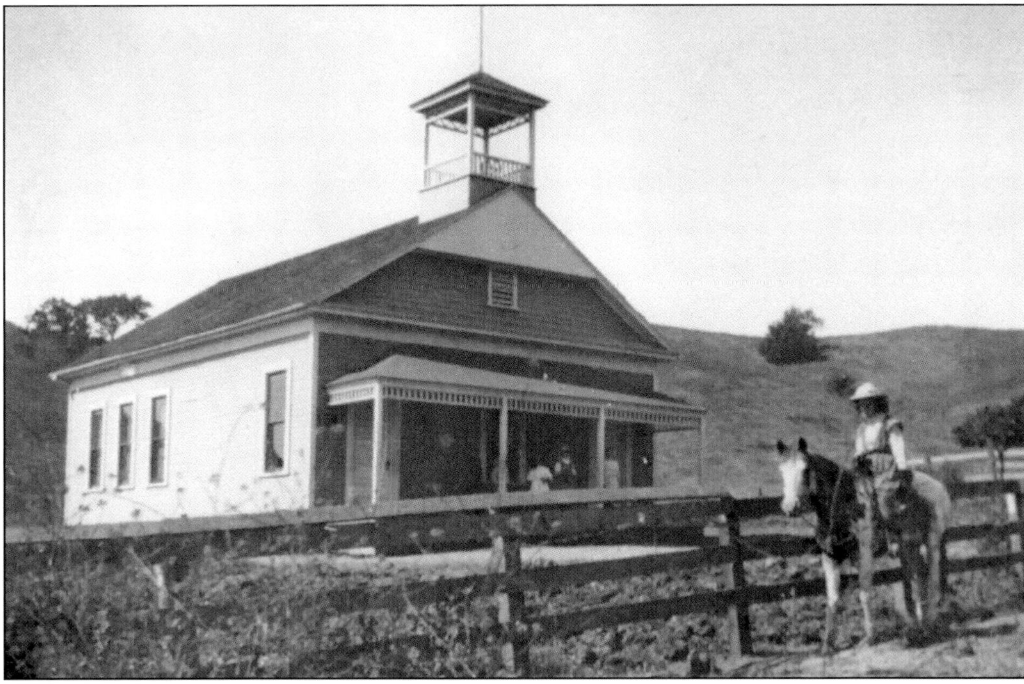

The Liberty School (south of Ventura Boulevard, west of Las Virgenes Road) was built in 1896. The land for the school was originally purchased for $1.87 from John Enos in May 1896. The Liberty School was the most affluent of the four small local schools. The horseback rider seen in the lower right-hand corner most likely rode her horse to school, which was common in those days.

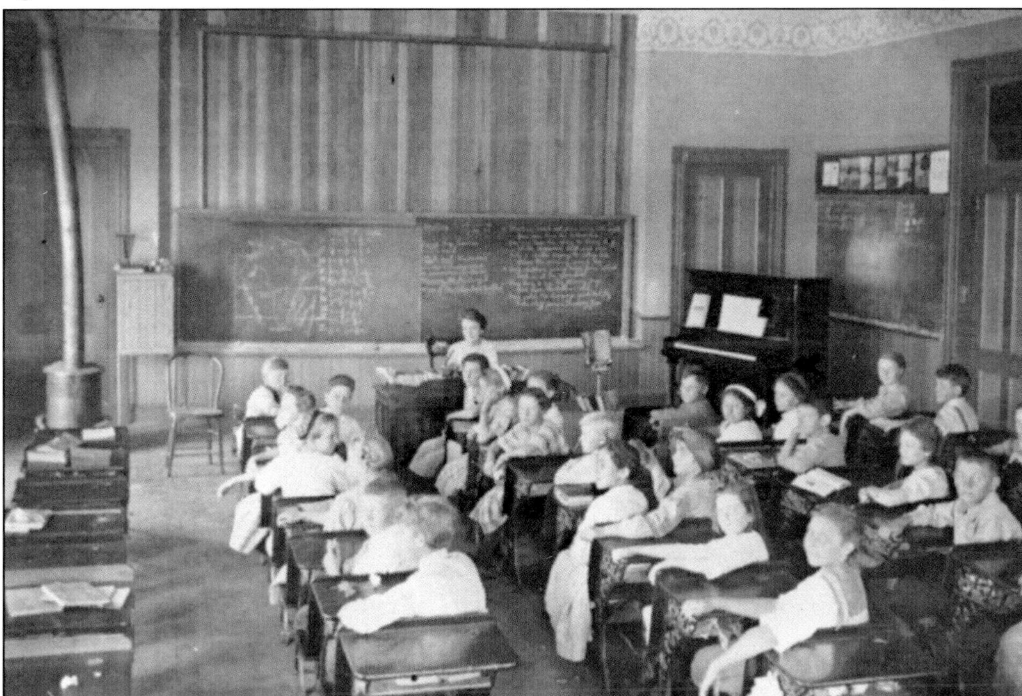

This is the interior of Liberty School's classroom as it appeared around 1910.

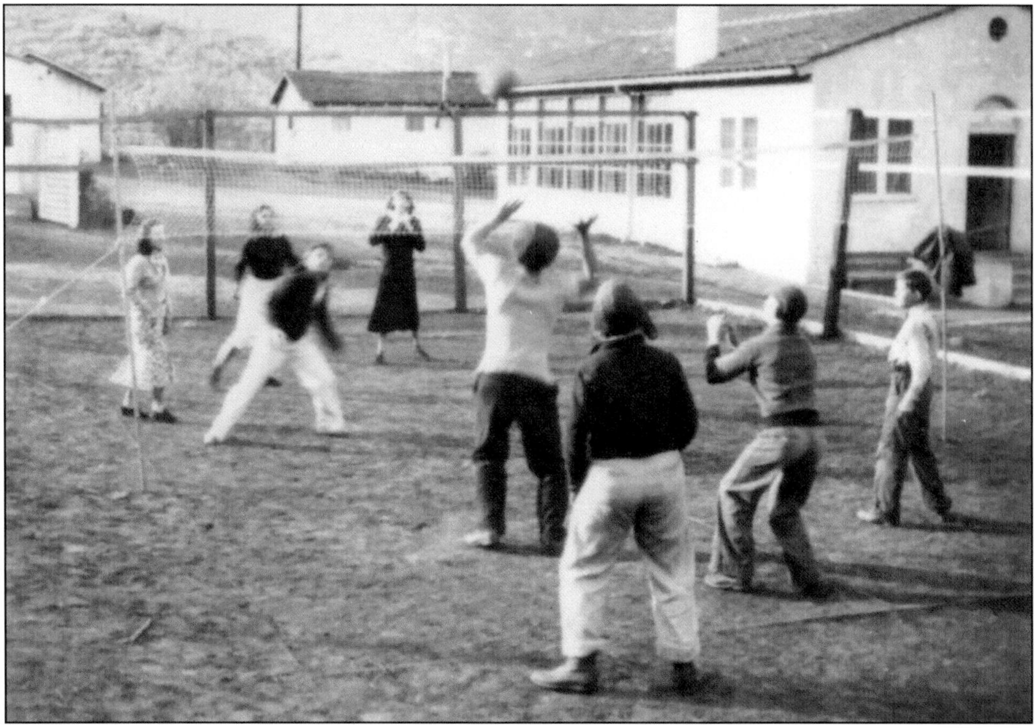

Las Virgenes School students play volleyball in front of the early buildings around 1936. The building at the top left housed the boys' and girls' restrooms. The little house in the back center was the teacher's house, and the building to the far right was the classroom. The children playing are, from left to right, Helen Reyes, Caroline Alvarez, Dorothy Combs, Dorothy Smith, George Smith, Tom Wernett, Clifford Frisk, and Leonard Combs.

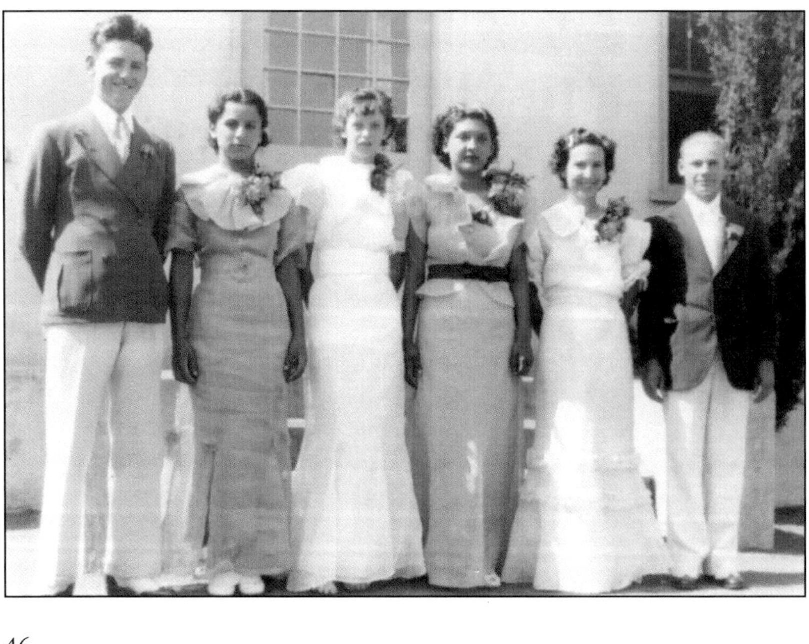

This photograph of the May 1936 Las Virgenes School eighth grade graduating class was taken at the east end of the library building. From left to right are George Smith, Dorothy Smith, Dorothy Combs, Caroline Alvarez, Helen Reyes, and Clifford Frisk.

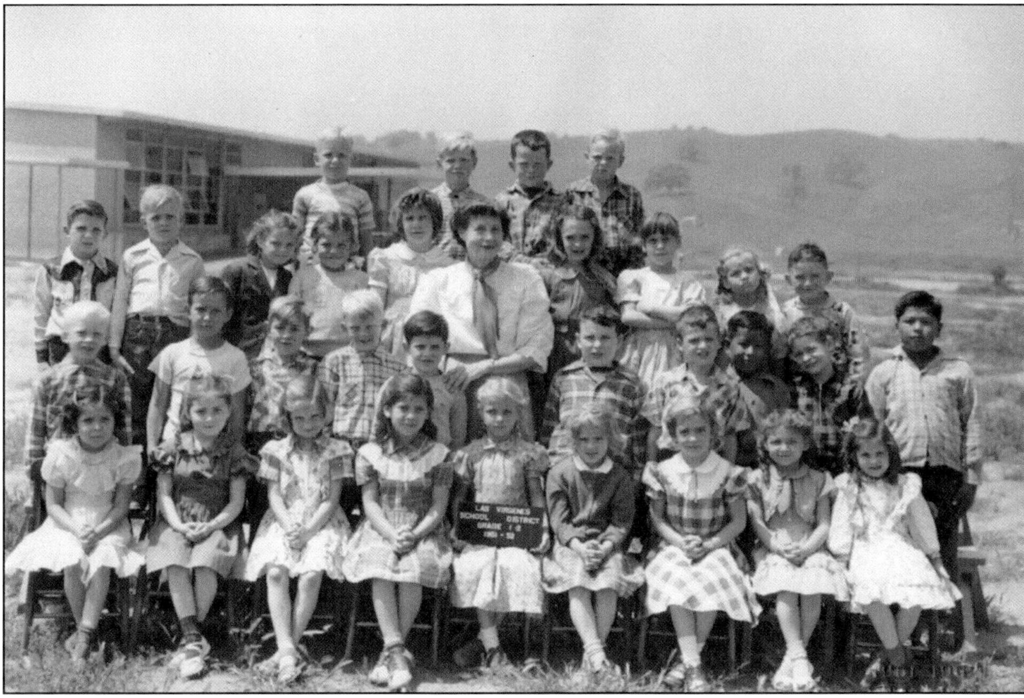

Here is revered teacher Theresa Thilmony and her 1951–1952 first and second grade class at the Las Virgenes School. The building in the background is still in use today at A.E. Wright Middle School. The hills seen in the background have now been developed into the residential communities of Calabasas View Estates, Deer Springs, and Steeplechase.

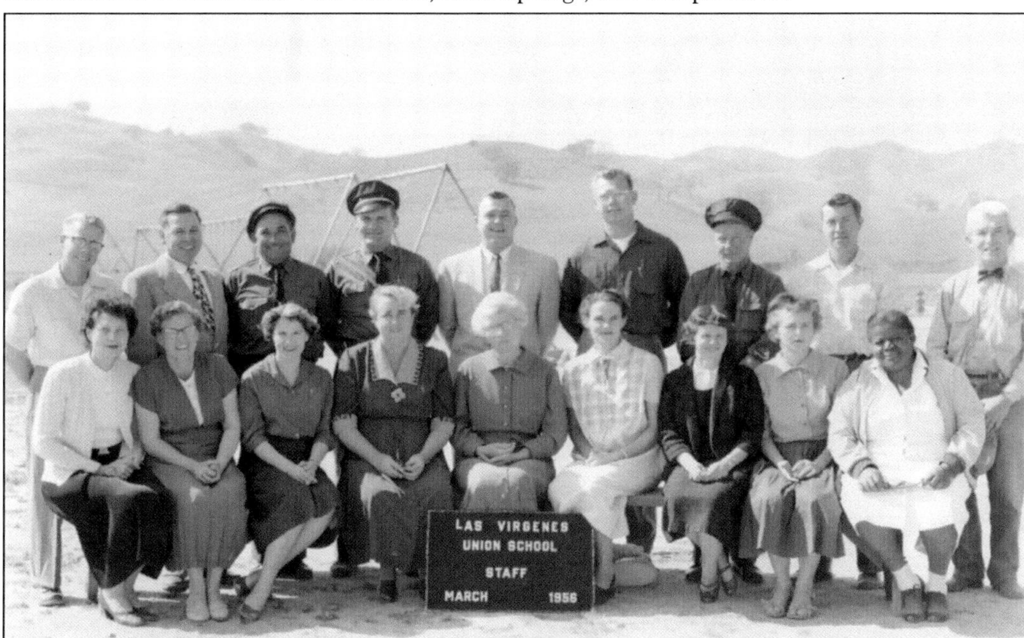

The Las Virgenes Union School faculty is pictured here on the school play yard in March 1956. Today, the rolling hills behind the staff have been developed into residential communities.

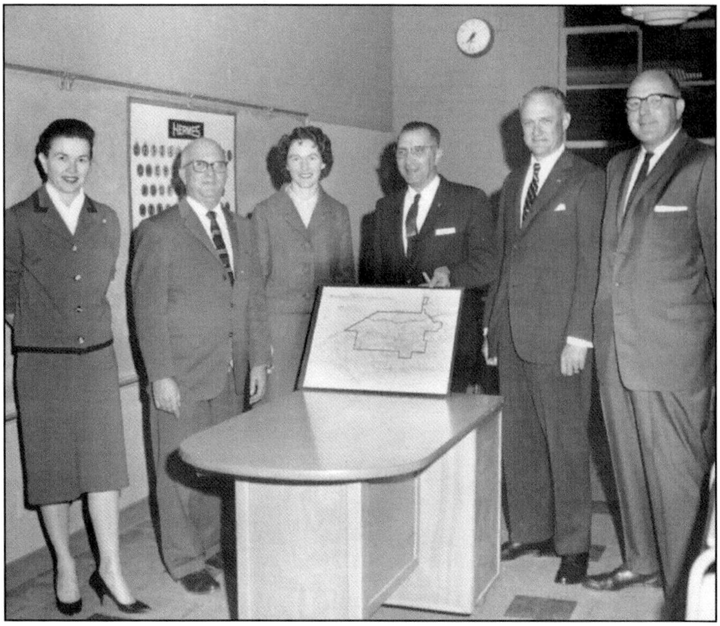

On July 1, 1962, the first Las Virgenes Unified School Board was elected, dissolving the Elementary and West County High School Board. On April 16, 1963, voters approved two propositions to finance the $2 million bond issue and $4 million state aid authorization needed to construct a high school and three elementary schools. From left to right are Jody White, Vern Martin, Arliss Wilhelm, Dr. Charles Carpenter, Wylie Drummond, and Don Courter.

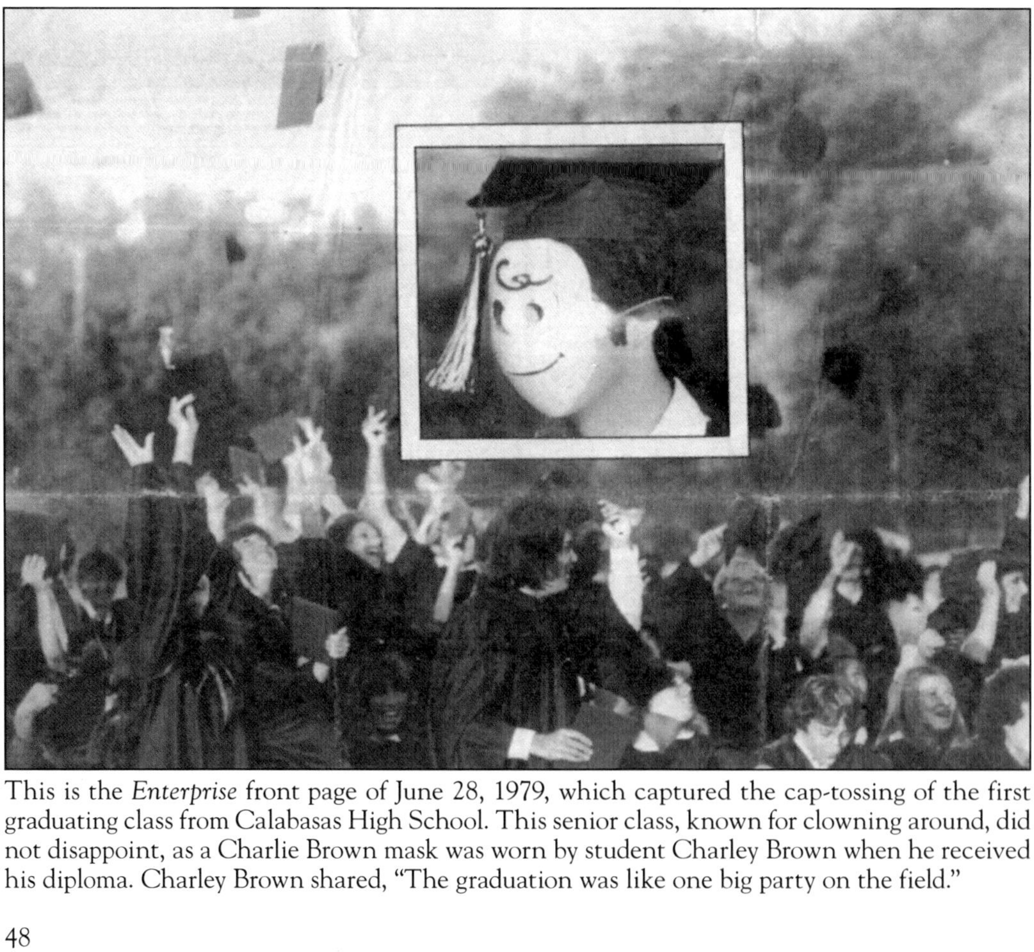

This is the *Enterprise* front page of June 28, 1979, which captured the cap-tossing of the first graduating class from Calabasas High School. This senior class, known for clowning around, did not disappoint, as a Charlie Brown mask was worn by student Charley Brown when he received his diploma. Charley Brown shared, "The graduation was like one big party on the field."

Four

A Tale of Two Communities

The city of Hidden Hills, a guard-gated community, is nestled in the westernmost foothills of the San Fernando Valley. The aesthetic is white three-rail fences, corrals, barns, and rustic equestrian trails. Street lights are limited to just one traffic signal, and bridle trails replace sidewalks.

Hidden Hills was first developed by A.E. Hanson, who, along with his son Archie, purchased the 1,000 acres to develop the community. Hanson involved his children in the process of naming the streets, hoping to inspire future generations to appreciate American history from 1805 to 1830. Two model homes were built in 1950, one of which was sold for $35,000 to one of the Dead End Kids, Leo Gorcy.

Lamond Chamberlain became the second major developer of Hidden Hills in 1956. A.E. Hanson turned over his declarant's rights and fee ownership of certain properties to the Hidden Hills Community Association and sold his undeveloped land to Hidden Hills Estates, Inc.

In 1961, the prospect of being annexed to the city of Los Angeles and having Burbank Boulevard extended through the community prompted Hidden Hills residents to rally and petition for cityhood. On October 19, 1961, Hidden Hills became the 73rd incorporated city in the county.

Park Moderne, also known as the Bird Streets, is believed to be the first planned subdivision in Calabasas. In 1927, William Lingenbrink, a patron of modern art, and his partner, C. Henry Taylor, acquired 140 acres of land northeast of Old Topanga Canyon Road from rancher Sam Cooper Jr. in exchange for a bathtub and plumbing for his ranch.

Lingenbrink commissioned architect Rudolph M. Schindler to design two community buildings on the site. Another architect, Jock Peters, known for creating the interior of the Los Angeles landmark and former Bullocks Wilshire Specialty store, created the Park Moderne clubhouse.

Lingenbrink's business model offered artists a portion of land in exchange for their art, which he then sold in a Sunset Boulevard gift shop. Among the colony's residents were portrait painter Paul von Kleiben, Dutch sculptor Jan de Swart, and Andy Anderson, a woodcarver whose figures were collected by presidents and actors.

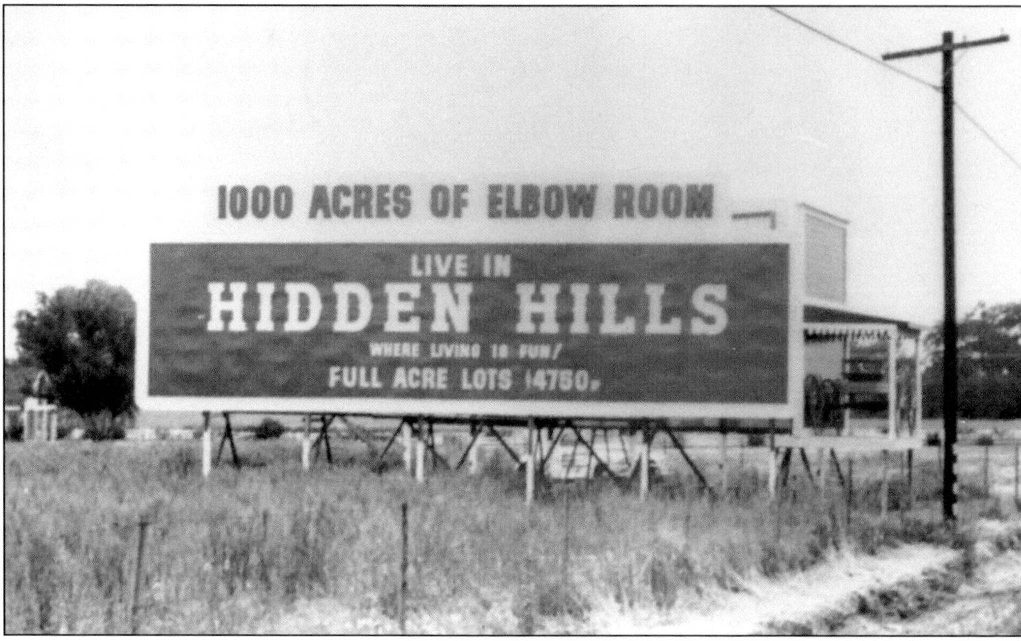

The development of Hidden Hills was advertised as "1000 Acres of Elbow Room, Live in Hidden Hills Where the Living is Fun." The development comprised 700 acres acquired in 1949 from E.E. Hurlbutt, 160 acres purchased in 1960 from Nace, et al, 20 acres from a Mrs. Lasher, 119 acres from the Straubinger family, and 5.6 acres from Spinks Realty Company. In 1950, acre lots in Hidden Hills sold for $4,750, which today are about 500 times that price. (Courtesy of the City of Hidden Hills.)

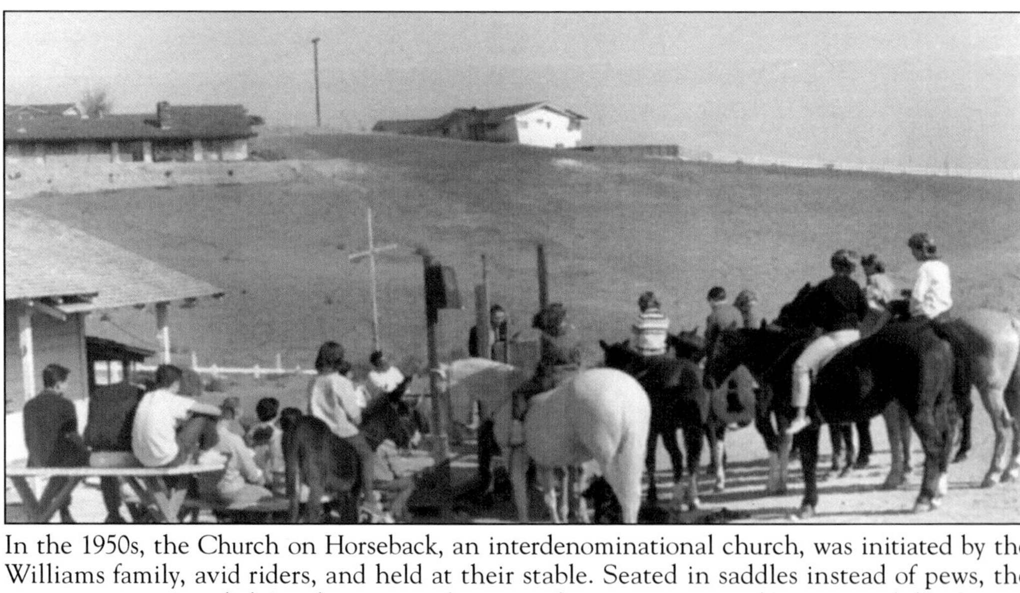

In the 1950s, the Church on Horseback, an interdenominational church, was initiated by the Williams family, avid riders, and held at their stable. Seated in saddles instead of pews, the congregation attended Sunday service for more than seven years. (Courtesy of the City of Hidden Hills.)

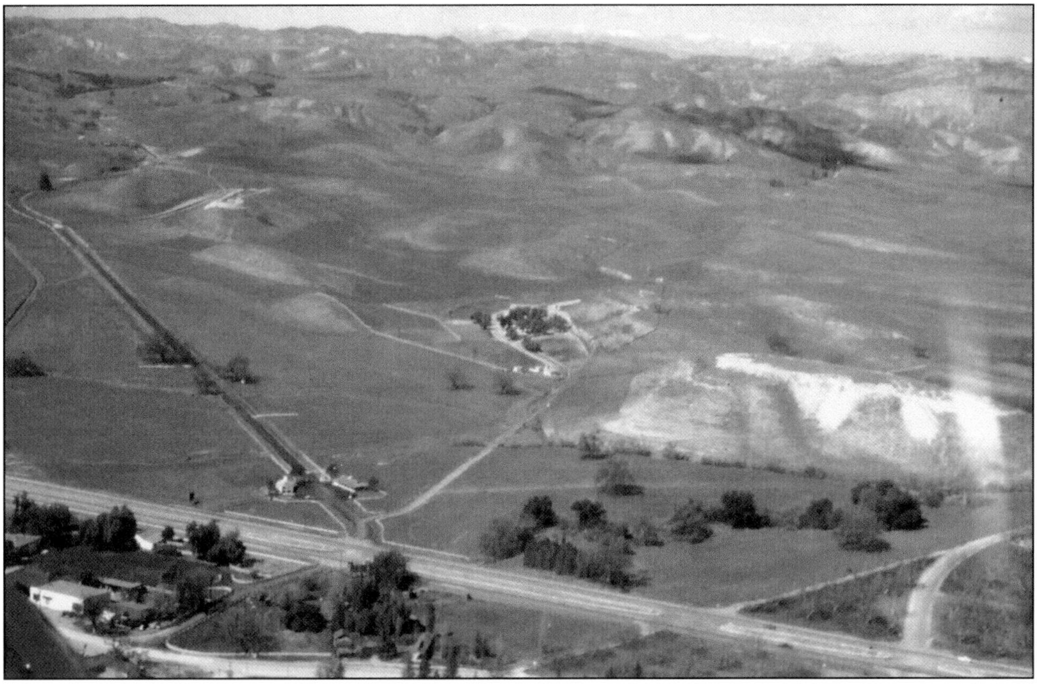

Above is an aerial view of Hidden Hills, Woodland Hills, and Calabasas in 1951. Ventura Boulevard is in the foreground, and Valley Circle is in the lower right corner. Two large oak trees (Twin Oaks Road) at the left of center identify Long Valley Road in Hidden Hills. "Wild Bill" Elliot Ranch, best remembered for the Red Ryder series of 16 movies about a famous comic strip cowboy, is at the right of center. "Wild Bill" also starred in the 1950s film production *The Homesteaders*, shot at Lasky Mesa. The photograph below shows an advertising billboard that was placed at the entrance to Hidden Hills in December 1965. (Both, courtesy of the City of Hidden Hills.)

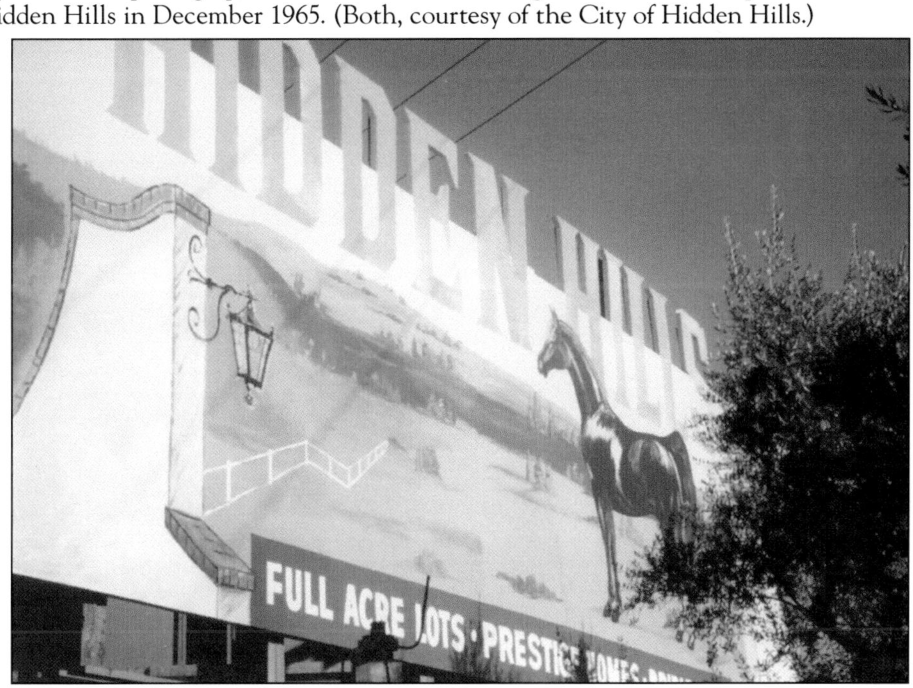

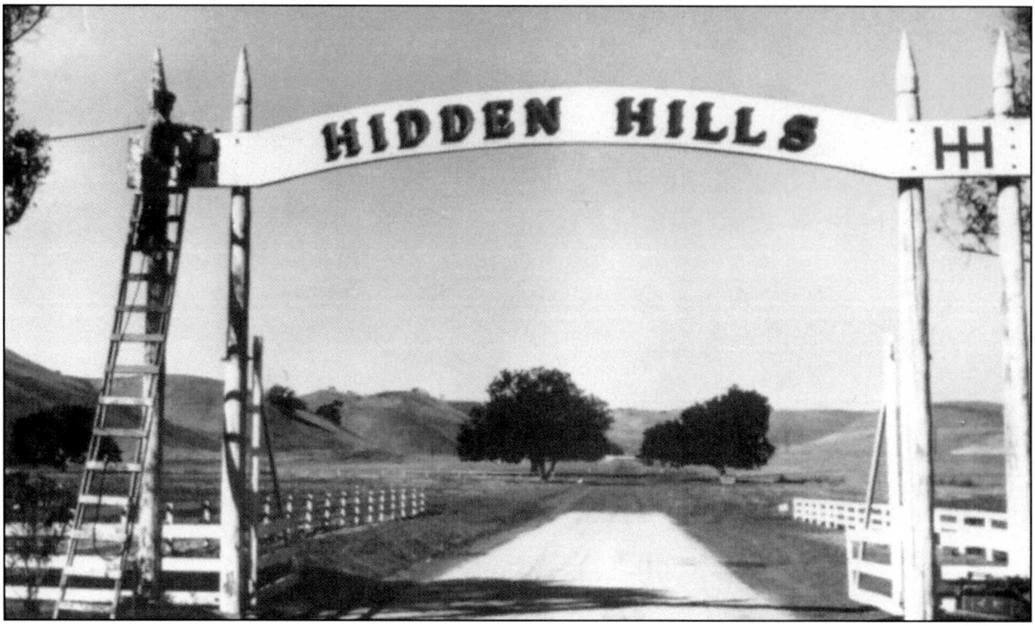

Pictured here is the entrance to the Hidden Hills community in 1950. A worker in the top left corner is putting the finishing touches on the main entrance. The first sections of the three-rail white fences have just been installed. (Courtesy of the City of Hidden Hills.)

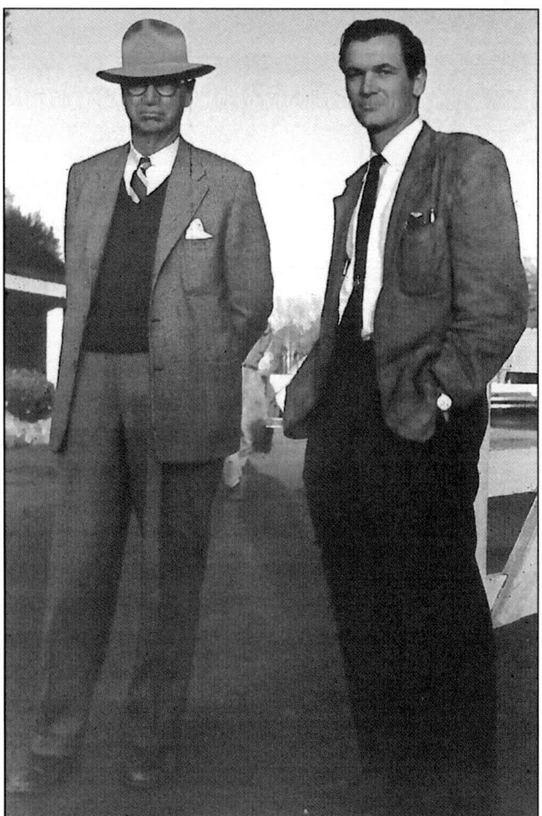

Here are Hidden Hills developers A.E. Hanson (left) and his son Archie Hanson (right). A.E. Hanson once said when describing their development philosophy, "We attempted to follow the natural contours of the land whenever possible." (Courtesy of the City of Hidden Hills.)

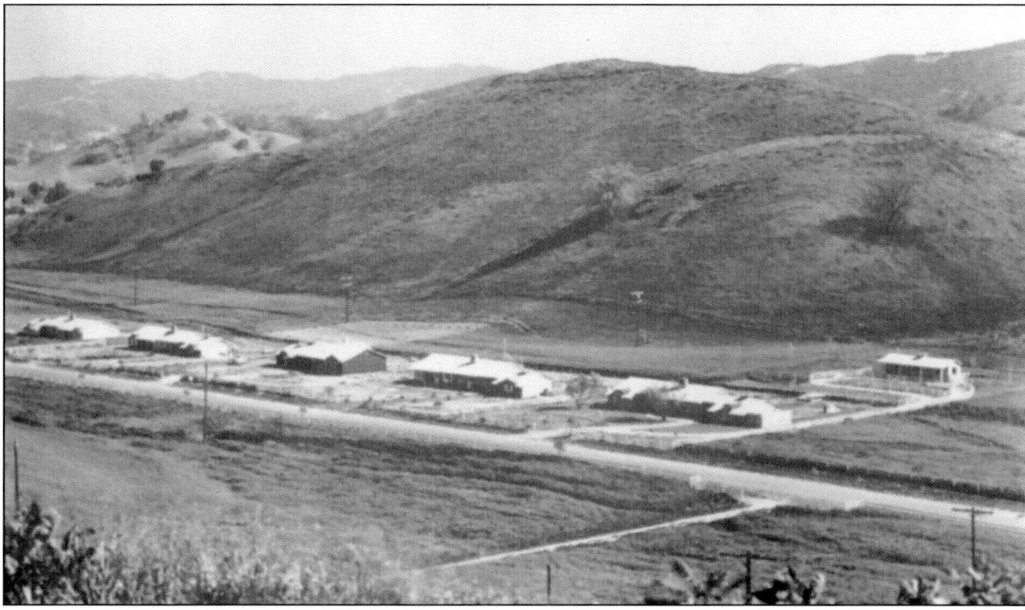

Pictured here is the early road construction of Long Valley Road in Hidden Hills, June 1950. While grading at the corner of Long Valley and Clear Valley Roads, a 20-foot-long whale skeleton, believed to be from the Late Miocene Era, was uncovered. Archie Hanson contacted paleontologists at the Los Angeles Natural History Museum to investigate. Unfortunately, locals absconded with many of the bones before the paleontologists arrived.

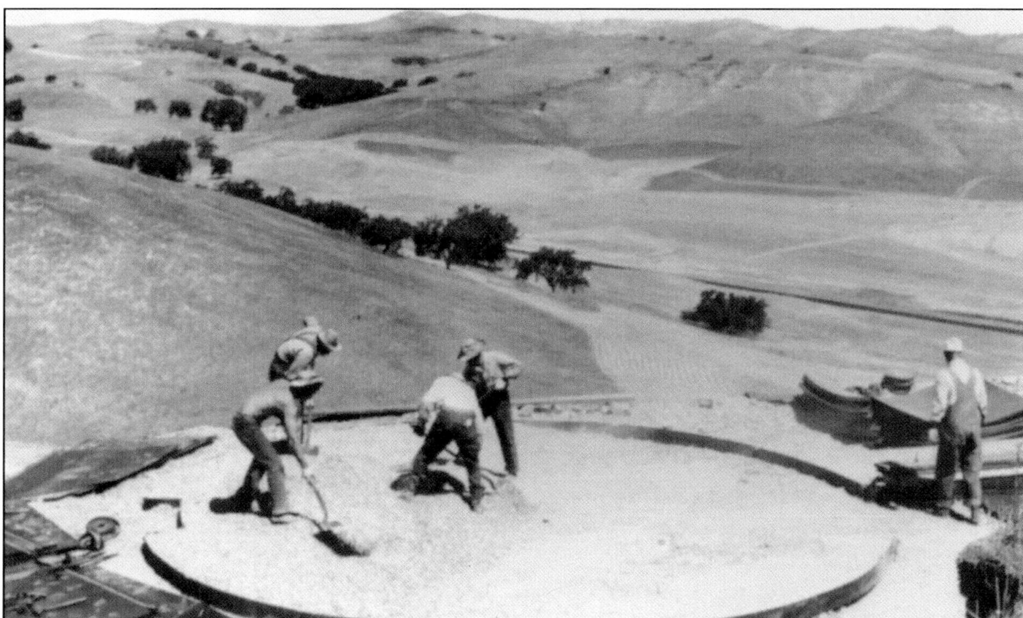

The construction of the No. 1 water tank took place in 1950. Long Valley Road is seen in the background and a view of Crummer Ranch is in the upper left corner. In 1949, R.E. Crummer bought George E. Barrett Jr.'s Malibu and Calabasas holdings, which included the land later known as the Ahmanson Ranch property. (Courtesy of the City of Hidden Hills.)

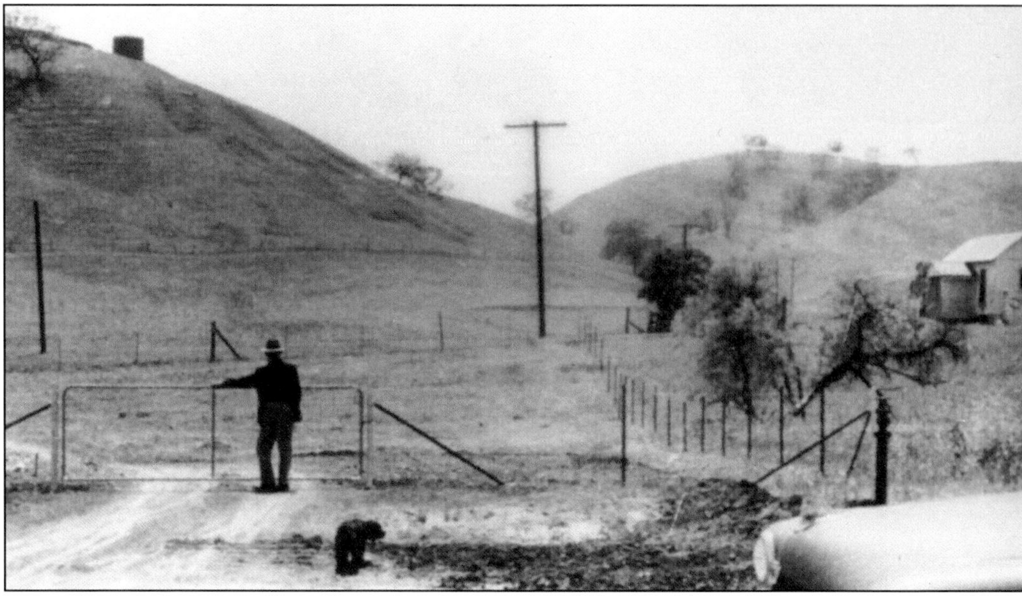

The old building on the right is the Leffingwell homestead. There was a local rumor that gold was buried under the house, but it was never found. Seen on the skyline is the No. 1 water tank. The car is on Long Valley Road, and the wire gate is the center line of what was to become Round Meadow Road in 1951. (Courtesy of the City of Hidden Hills.)

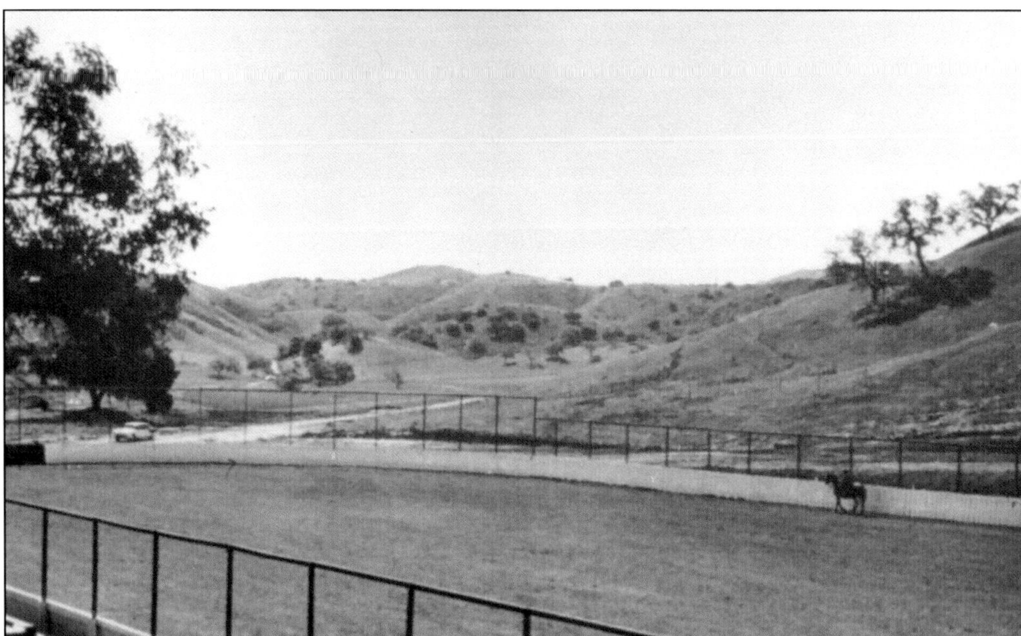

Pictured here is the polo field, now the home at 24925 Lewis and Clark Road. The car is parked on what is today Jed Smith Road. The trees in the foreground are at the intersection of Jed Smith and Round Meadow Road. The road was named after the obvious round meadow above the field. Long Valley Road was named because it was a lengthy thoroughfare through a valley. (Courtesy of the City of Hidden Hills.)

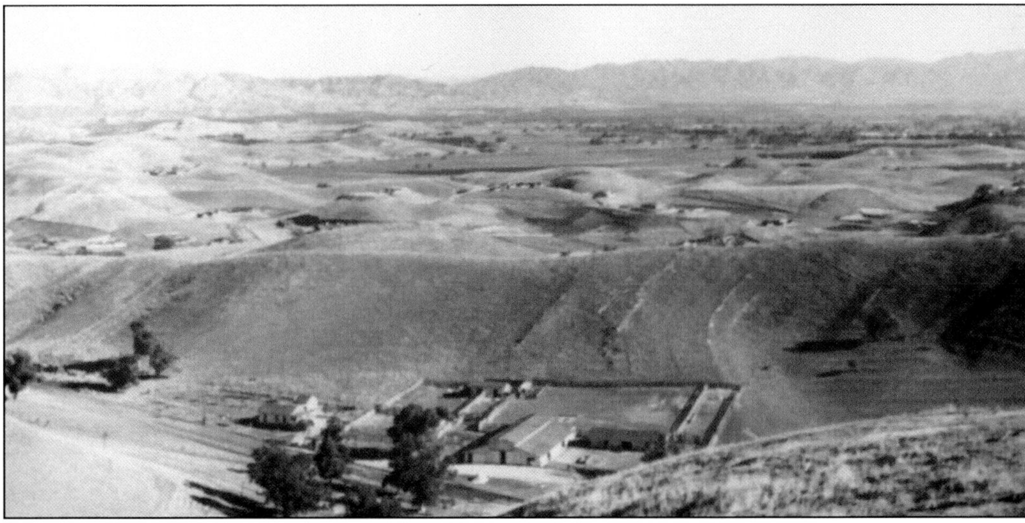

The Calarbia Ranch, a 700-acre ranch owned by Mrs. E.E. Hurlbutt, is pictured here in 1954. Shown is the intersection of today's Jed Smith Road and Lewis and Clark Road; the large barn is located at about 5494 Jed Smith Road. The Hurlbutt home, the last building in the group on the left, is located at about 5546 Jed Smith Road. The polo field was located to the right of the eucalyptus trees.

The Glory Ranch was located at the northwest corner of Hidden Hills, off Jed Smith Road. The ranch was a dude ranch for children, "to provide the opportunity for young folks to enjoy a Western vacation." Children could be sent to camp for a week at the cost of $60. The ranch star was Top Hat, a registered Palomino that won reserve champion in 1953 and champion in 1954.

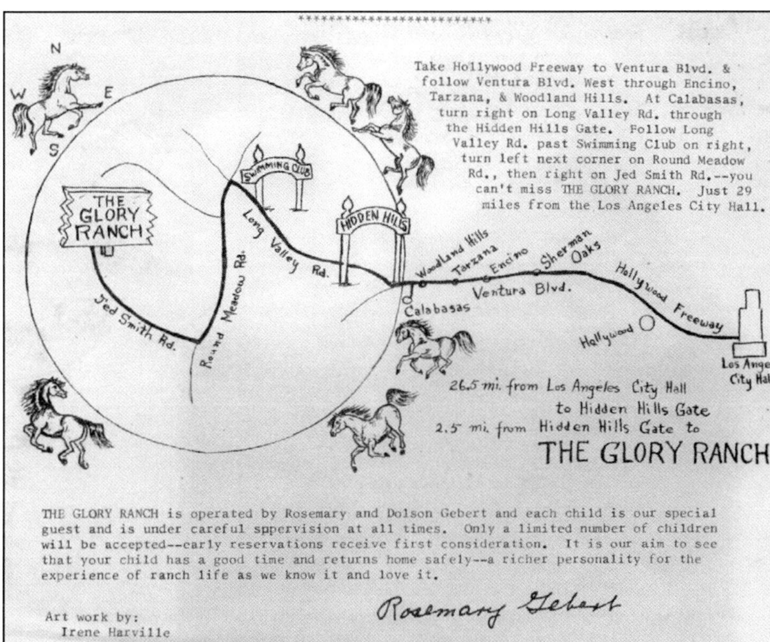

Take Hollywood Freeway to Ventura Blvd. & follow Ventura Blvd. West through Encino, Tarzana, & Woodland Hills. At Calabasas, turn right on Long Valley Rd. through the Hidden Hills Gate. Follow Long Valley Rd. past Swimming Club on right, turn left next corner on Round Meadow Rd., then right on Jed Smith Rd.--you can't miss THE GLORY RANCH. Just 29 miles from the Los Angeles City Hall.

N
W
E
S
THE GLORY RANCH
SWIMMING CLUB
HIDDEN HILLS
Long Valley Rd.
Round Meadow Rd.
Jed Smith Rd.
Woodland Hills
Tarzana
Encino
Sherman Oaks
Ventura Blvd.
Calabasas
Hollywood Freeway
Hollywood
Los Angeles City Hall

26.5 mi. from Los Angeles City Hall to Hidden Hills Gate
2.5 mi. from Hidden Hills Gate to
THE GLORY RANCH

THE GLORY RANCH is operated by Rosemary and Dolson Gebert and each child is our special guest and is under careful sppervision at all times. Only a limited number of children will be accepted--early reservations receive first consideration. It is our aim to see that your child has a good time and returns home safely--a richer personality for the experience of ranch life as we know it and love it.

Rosemary Gebert

Art work by:
Irene Harville
Spring Valley, Cal.

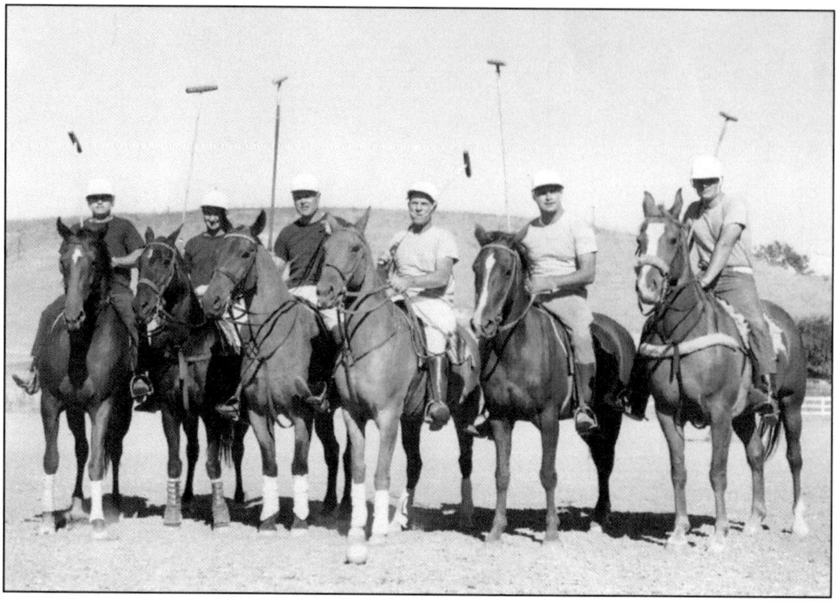

At one time, Hidden Hills was said to be the community that was thc home to more horses than residents. Here are members of the polo team dressed in uniform. (Courtesy of the City of Hidden Hills.)

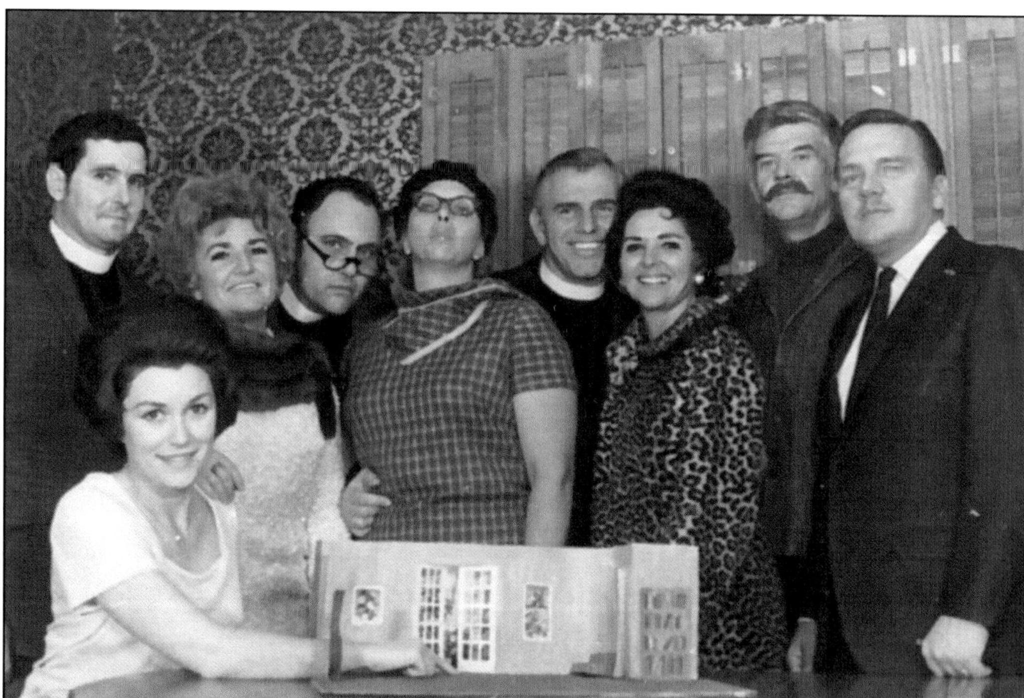

Pictured here is the cast from the first Hidden Hills Players production of *Curse You Jed Smith*, an original adaptation of the melodrama *Curse You, Jim Dalton!* The performance was at the Round Meadow Elementary School auditorium in the late 1960s. The cast included Hidden Hills residents Ronald Gero, Sandra Donham (director), Shelia Bryan, Norman Sellinger, Elinor Beckman, Tom Lindholm, Gina Mooneyham, Chuck Brown, and Mel McKeller. (Courtesy of the City of Hidden Hills.)

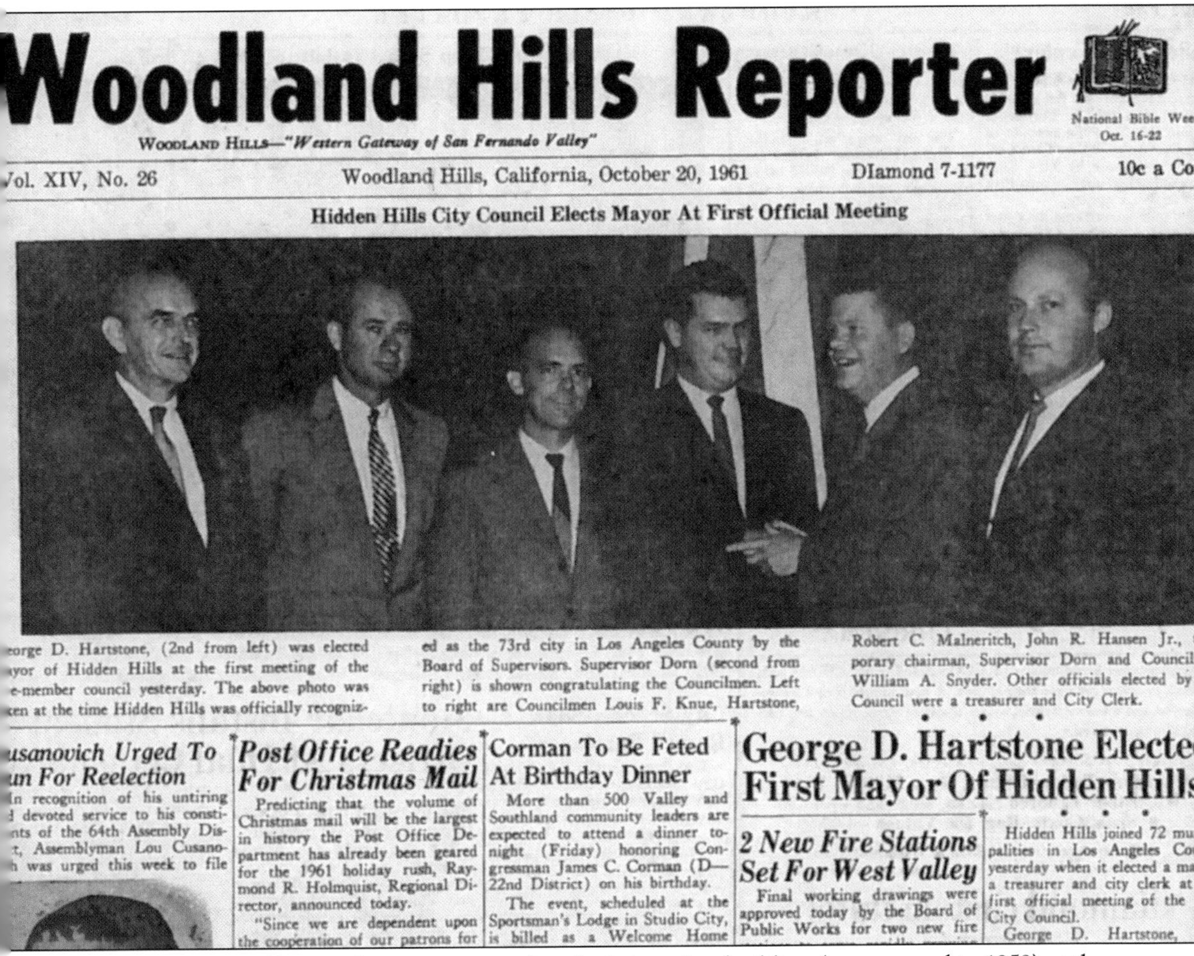

Woodland Hills Reporter

WOODLAND HILLS—"*Western Gateway of San Fernando Valley*"

National Bible Week Oct. 16-22

Vol. XIV, No. 26 | Woodland Hills, California, October 20, 1961 | DIamond 7-1177 | 10c a Co

Hidden Hills City Council Elects Mayor At First Official Meeting

eorge D. Hartstone, (2nd from left) was elected ayor of Hidden Hills at the first meeting of the e-member council yesterday. The above photo was en at the time Hidden Hills was officially recogniz- ed as the 73rd city in Los Angeles County by the Board of Supervisors. Supervisor Dorn (second from right) is shown congratulating the Councilmen. Left to right are Councilmen Louis F. Knue, Hartstone, Robert C. Malneritch, John R. Hansen Jr., t porary chairman, Supervisor Dorn and Councilr William A. Snyder. Other officials elected by Council were a treasurer and City Clerk.

usanovich Urged To un For Reelection

In recognition of his untiring d devoted service to his consti- nts of the 64th Assembly Dis- t, Assemblyman Lou Cusano- h was urged this week to file

Post Office Readies For Christmas Mail

Predicting that the volume of Christmas mail will be the largest in history the Post Office Department has already been geared for the 1961 holiday rush, Raymond R. Holmquist, Regional Director, announced today.

"Since we are dependent upon the cooperation of our patrons for

Corman To Be Feted At Birthday Dinner

More than 500 Valley and Southland community leaders are expected to attend a dinner tonight (Friday) honoring Congressman James C. Corman (D—22nd District) on his birthday.

The event, scheduled at the Sportsman's Lodge in Studio City, is billed as a Welcome Home

George D. Hartstone Electe First Mayor Of Hidden Hills

2 New Fire Stations Set For West Valley

Final working drawings were approved today by the Board of Public Works for two new fire

Hidden Hills joined 72 mur palities in Los Angeles Cou yesterday when it elected a ma a treasurer and city clerk at first official meeting of the City Council.

George D. Hartstone,

On August 21, 1962, at its first meeting in the administration building (constructed in 1959) at the Hidden Hills Swim Club on Long Valley Road, the new Hidden Hills City Council adopted its first budget of $18,088. The first Hidden Hills Fiesta was held on October 20, 1962, to celebrate the first anniversary of the city's incorporation on October 19, 1961. Monte Montana Jr. was the first grand marshal of the parade that started at 12:00 p.m. on Long Valley Road at Oakfield Road. Other activities included a horse show with a roping exhibition by Monte Montana, a barbecue dinner, and a teenagers' dance and entertainment, recruited from local talent. The annual celebration has continued over the years, growing into a huge party and gathering of neighbors honoring the birth of this unique little city. The 1961 *Woodland Hills Reporter* headline above shows, from left to right, Councilmember Louis F. Knue, Mayor George Hartstone, Councilmember Robert C. Malneritch, Councilmember John R. Hansen Jr., William Dorn (Los Angeles County Board of Supervisors), and Councilmember William A. Snyder. (Courtesy of the City of Hidden Hills.)

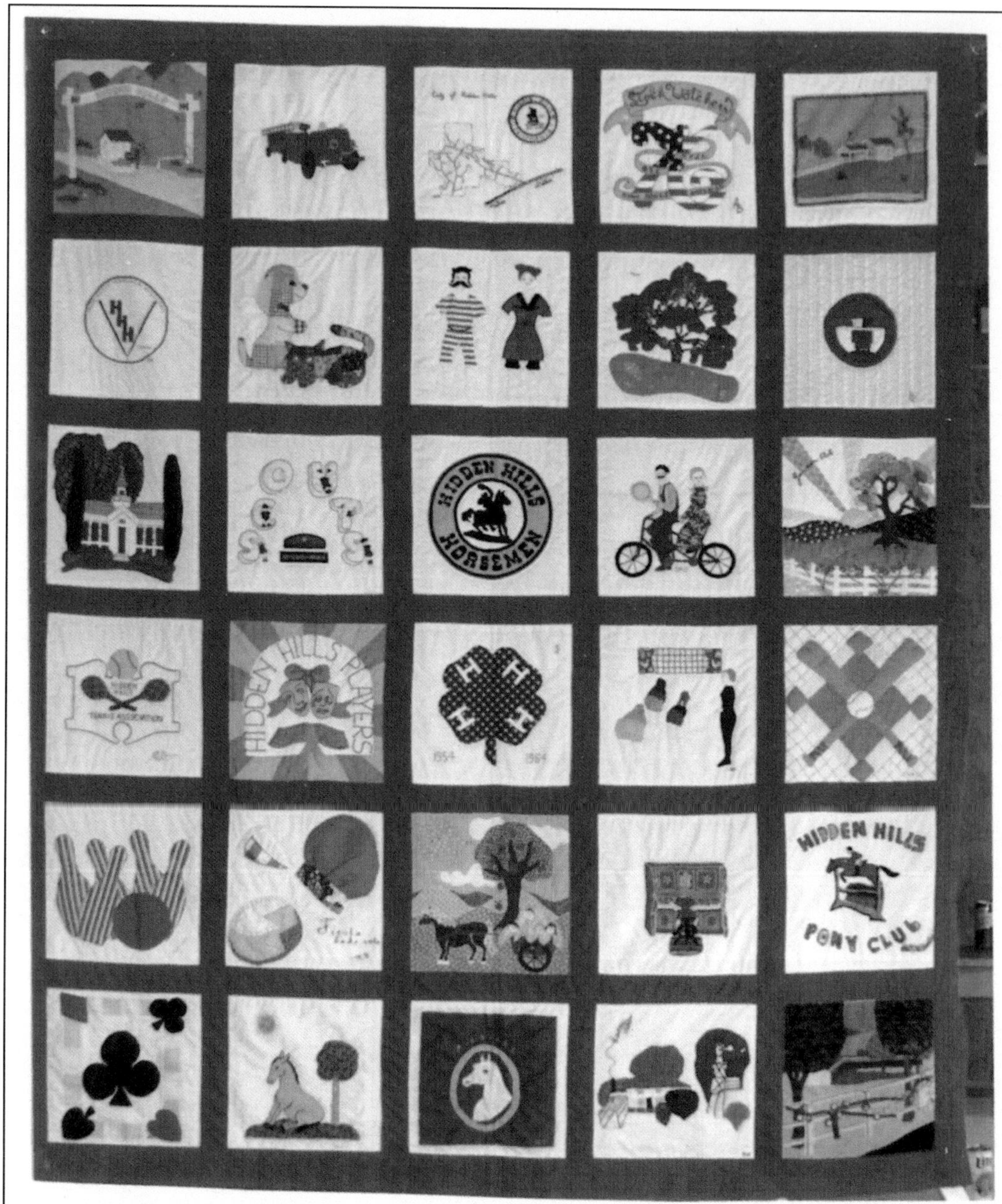

This is a quilt that was created for the 1976 Hidden Hills Fiesta. Each section represents a community landmark or organization. Sewers included Bunny Herdeg, Margaret Fredricks, Frieda Boyle, Coleen and Amy Hartman, Ann Bruskrud, Sara LeBien, Suzanne Kovner, Erin Herdeg, Linda Higgins, Nancy Faner, Stella Lindholm, Margaret Hampton, Doris Shephard, Rita Jewell, Girl Scouts, The Hidden Hills Horsemen Association, Gloria Spencer, Betsy Moore, Rita Green, Judy Leach, Agnes Kurzeka, Eleanor DeCarteret, Susie DeMott, Marilyn Yetter, Gertrude Reed, Mel Blackwell, Susan Black, Lyla Grant, Lola Warner, Gusti Snapp, Gray Burro, Margaret Teagle, Arliss Wilhelm, and Mary Hrabe. (Courtesy of the City of Hidden Hills.)

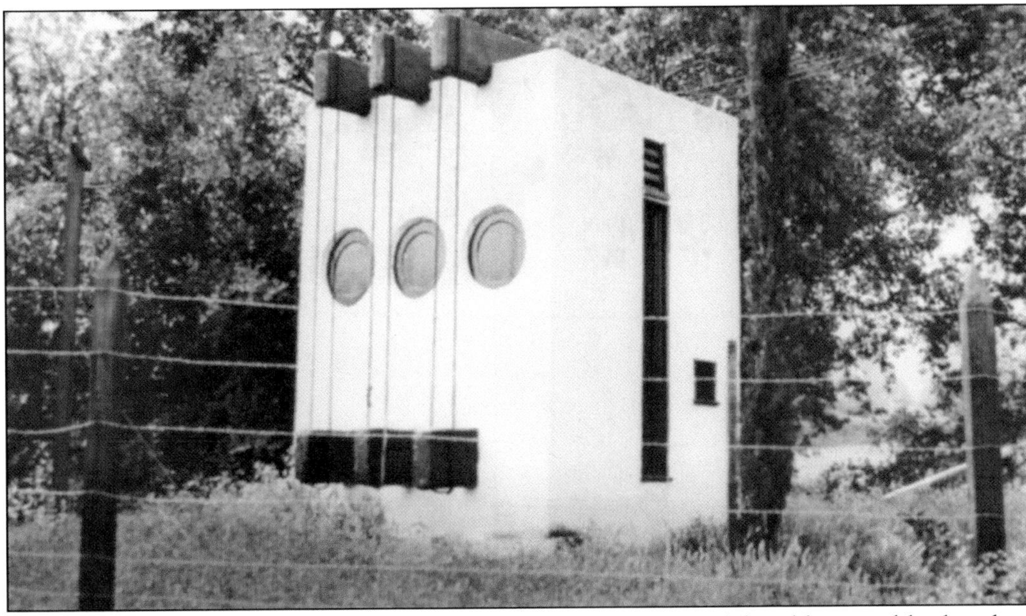

This is the pump house in the Park Moderne development, one of the oldest neighborhoods in Calabasas. Remnants remain of the clubhouse, pool, and cabins scattered across streets with bird names such as Meadow Lark Drive, Black Bird Way, Blue Bird Drive, and Humming Bird Way.

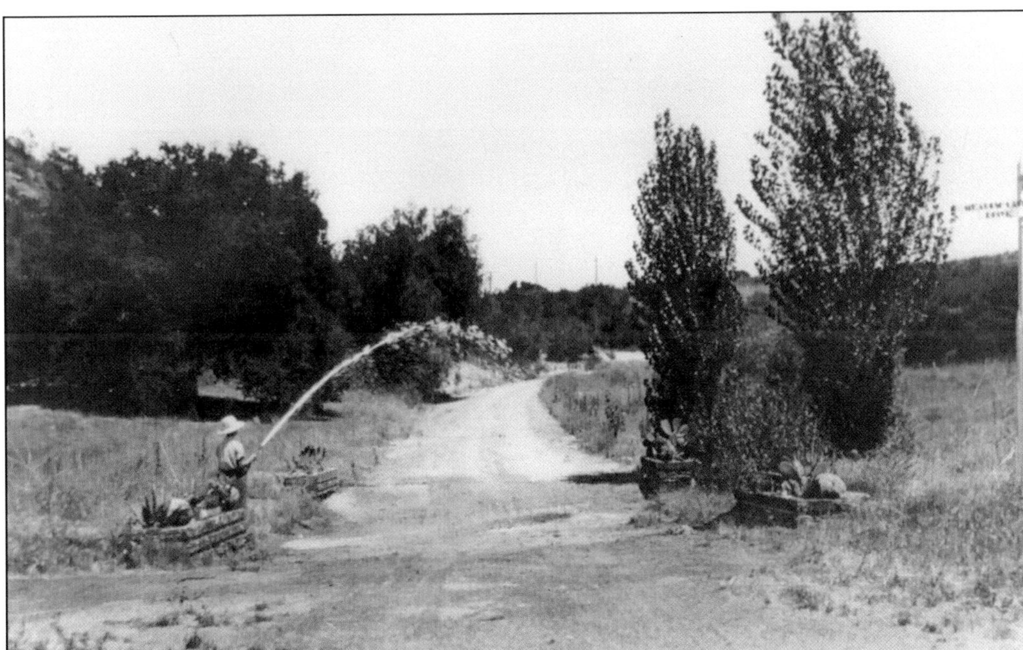

This photograph, taken by C. Henry Taylor and dated May 4, 1949, features the corner of Meadow Lark Drive at Blue Bird Drive.

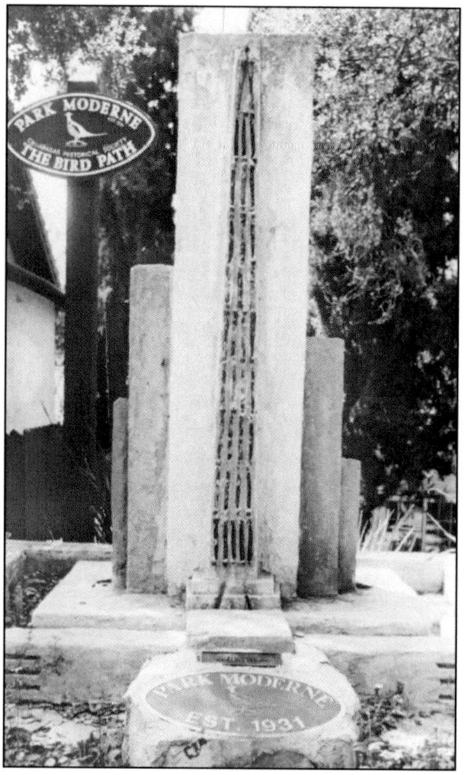

This Park Moderne fountain, built by Jock Peters in the 1920s, is the last remaining fountain in this artist community that was envisioned to feature walking paths, pools, and artistic fountains throughout. The Zigzag fountain is located on a Native American footpath that can still be enjoyed in what are now called "the bird streets." In 2011, the City of Calabasas dedicated the Zigzag fountain and the Bird Path as Calabasas Historical Landmark No. 5.

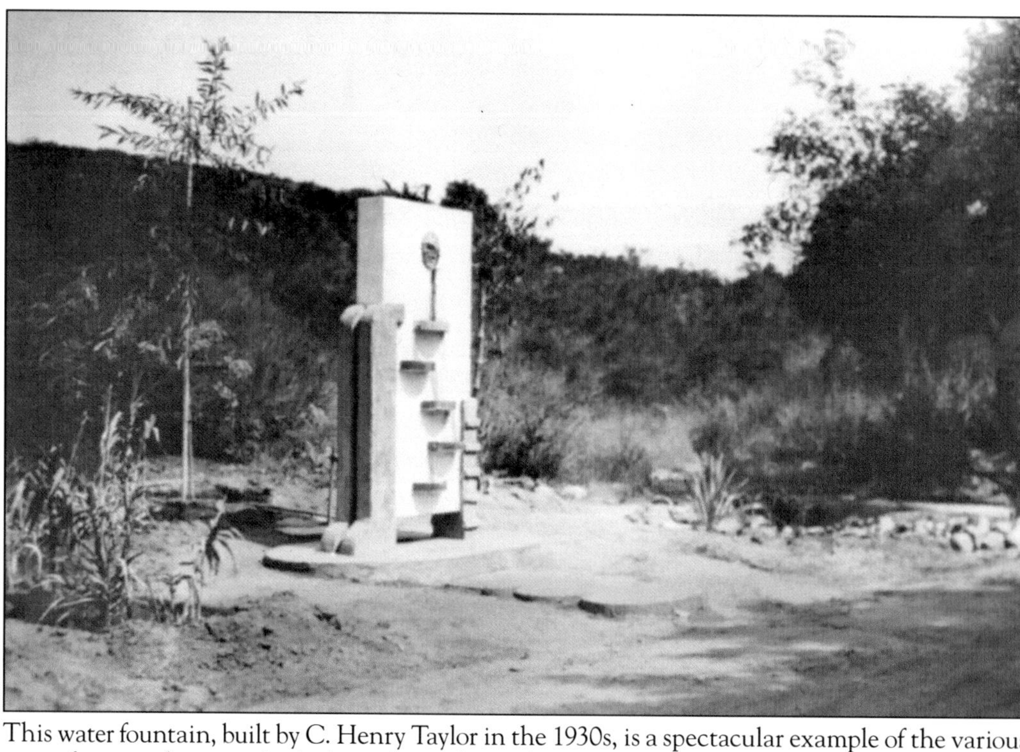

This water fountain, built by C. Henry Taylor in the 1930s, is a spectacular example of the various water features that were built throughout the park.

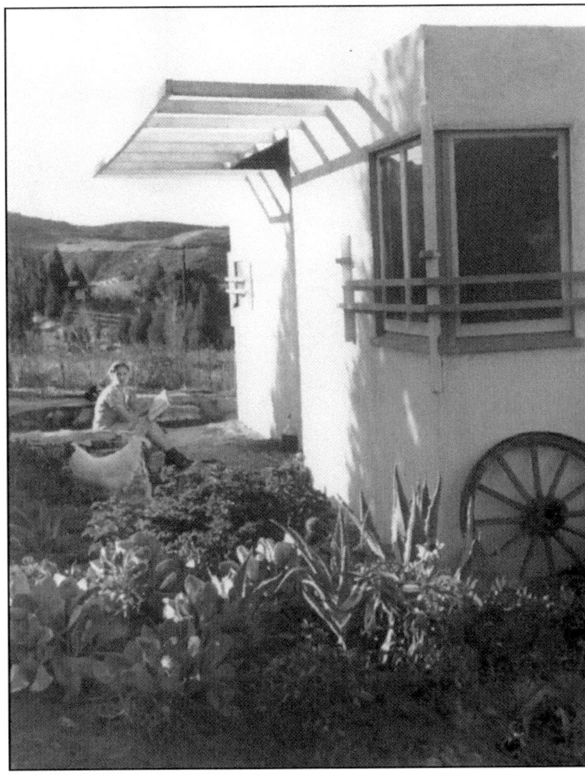

Pictured at right around 1930 is the second home of Jan de Swart. Artist de Swart, a famous sculptor working in concrete, metal, and plastic, was the first resident in Park Moderne. Below, Jock Peters's daughters are clasping hands around the artist's totem pole, which was hand-carved from a telephone pole.

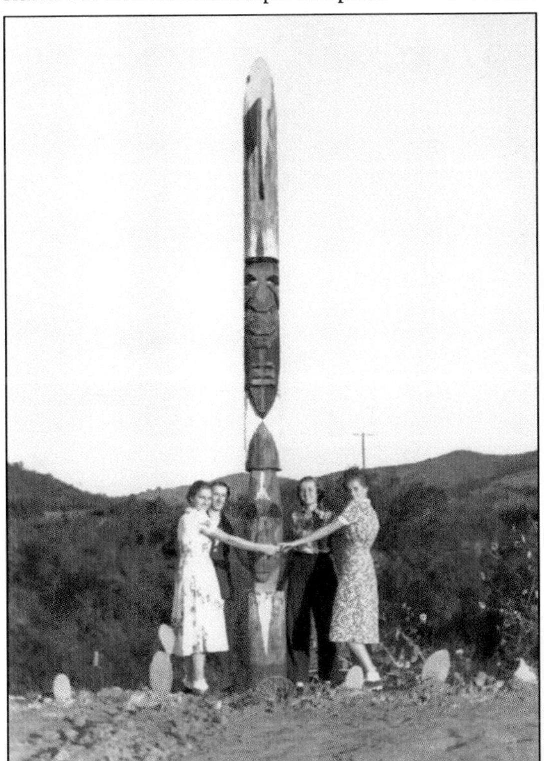

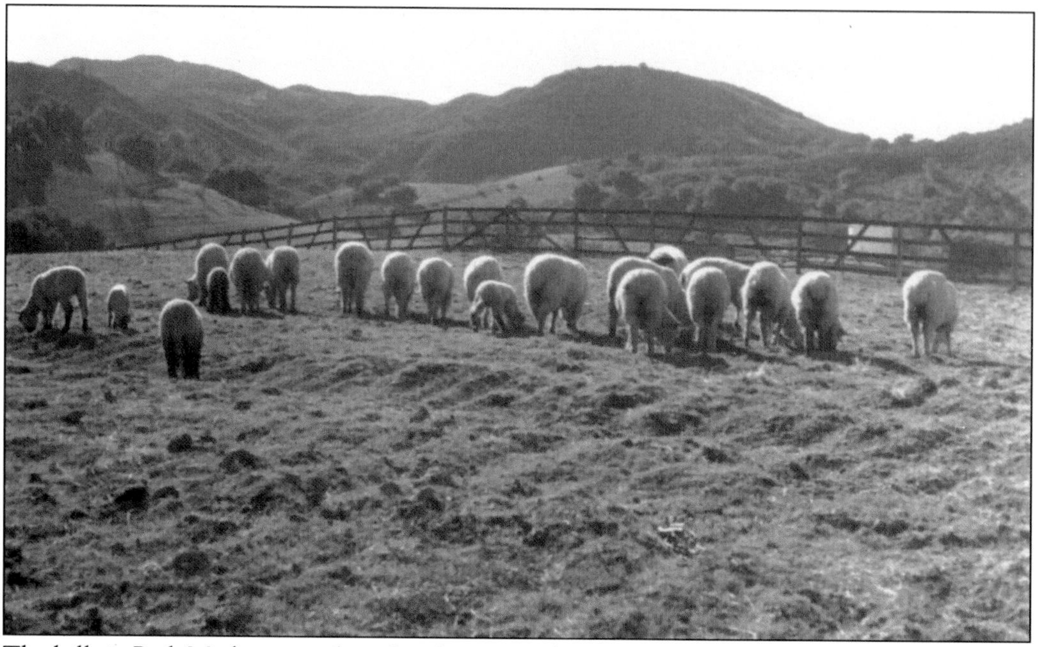

The hills in Park Moderne are dotted with grazing sheep, most likely on the Fosters Ranch. This view from around 1940 is close to the current location of Calabasas High School.

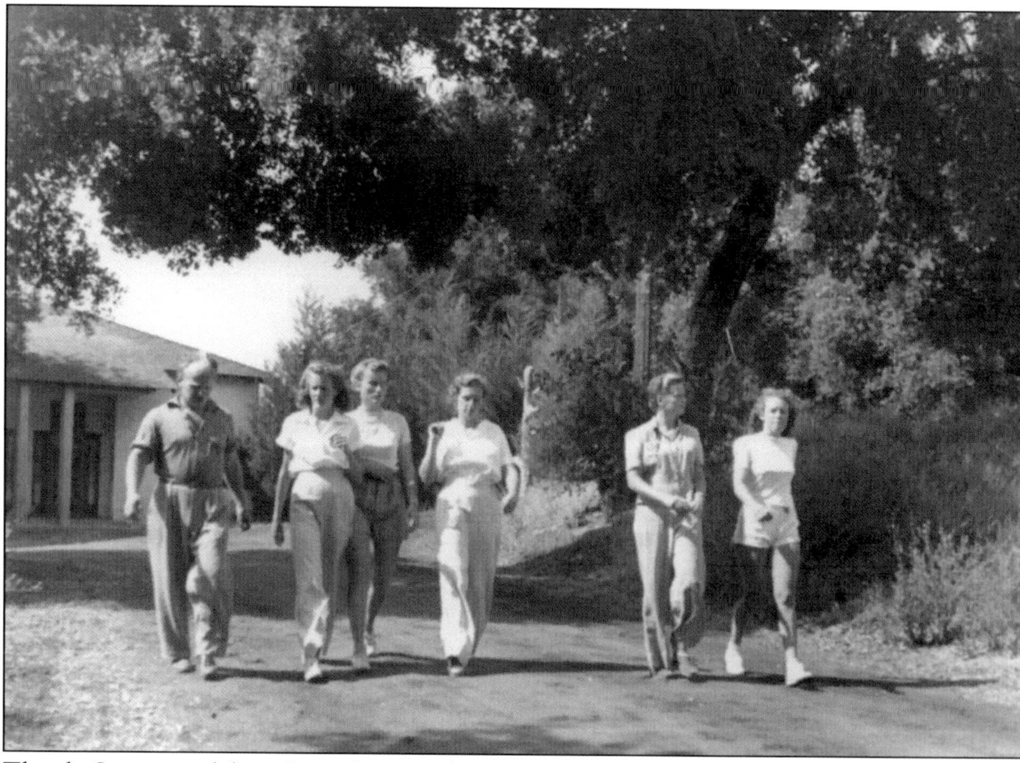

The de Swarts and friends stride past the Park Moderne clubhouse on an afternoon walk around 1930.

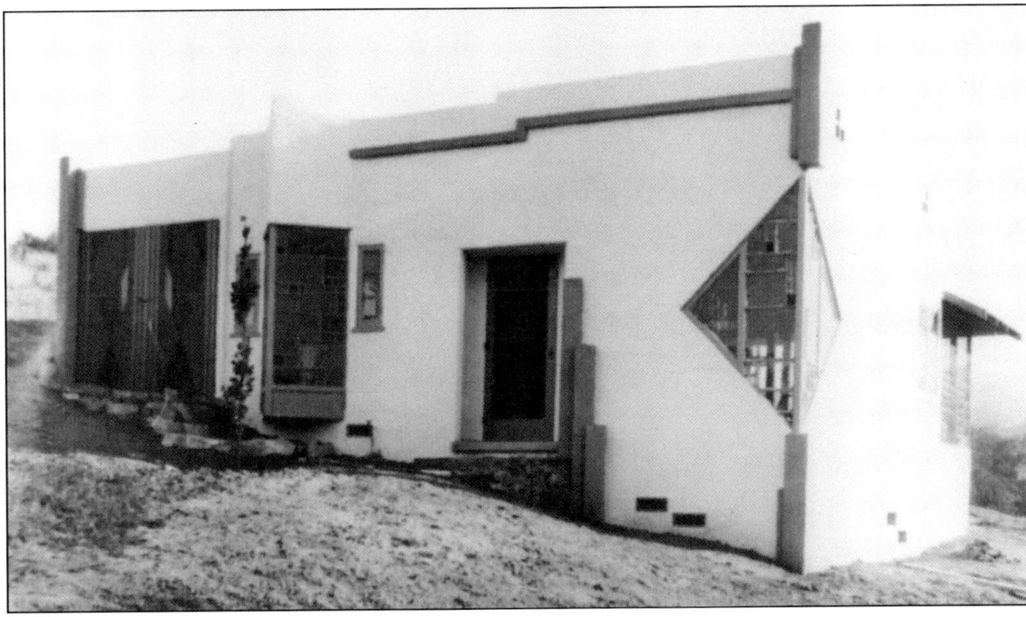

This is an example of architect Rudolph Schindler's design at 3993 Blackbird Way. There are still trace remains from the original studio seen today.

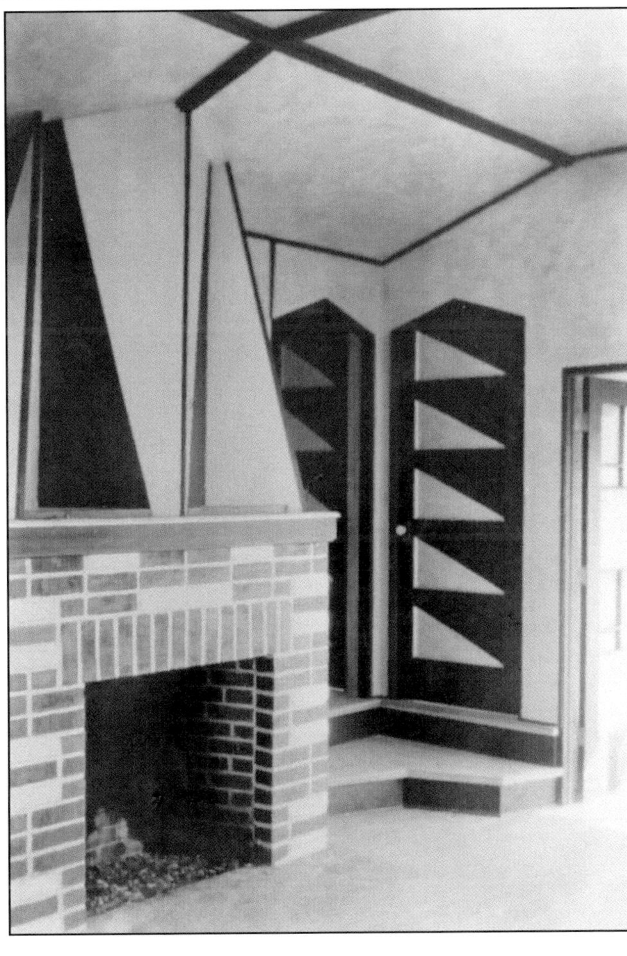

The interior of the Larson home, designed by Schindler in Park Moderne, is featured here around 1930.

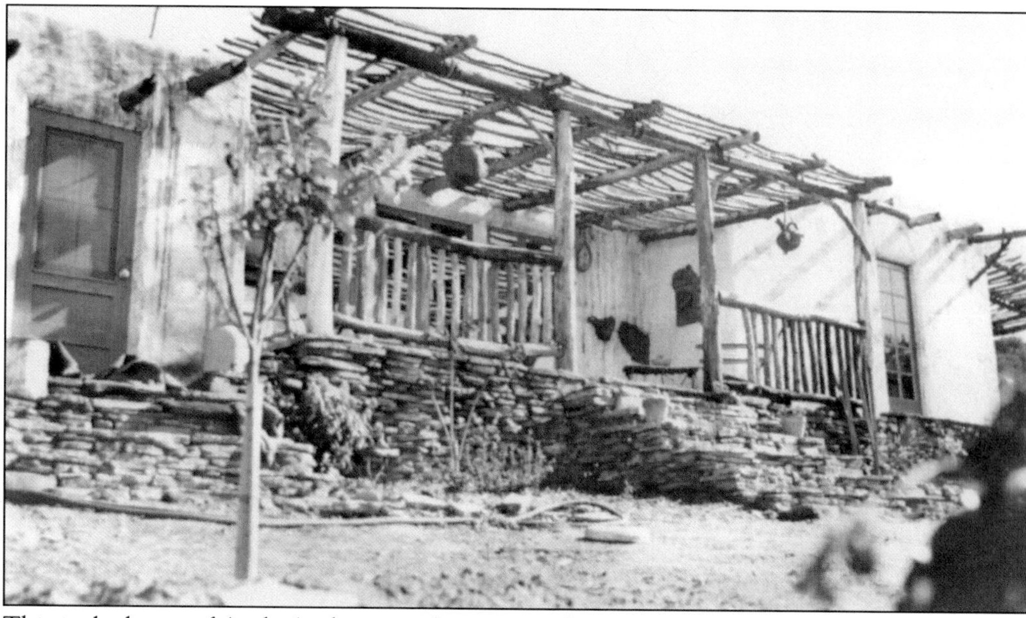

This is the home of Andy Anderson, a famous wood carver, who hand-built his house. Among the stream of celebrities who visited him was Jimmy Durante; he would come with his wife, who often refused to go back home with him. She loved the atmosphere of Park Moderne. Durante would return several days later to look for her. Thus came the famous line with which he closed *The Jimmy Durante Show*: "Goodnight, Mrs. Calabash, wherever you are."

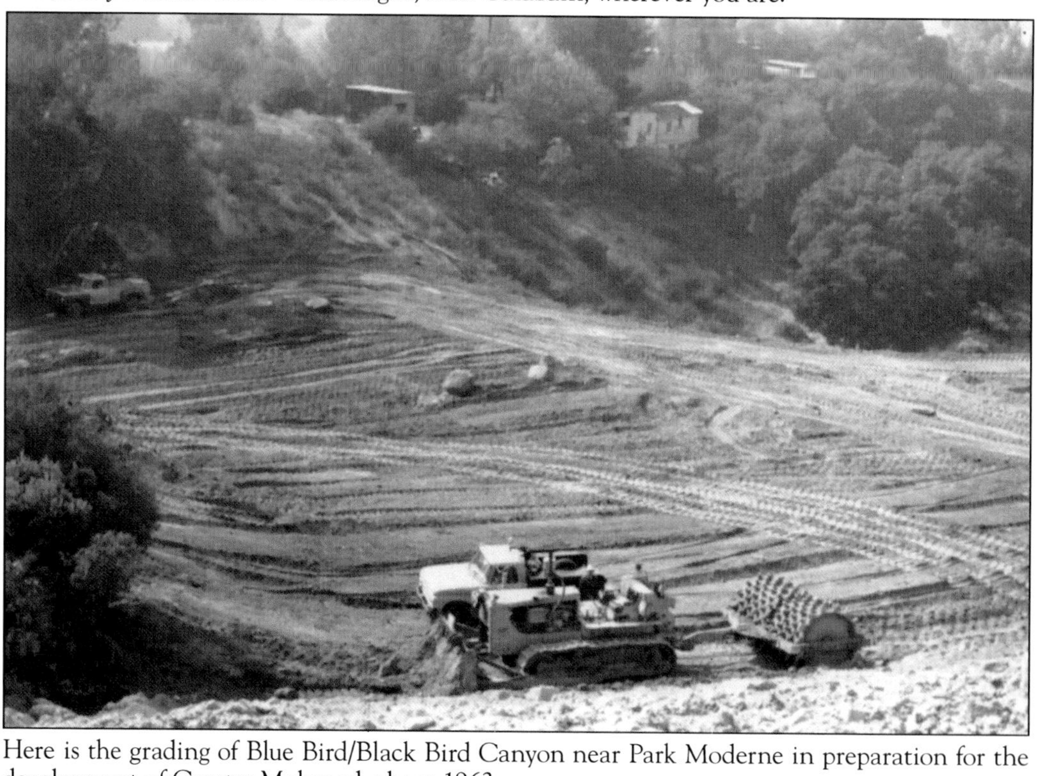

Here is the grading of Blue Bird/Black Bird Canyon near Park Moderne in preparation for the development of Greater Mulwood, about 1963.

Five

Filming on the Landscape That Transformed

As Carolyn Welke and Ruth Loring, historical society members, put it best, "No chapter in Calabasas history is more glorious than its major role in the movies." Since the 1920s, films have been made using Calabasas's unique landscape as the background; the land was a chameleon conforming to the various movie themes.

Motion picture pioneer Jesse L. Lasky started using the property now known as Lasky Mesa in 1914 as a location for filming. In the late 1930s, George E. Barrett Jr., a wealthy financier and landholder, purchased the Lasky Mesa property. The Barrett Ranch raised horses, allowed filming, and was a vacation retreat for Barrett and his family. Through the late 1930s and 1940s, a number of bigger-budget semi-historical movies were filmed at the ranch, including *Gone with the Wind*, *They Died with Their Boots On*, *Duel in the Sun*, *Adventures of Don Juan*, *The Charge of the Light Brigade*, and *The Thundering Herd*, and television shows such as *Petticoat Junction*.

Warner Bros. purchased 500 acres near Calabasas Creek in the vicinity of Mulholland Drive and Valmar Road in 1935. Dubbed Warner Ranch, it eventually grew to 2,800 acres with numerous outdoor sets. Warner Ranch was located in Calabasas until 1961 and was one of the largest Hollywood movie lots. Among the films shot at the ranch were *Casablanca*, *Santa Fe Trail*, and *Sergeant York*. The Monte Nido area was the site for scenes from great classic films such as *Tarzan*, *Stalag 17*, and *The Adventures of Robin Hood*.

Purchased in 1952, the Ingram Movie Ranch in Calabasas was owned by the early-1930s cowboy star Lloyd Ingram. Some of the films shot there include *Mark of The Lash*, *Kansas Territory*, and *The Desperado*. Television shows filmed were *The Lone Ranger*, *The Roy Rogers Show*, and *The Cisco Kid*.

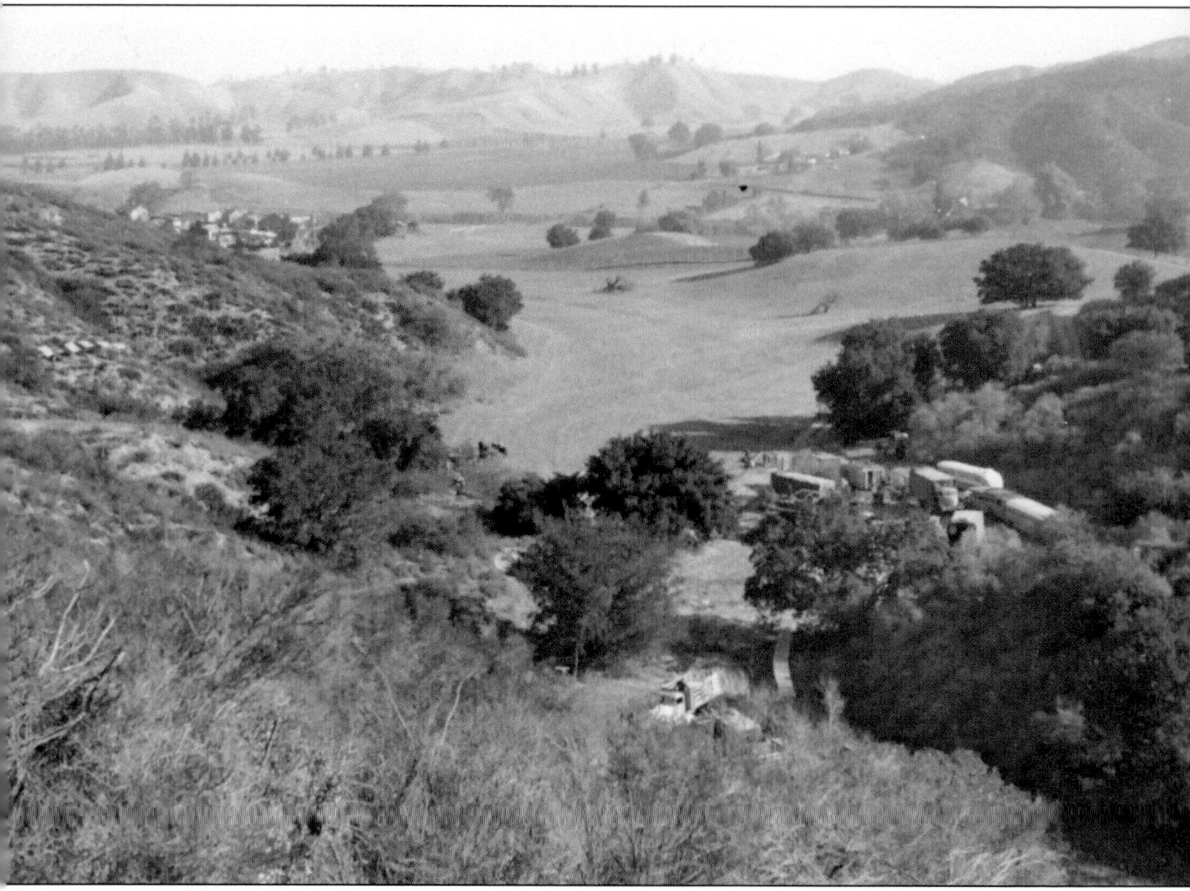

This is Warner Ranch in 1949, south of Ventura Boulevard at Mulholland Drive. Jack Warner built a home where the present-day Calabasas Country Club sits. The 18-hole golf course nostalgically named each hole after the films created there. During World War II, the ranch was used by the armed forces for training films. (Courtesy of Bison Archives.)

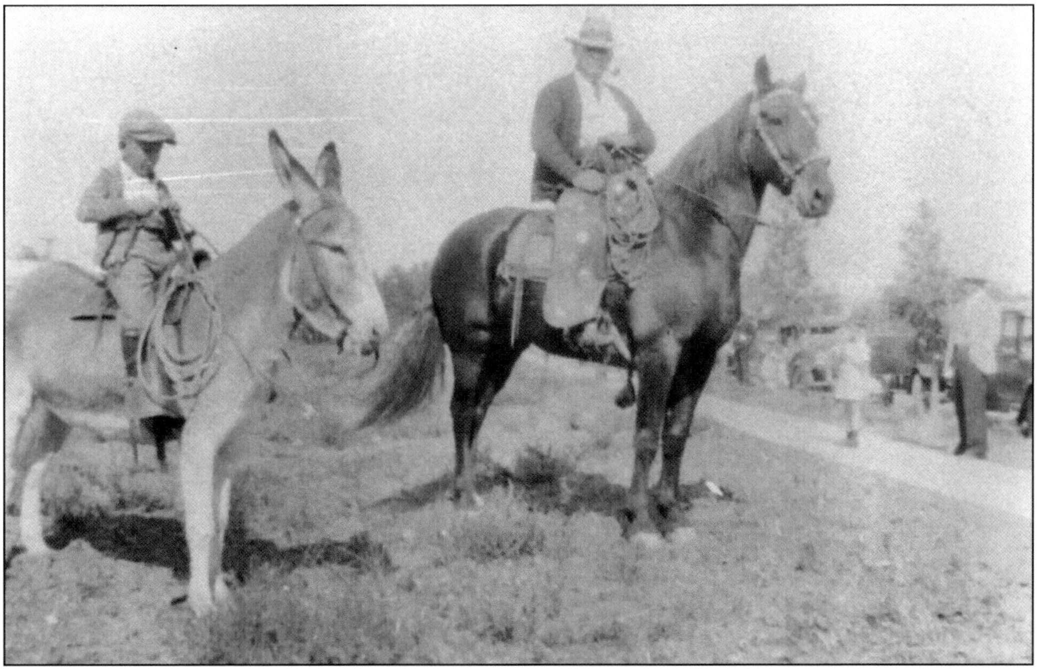

Calabasas locals frequently found themselves in movies as extras, particularly if they rode horses. Pictured here are Frank Farmer, on a mule, with Don Poyer, on his horse. Farmer's home backed up to the Warner Ranch, and Poyer lived on Calabasas Road. Their proximity to Warner Ranch made it easy for the studios to call on them for odd jobs and small acting roles.

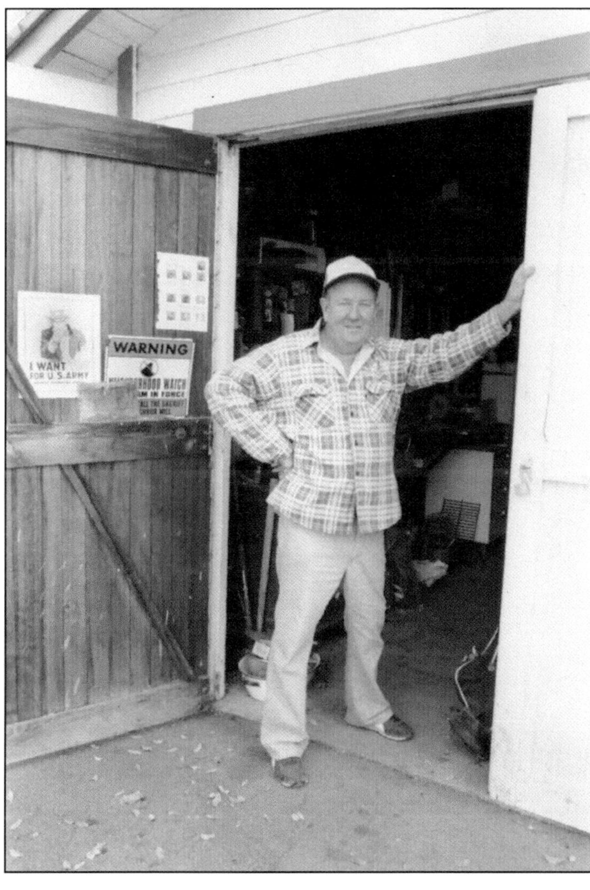

An older Frank Farmer stands in the threshold of his barn located in Calabasas Junction in 1990. Farmer witnessed filmmaking in the 1930s and 1940s in his own backyard, meeting Robert Mitchum, Errol Flynn, and Clark Gable. Farmer was also recruited for the films *Mrs. Wigg's Cabbage Patch*, *The Charge of the Light Brigade*, *Dragon Seed*, and *Dawn Patrol*.

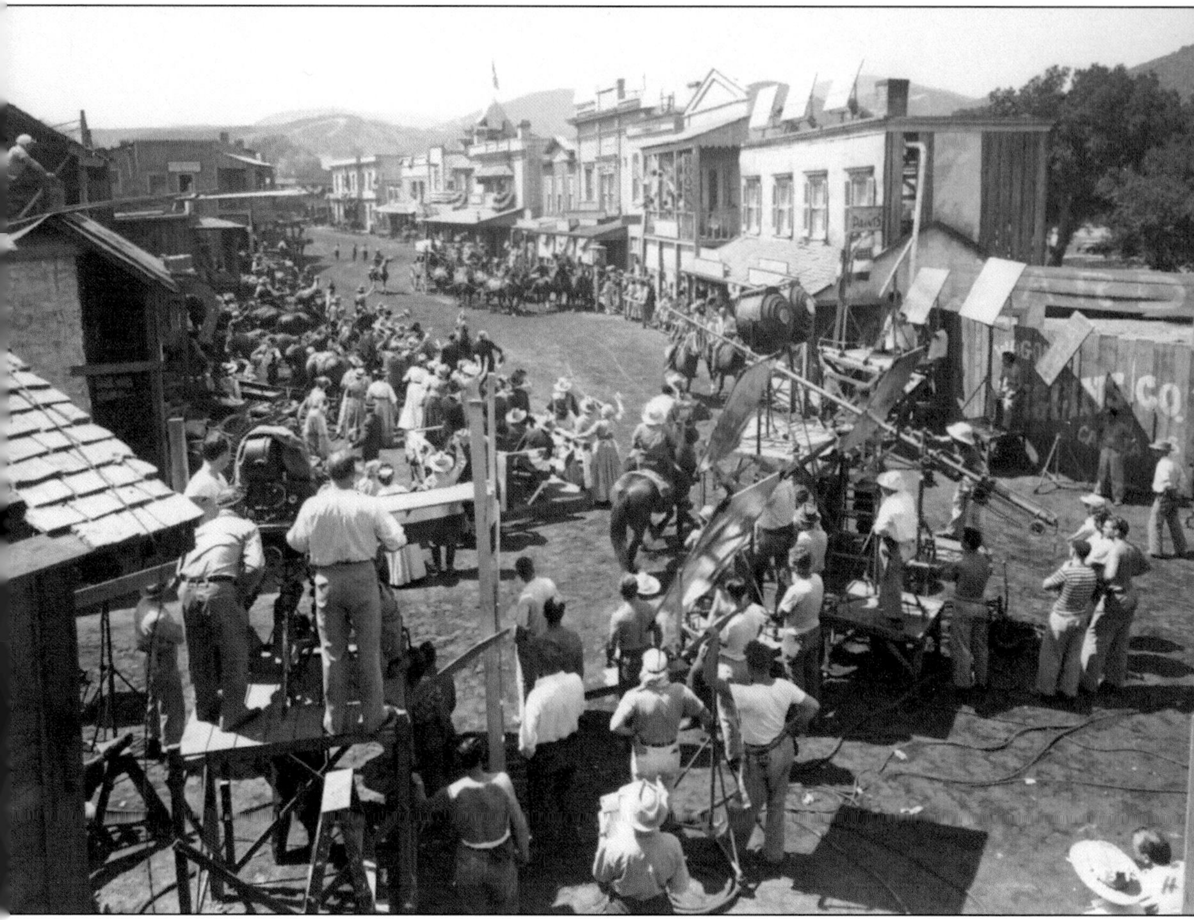

Warner Ranch was the location of many outdoor sets that were used in various films. Shown is the Warner Ranch during the filming of the movie *Pursued* (1947), starring Robert Mitchum, Teresa Wright, and Judith Anderson. The plot is about an orphan boy brought up by a ranch family in the 1880s who is haunted by nightmares of a childhood trauma. Two other films starring Errol Flynn used this Western town movie set, *Dodge City* and *Virginia City*. (Courtesy of Bison Archives.)

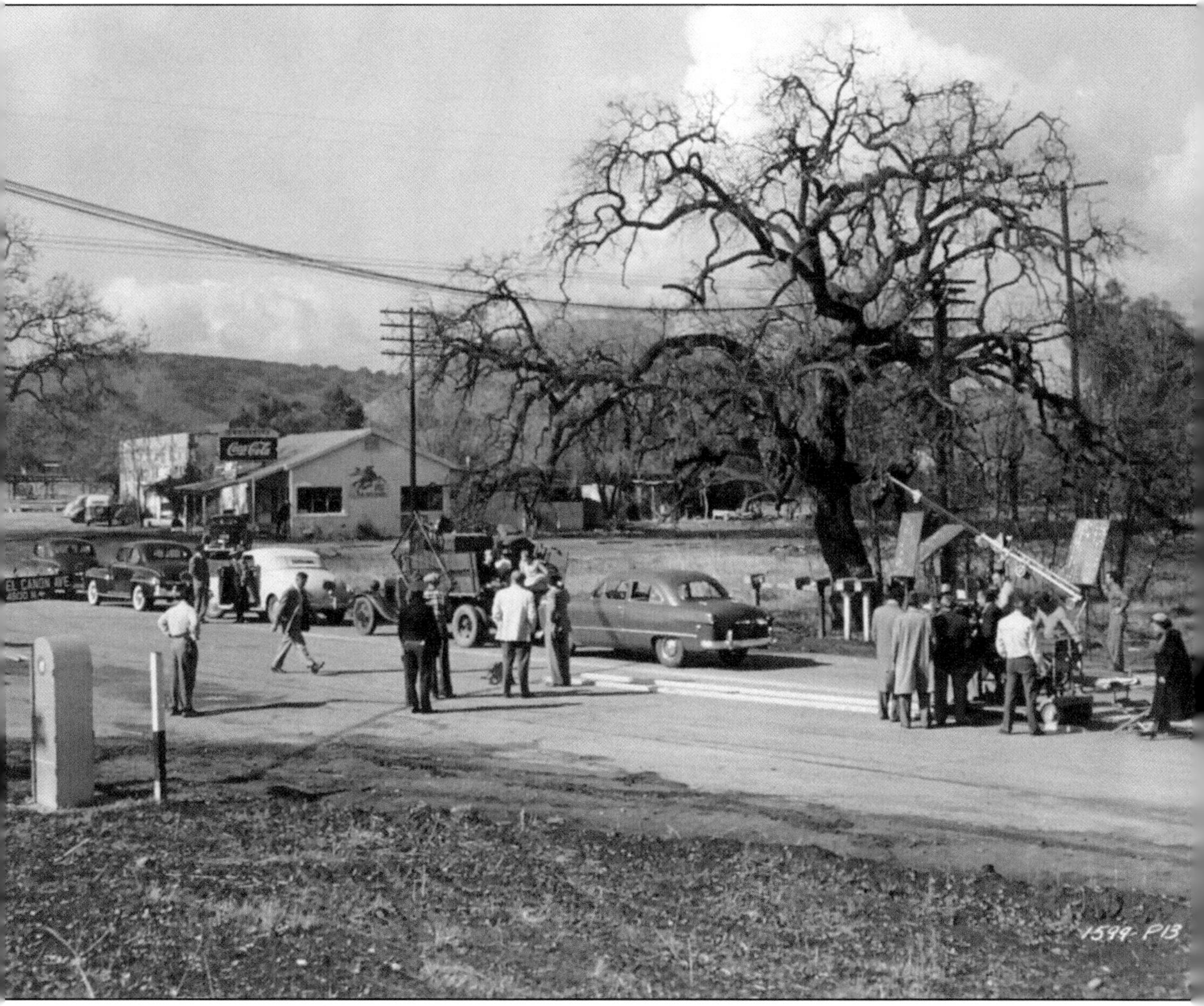

This photograph was taken in Old Town Calabasas on the set location for the Universal Studios film *Take One False Step*, starring William Powell and Shelley Winters. This 1949 film features the story of a professor in Los Angeles who is inveigled by an old flame into taking a midnight drive. The next day the girl is missing, believed killed, and the professor is the prime suspect. (Courtesy of Bison Archives.)

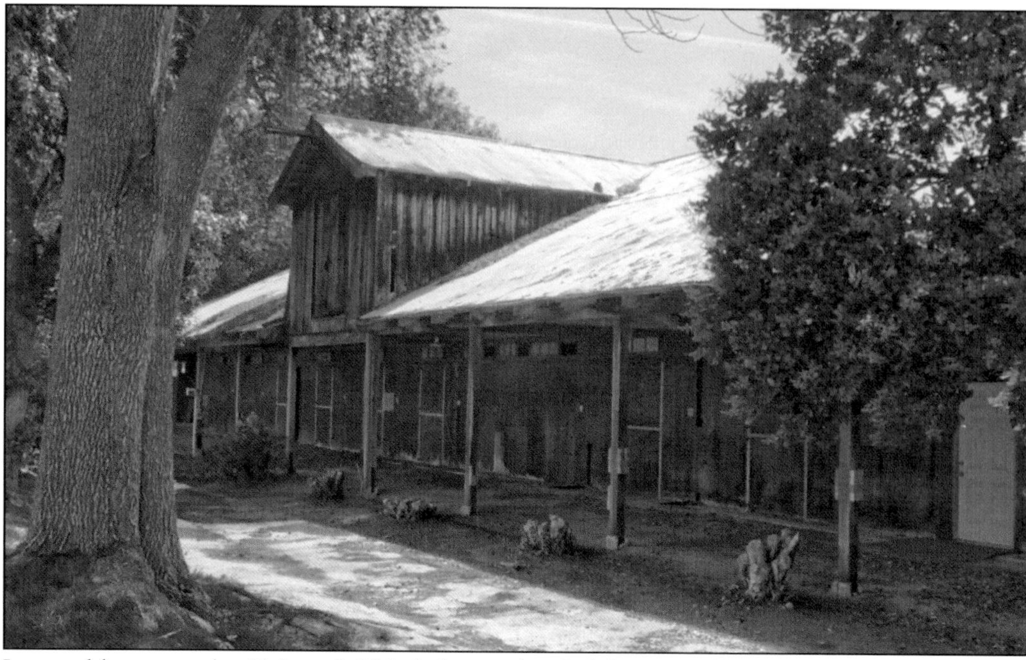

Located between the 11th and 15th holes at the Calabasas Golf and Country Club are the structures remaining from the Warner Ranch. Shown is the barn used in the movie *National Velvet*, released in 1944, starring Elizabeth Taylor and Mickey Rooney. Today, the barn is used as a headquarters for the golf course's landscaping company. (Photograph by Karlo Gorgin; courtesy of the Calabasas Media Department.)

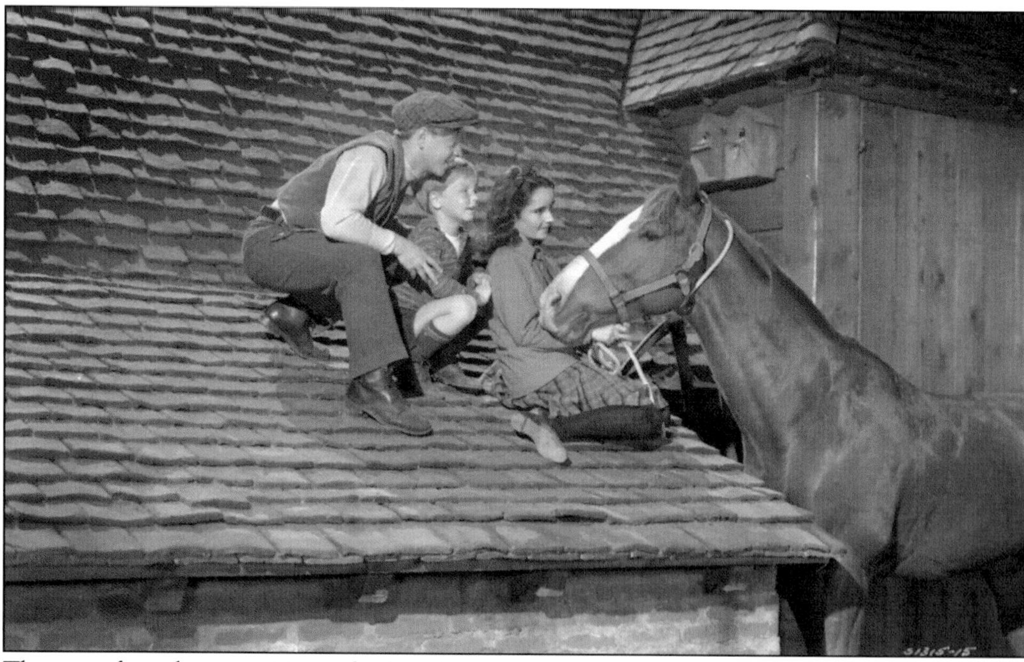

This scene from the movie *National Velvet*, shot on what now is the site of the Calabasas Country Club, captures a young penniless drifter named Mi Taylor (Mickey Rooney) and Velvet Brown (Elizabeth Taylor) secretly planning a win at the racetrack. (Courtesy of the Warner Bros. Library.)

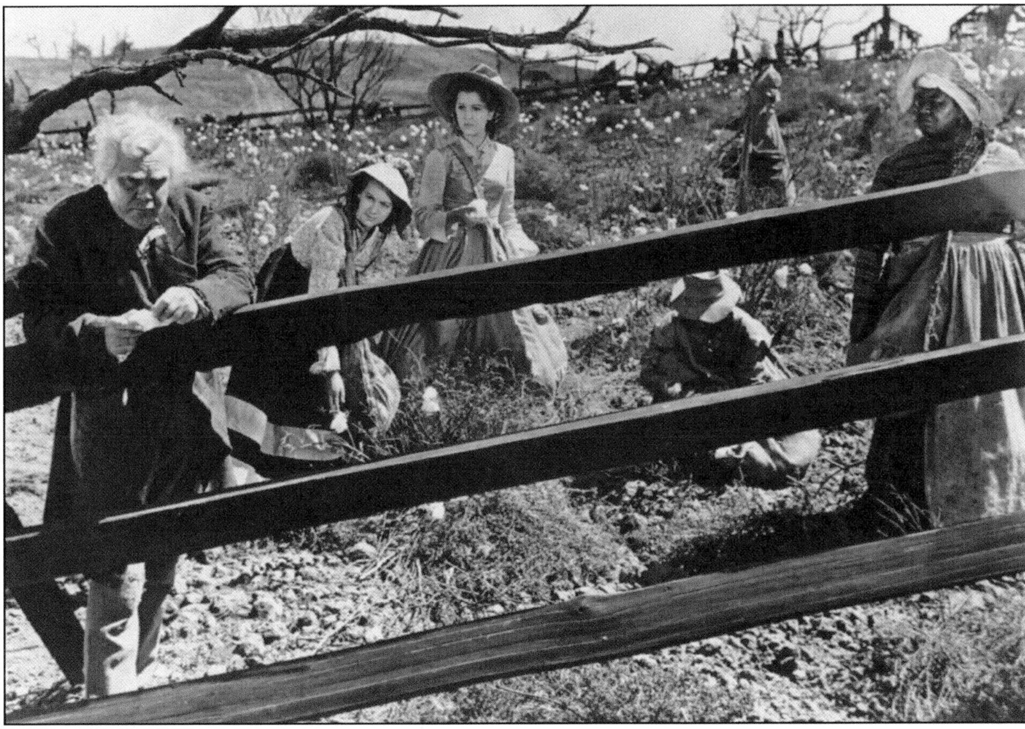

Here is a scene from the 1939 classic *Gone with the Wind*, which was filmed on Lasky Mesa. Other Lasky Mesa films include *Santa Fe Trail*, *They Died with Their Boots On*, *Duel in the Sun*, and *Adventures of Don Juan*. (Courtesy of Bison Archives.)

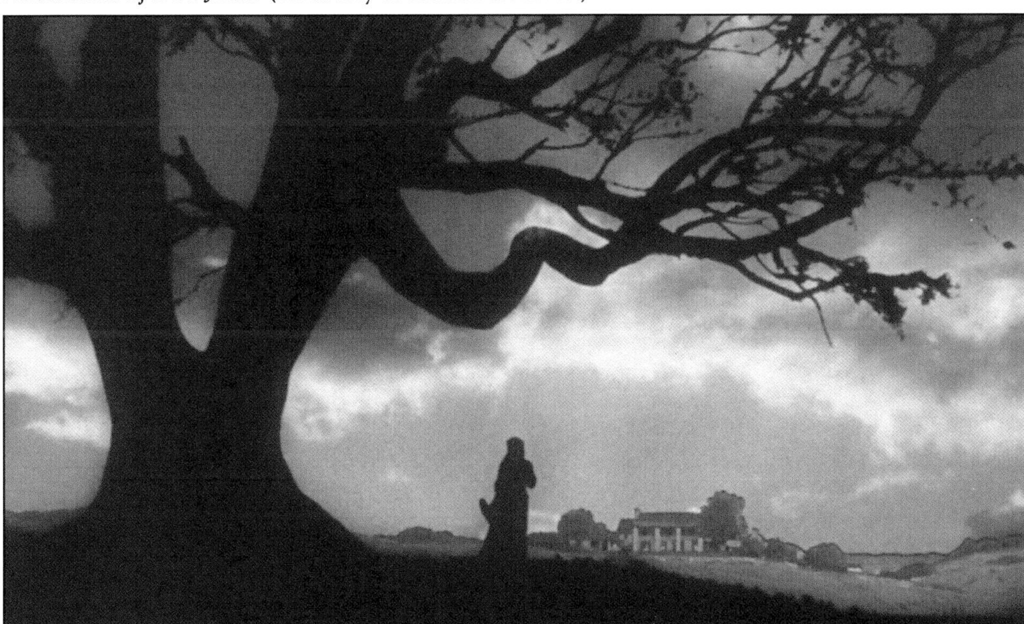

Many memorable scenes from *Gone with the Wind*, including when Katie Scarlett O'Hara (Vivien Leigh) vows never to go hungry again, were filmed on a hilltop in Lasky Mesa. (Courtesy of the Warner Bros. Library.)

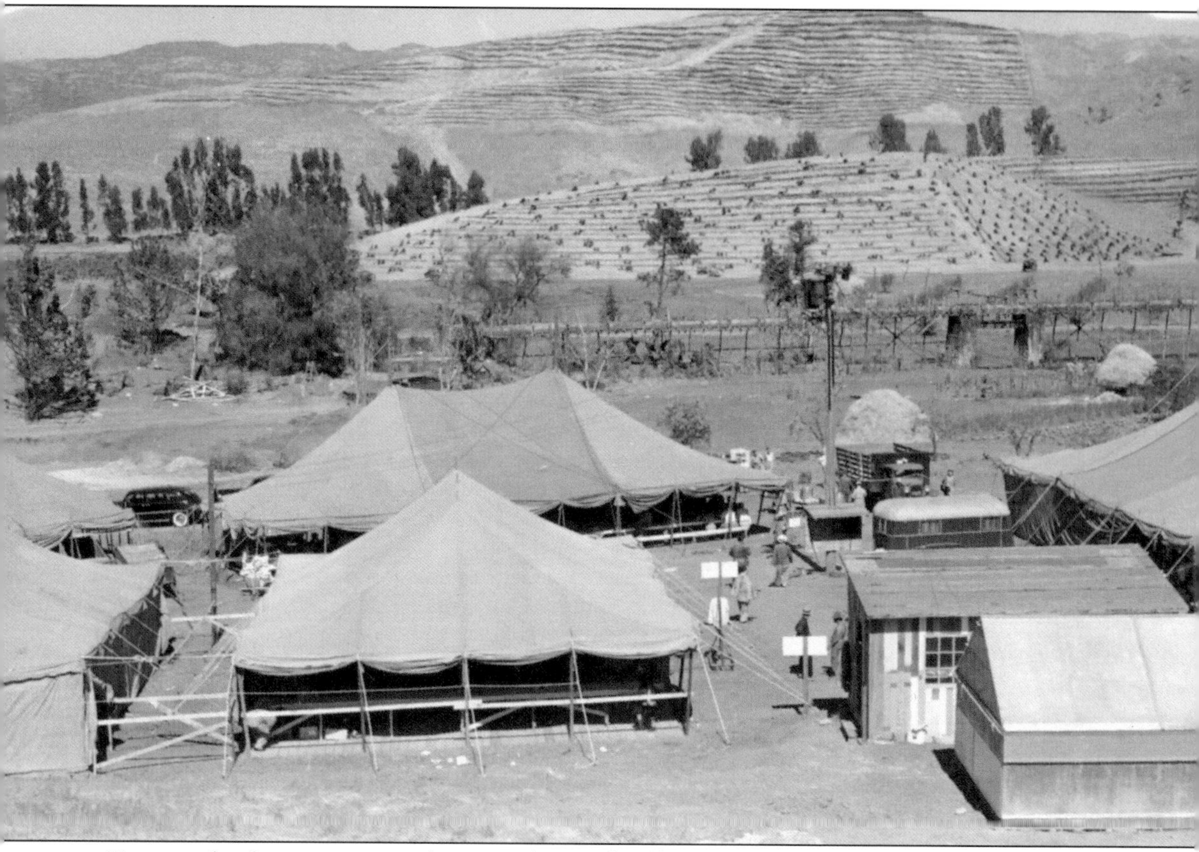

Here are the dressing tents on location during the filming of *Dragon Seed*. In 1944, MGM picked up the screen rights to *Dragon Seed*, Pearl S. Buck's popular 1942 tale of Chinese peasants fighting off Japanese invaders during World War II. Turner's website describes the movie as follows: "*Dragon Seed* managed to be both ahead of its time and behind the times simultaneously; it pointed to new roles for women while also demonstrating an amazing lack of sensitivity on racial issues." *Dragon Seed* ranks as the strangest film in Katharine Hepburn's career. (Courtesy of Bison Archives.)

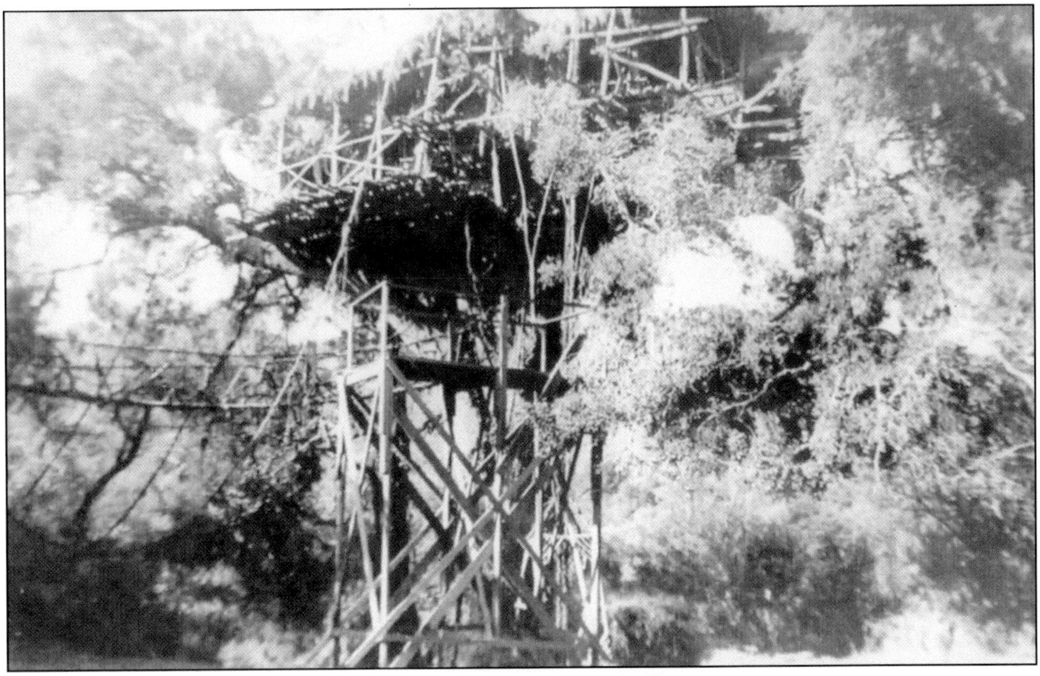

Monte Nido, which borders Calabasas and Malibu, was the location for the great classic Tarzan films in the late 1930s. Here, the Tarzan tree is seen located off Piuma Road. The area was so well suited for filmmaking that Warner Ranch was located in Monte Nido until 1961. Even today, location scouts often seek out the area. (Courtesy of Warner Bros. Library.)

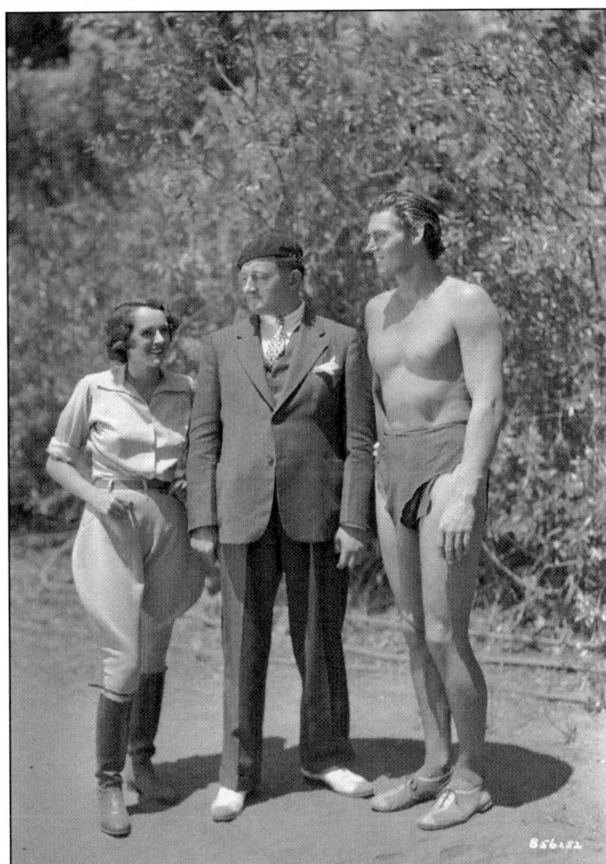

Warner Ranch was located in Calabasas until 1961, one of the largest of Hollywood movie lots. Among the films shot at the ranch were *Casablanca*, *The Santa Fe Trail*, and *Sergeant York*. The Monte Nido area was the site for scenes from great classic films such as *Stalag 17* and *The Adventures of Robin Hood*. This shot features, from left to right, Maureen O'Sullivan, John Buckler, and Johnny Weissmuller from *Tarzan Escapes*, shot in Monte Nido. (Courtesy of Warner Bros. Library.)

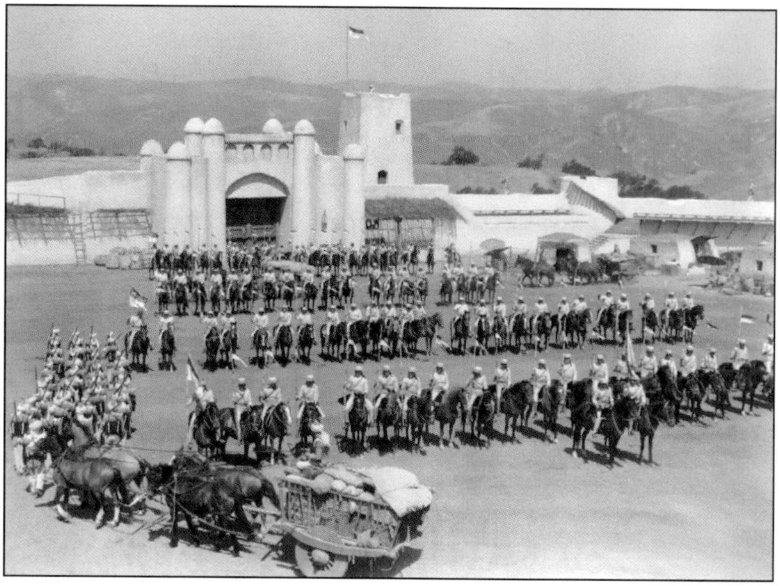

Here is a scene at Lasky Mesa from *The Charge of the Light Brigade* (1936), starring Errol Flynn, Olivia de Havilland, and Patric Knowles. The story is loosely based on the famous Charge of the Light Brigade, which took place during the Crimean War (1853–1856) and was memorialized in a poem by Alfred Tennyson. (Courtesy of Bison Archives.)

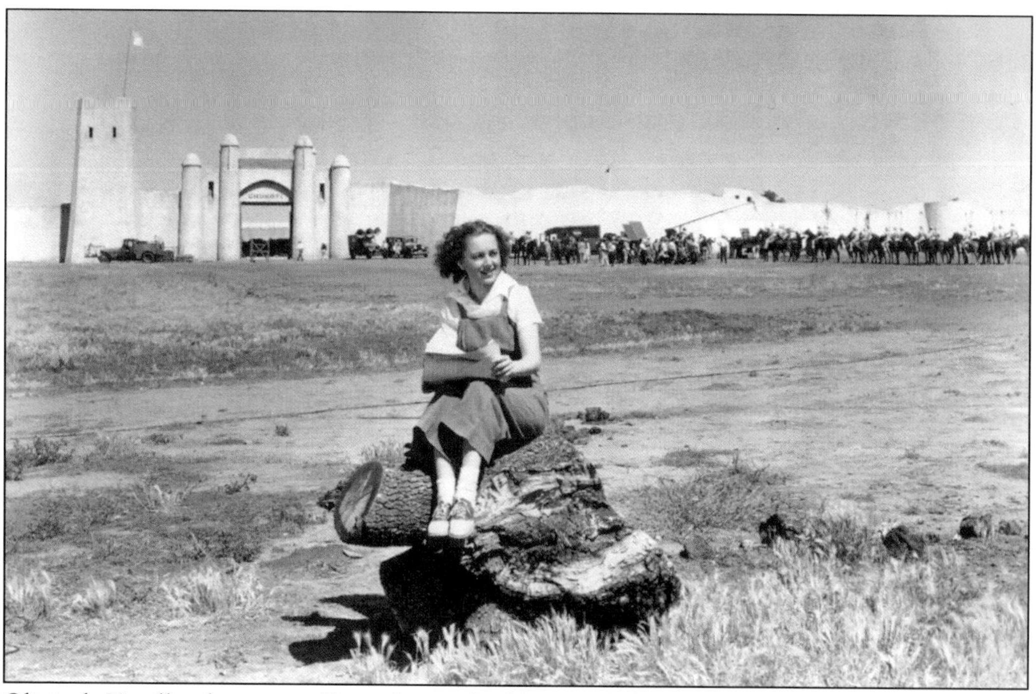

Olivia de Havilland is pictured here during the filming of *The Charge of the Light Brigade* at Lasky Mesa. The battlefield set was lined with trip wires to hobble the cavalry horses. According to the website IMDb, "For the filming of the climactic charge, 125 horses were trip-wired. Of those, 25 were killed outright or had to be put down afterward. The resulting public furor caused the U.S. Congress to pass laws to protect animals used in motion pictures." (Courtesy of Bison Archives.)

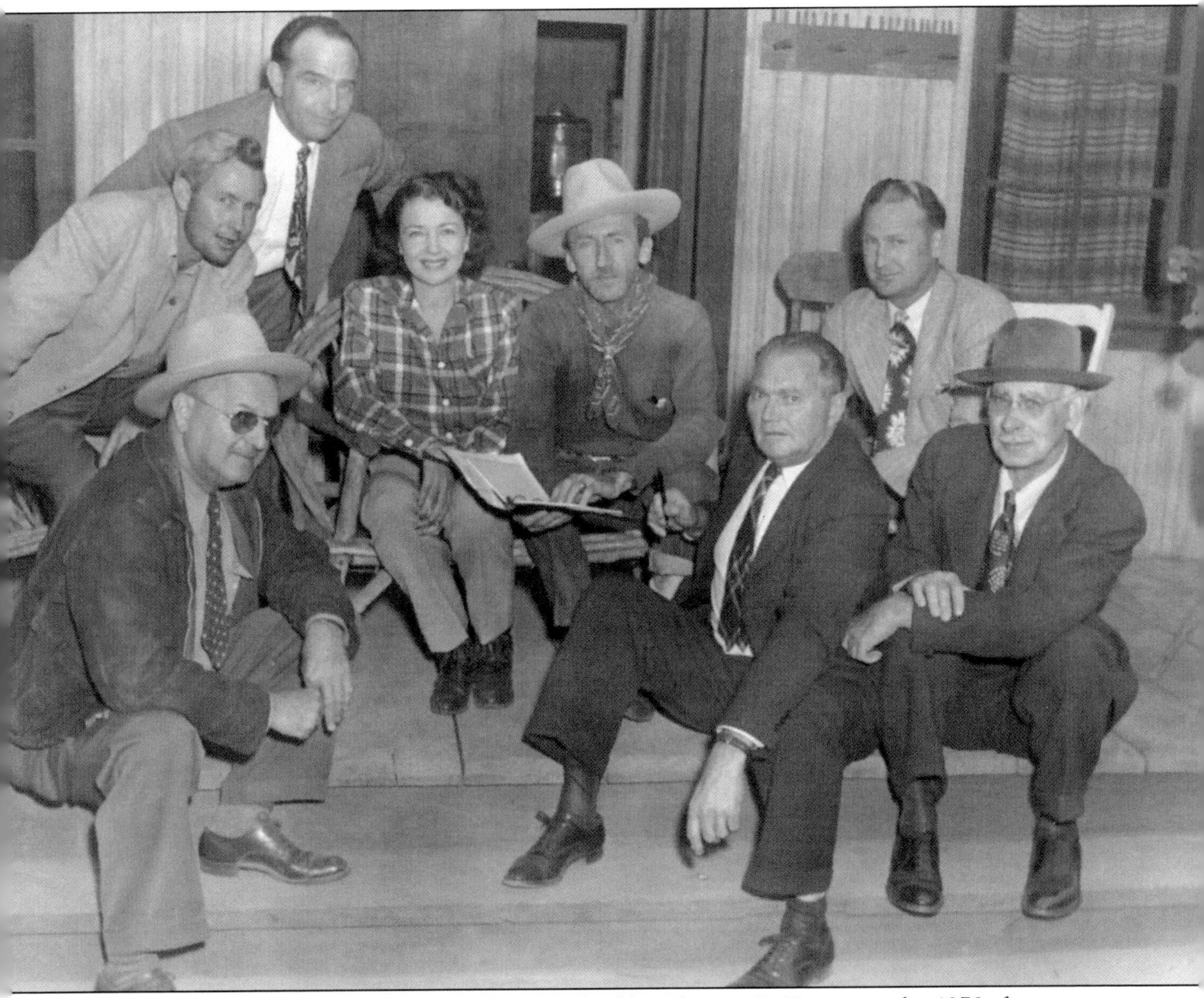

This group of Calabasas citizens was photographed by Christy G. Turner in the 1970s for a press release during their meeting to plan the Western Jamboree celebration. Pictured here are, from left to right, (first row) Glen MacMillian, Hugh Harlan (publicity), and L.B. "Pat" Murphy (master of ceremonies); (second row) Bill Rall, John Labig, actress Vera Vague (honorary mayor), Paul Cruder (general chairman), and Bud Bently.

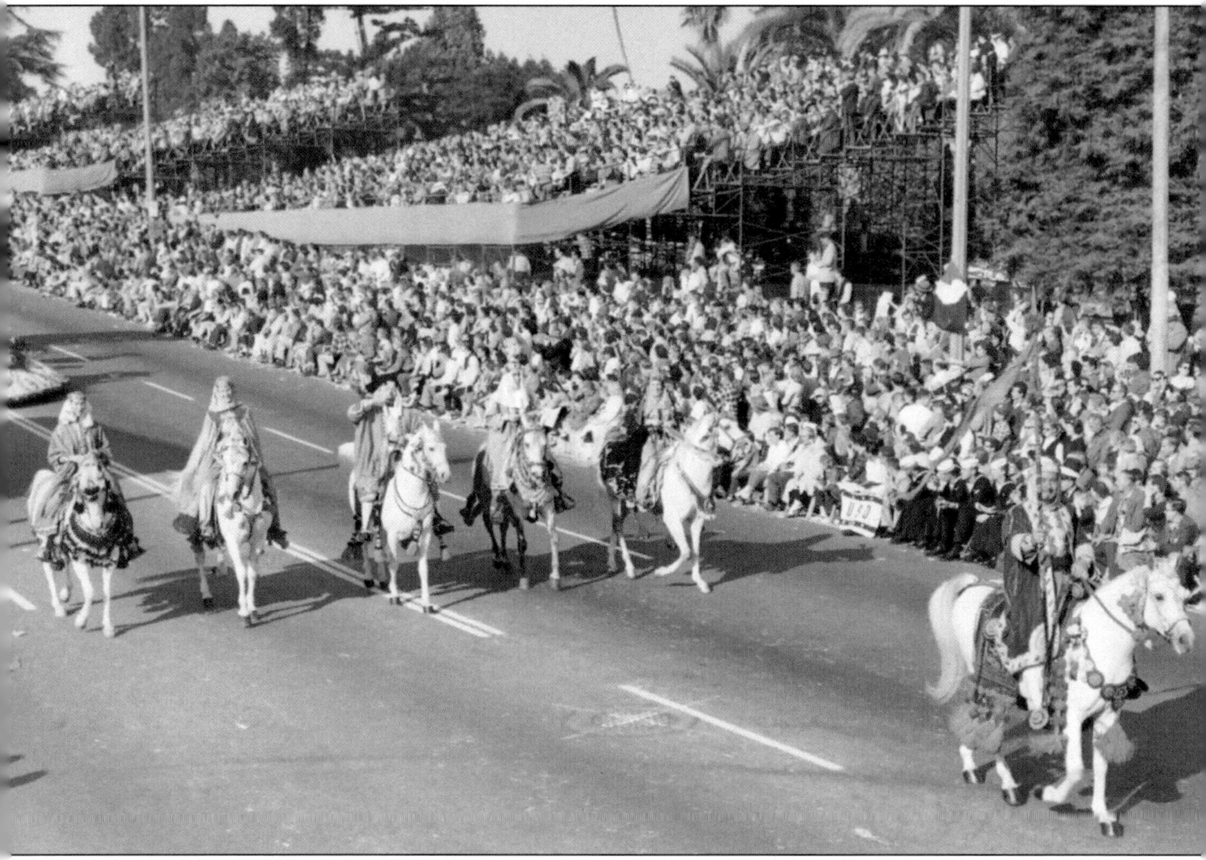

The Rose Parade is not only narrated by longtime Hidden Hills resident Bob Eubanks, but one of the parade entries for many years was the Hidden Hills Glory Ranch professional riders. Seen here during the 1969 parade are, from left to right, Ollie Prasser, Pearl Larsen, Rosemary Gebert (the Glory Ranch operator), Gene Parks, and Dr. Lu Prell Williams.

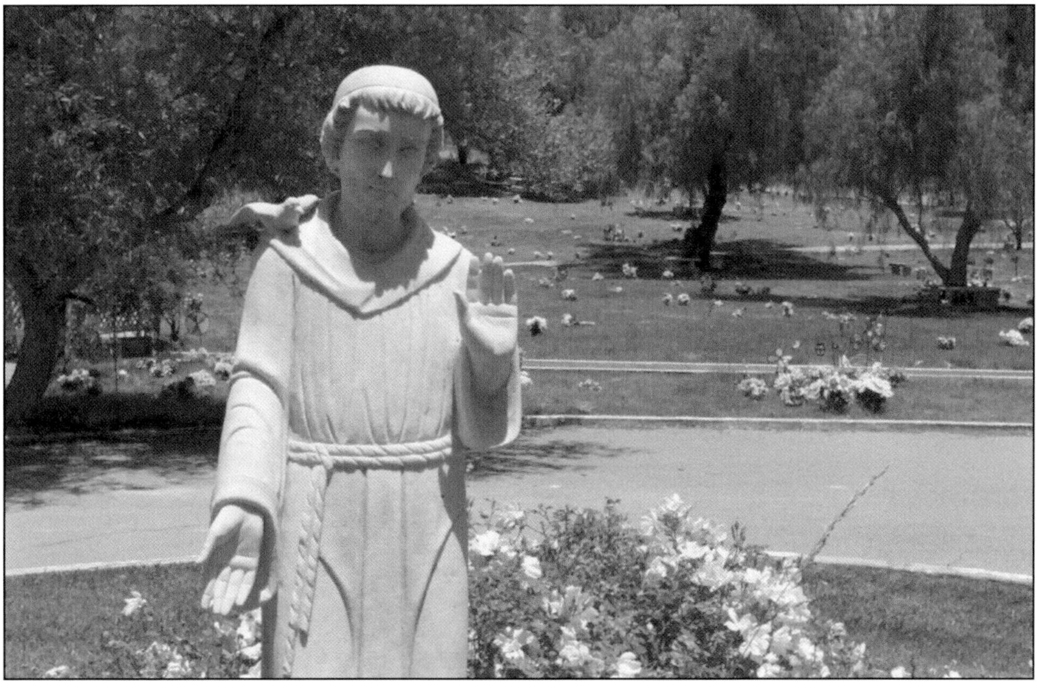

In Calabasas, one can pay homage to famous animals buried in the Los Angeles Pet Memorial Park. Established in 1928, the park, originally called the Los Angeles Pet Cemetery, is one of the oldest facilities of its kind on the West Coast. Animal celebrities memorialized include Pete the dog (featured in *The Little Rascals*), Topper (Hopalong Cassidy's horse), Good Scout (Tonto's horse), and Kabar (Rudolph Valentino's dog). In 1973, the owners, the Rollins and the Dr. Eugene Jones family, donated the cemetery to the Los Angeles Society for the Prevention of Cruelty to Animals (SPCAla). On September 12, 1986, the nonprofit group of pet owners who established SOPHIE (Save Our Pets History In Eternity) purchased the property to prevent the sale of the park to a developer. The elaborate headstone is the memorial marker for Tawny, the MGM lion. (Both, photograph by Karlo Gorgin; courtesy of the Calabasas Media Department.)

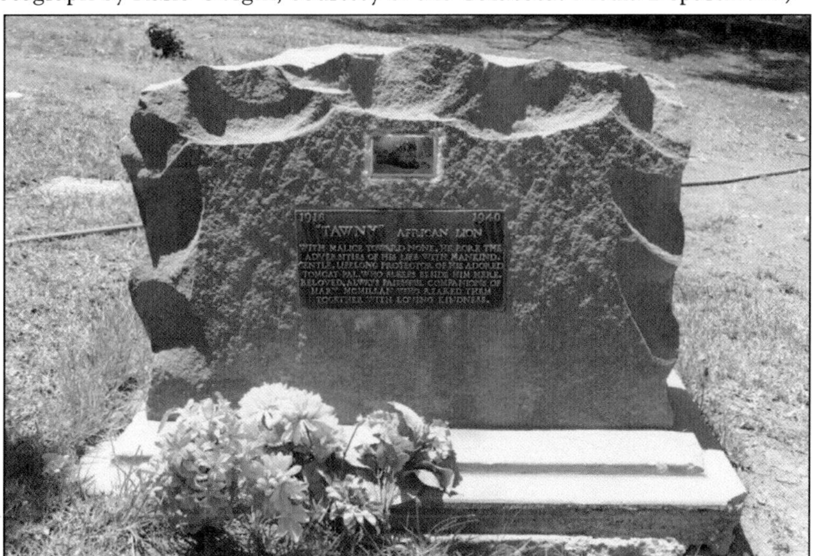

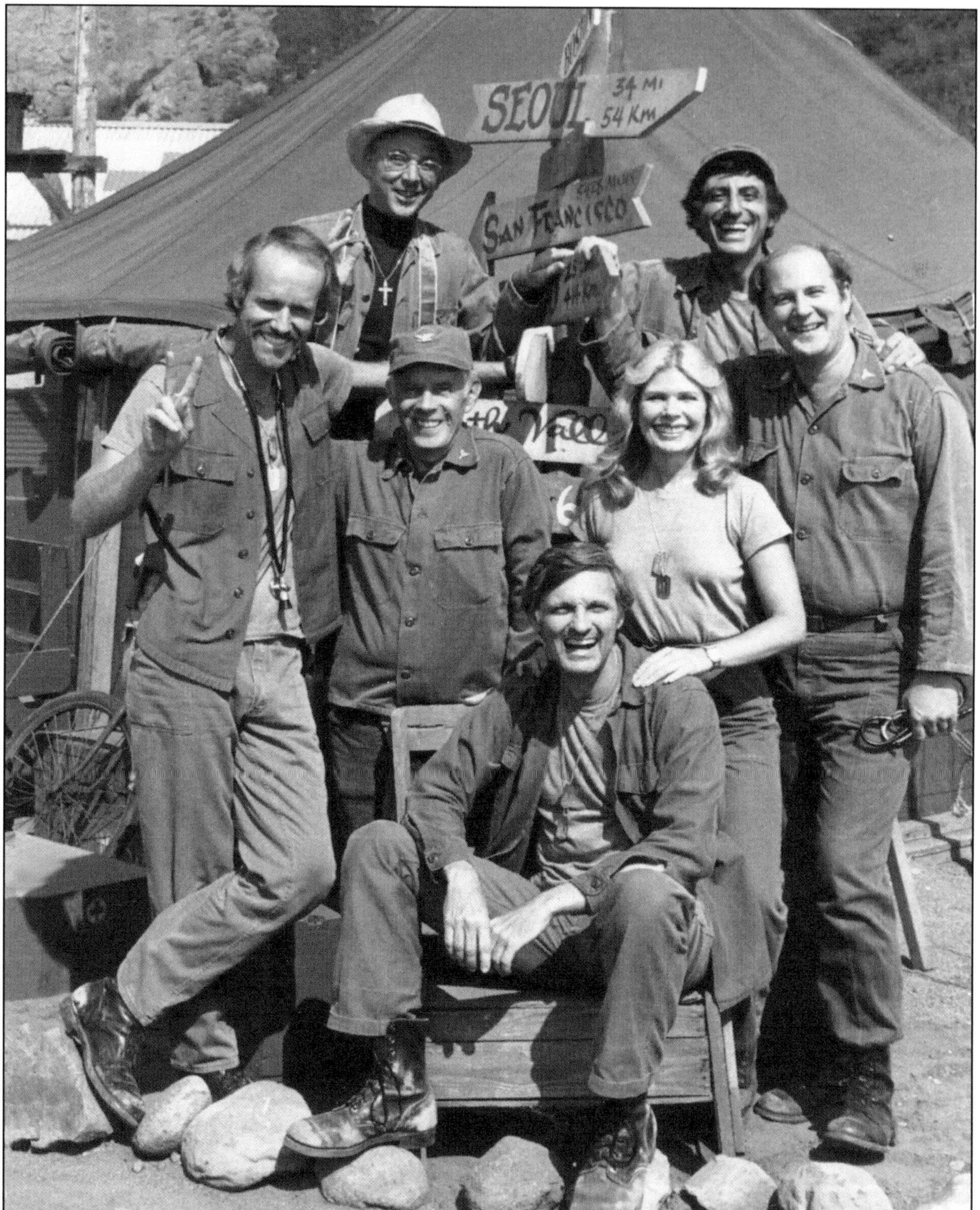

In 1946, film studio 20th Century Fox bought 2,000 acres of the Crags Mountain Lodge property for Century Ranch, later known as Fox Ranch. This location was used by other studios that would rent the property to use the landscape for dozens of films, including a number of the Tarzan movies, the original *Planet of the Apes* and subsequent television series, and the long-running series *M*A*S*H*. *Butch Cassidy and the Sundance Kid* and *The Sand Pebbles* were also filmed there. A portion of the Fox property was preserved and turned into today's Malibu Creek State Park. Here is a promotional shot of the cast from the hit show *M*A*S*H*. (Courtesy of Bison Archives.)

Six

Cityhood

On April 5, 1991, the City of Calabasas became the 466th incorporated municipality in the State of California. After overcoming the many hurdles to achieving cityhood, the first city council faced the enormous task of building the infrastructure of a modern city from the ground up. Like most other smaller municipalities, Calabasas is a "contract city," meaning that it contracts with outside public and private entities for most services (such as police and fire protection).

Starting with no staff, supplies, or facilities aside from one neighborhood park, the council moved quickly to stabilize the fledgling government. Complicating matters was the unavoidable circumstance of having to do so on the precipice of a steep national economic downturn.

For the first city hall, the council selected a modest suite on the second floor of a nondescript office building. A skeleton crew of staff was hired to manage the daily operations of the city. Early meetings were always long and often contentious, as the council carefully laid the foundation for the new government.

Opportunities to obtain land for municipal purposes were severely limited because much of the city had been built out and most of the available space allocated to other uses by the time of incorporation. But over the years, city officials were highly creative in acquiring parkland and other properties, and today the city owns and/or operates 12 facilities devoted to various educational and recreational uses. Chief among these is the Calabasas Civic Center, completed in 2008 and home to city hall and the municipal library.

The city presently employs approximately 100 full-time and many part-time employees, divided into nine separate departments covering a wide range of municipal services. The city's annual budget has quadrupled, now standing at about $22.5 million. From its modest origins, Calabasas looks to have a bright future.

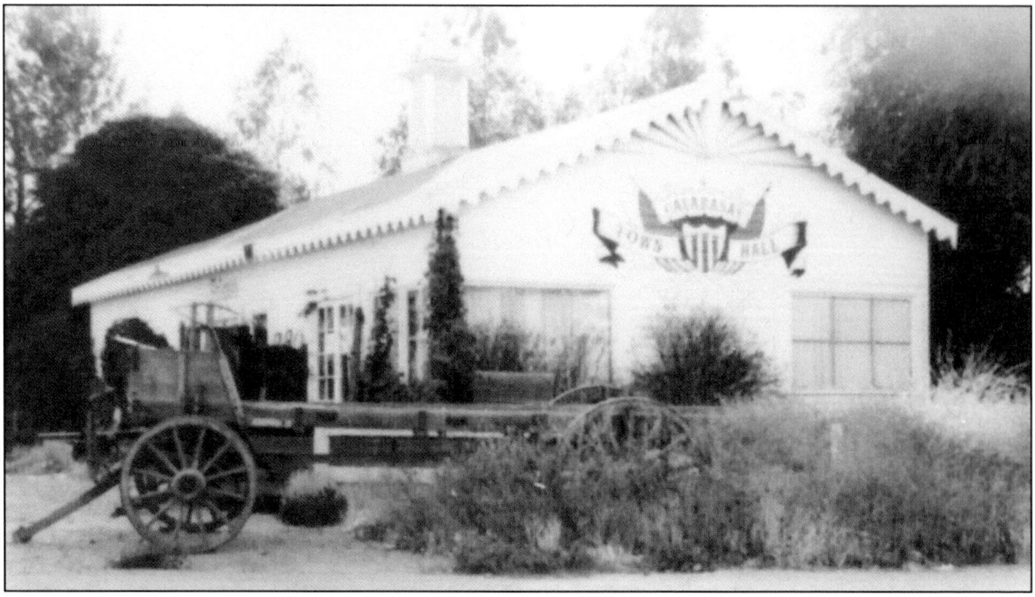

Pictured here is the original Calabasas Town Hall located in Old Town on Calabasas Road in 1958. Wally's Store had previously been at this location.

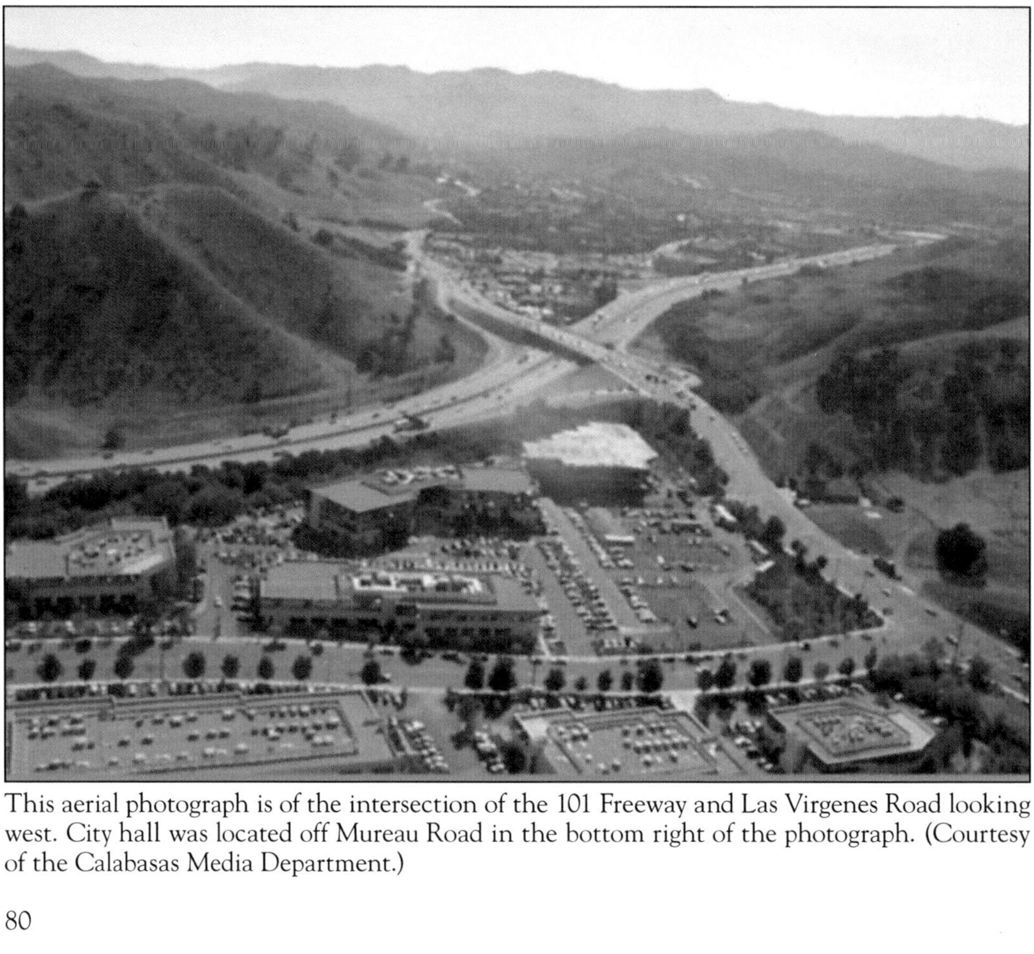

This aerial photograph is of the intersection of the 101 Freeway and Las Virgenes Road looking west. City hall was located off Mureau Road in the bottom right of the photograph. (Courtesy of the Calabasas Media Department.)

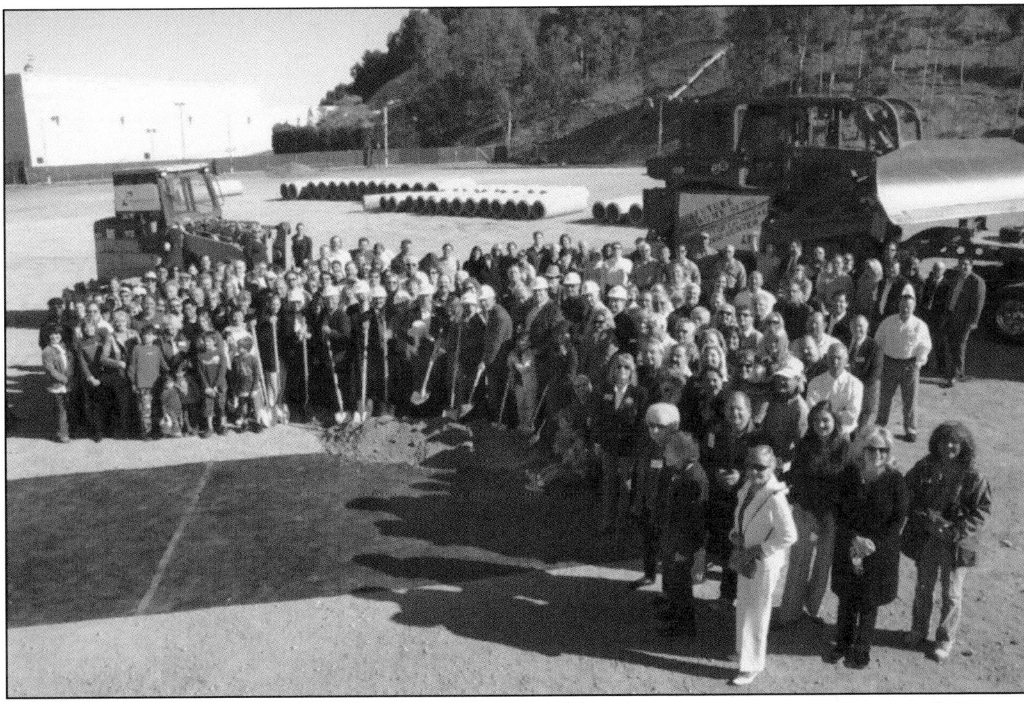

Calabasas city officials and staff pose at the ground-breaking ceremony on the site of the new Calabasas Civic Center in January 2007. (Courtesy of the Calabasas Media Department.)

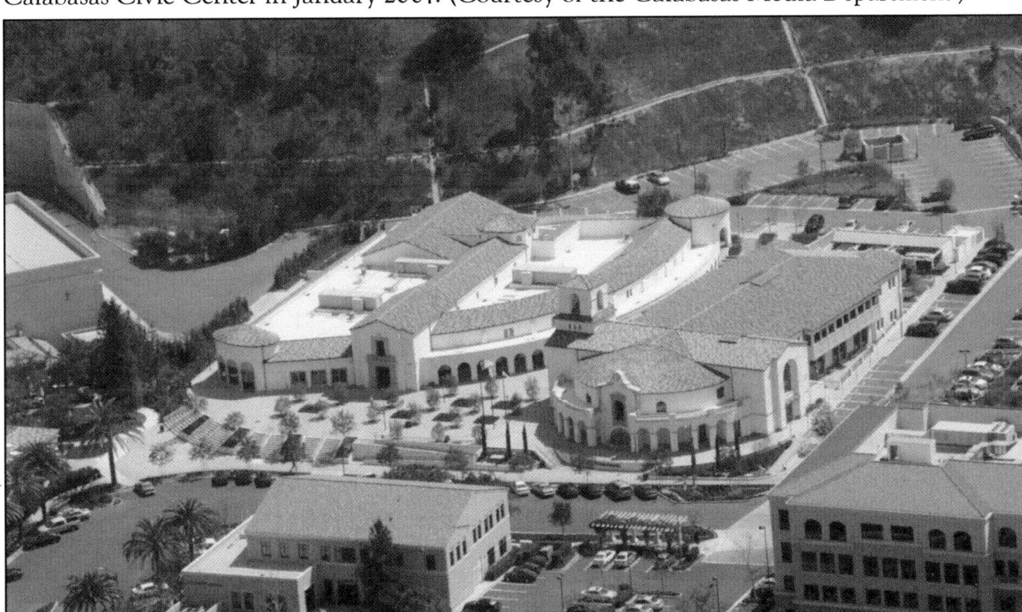

This aerial photograph was taken days after the Calabasas Civic Center was completed in 2008. The architect was Robert A.M. Stern, whose design received a Gold LEED certification. The library (left) was built with the help of an $8.2 million grant. This wing of the facility has a multipurpose meeting space with an amphitheater and adjacent patio. City hall (right) includes a grand lobby, council chamber vestibule, and staff offices.

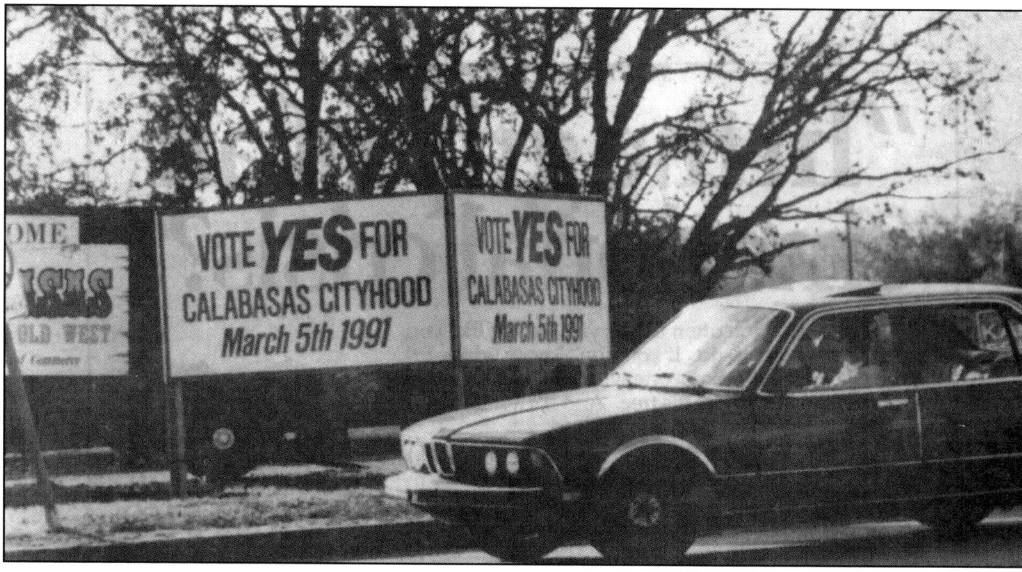

Billboard signage on Calabasas Road near the busy corner at Mulholland Drive solicits votes for Calabasas cityhood at the election scheduled for March 5, 1991.

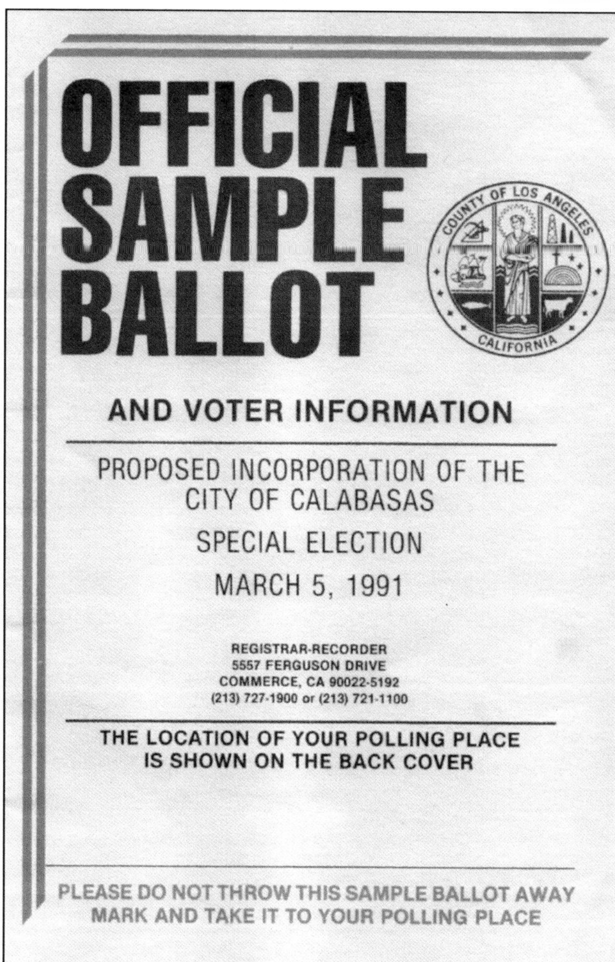

OFFICIAL SAMPLE BALLOT

COUNTY OF LOS ANGELES CALIFORNIA

AND VOTER INFORMATION

PROPOSED INCORPORATION OF THE CITY OF CALABASAS

SPECIAL ELECTION

MARCH 5, 1991

REGISTRAR-RECORDER
5557 FERGUSON DRIVE
COMMERCE, CA 90022-5192
(213) 727-1900 or (213) 721-1100

THE LOCATION OF YOUR POLLING PLACE IS SHOWN ON THE BACK COVER

PLEASE DO NOT THROW THIS SAMPLE BALLOT AWAY
MARK AND TAKE IT TO YOUR POLLING PLACE

Here is the ballot cover for the March 5, 1991, special election. (Courtesy of former mayor Bob Hill.)

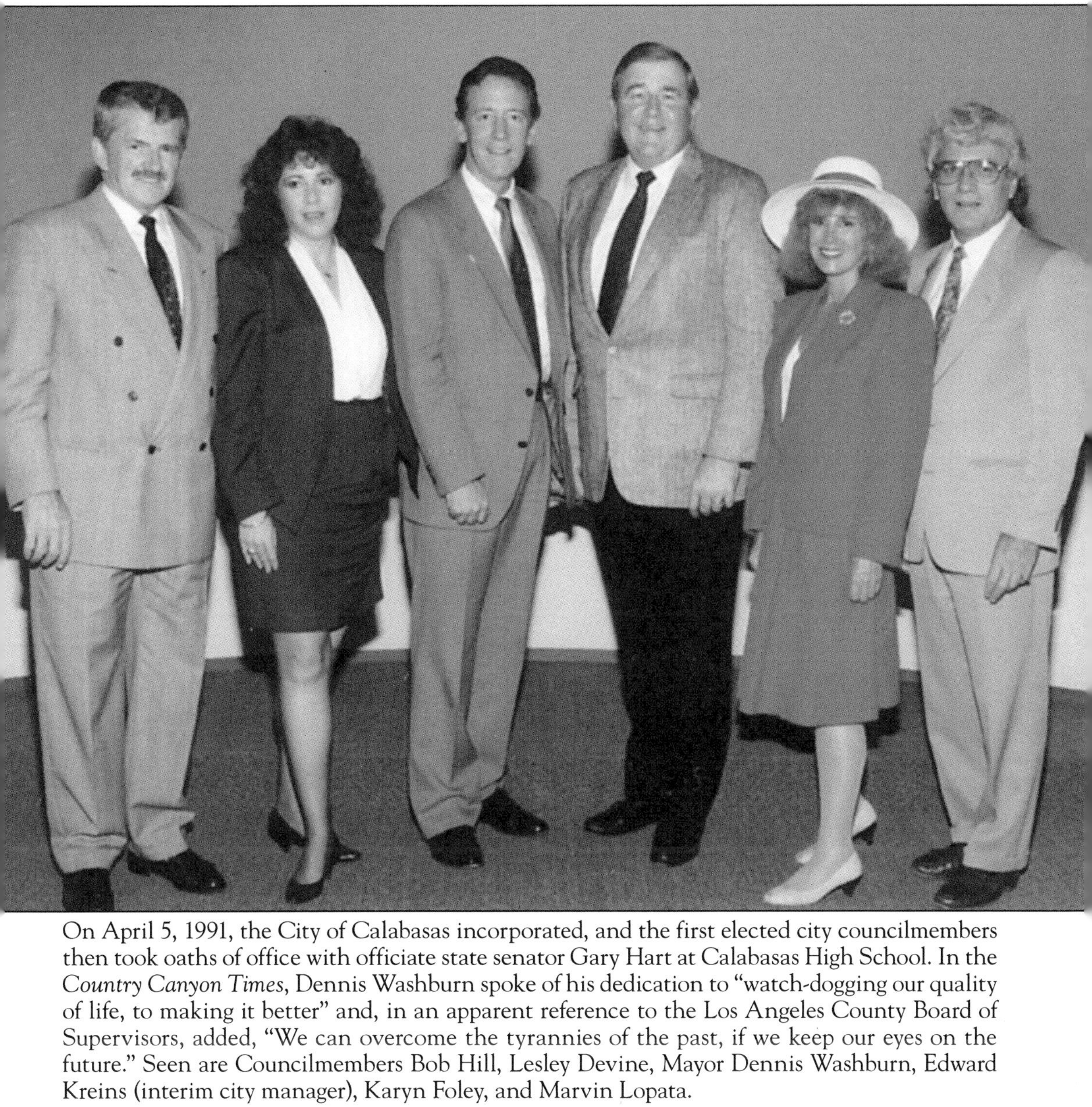

On April 5, 1991, the City of Calabasas incorporated, and the first elected city councilmembers then took oaths of office with officiate state senator Gary Hart at Calabasas High School. In the *Country Canyon Times*, Dennis Washburn spoke of his dedication to "watch-dogging our quality of life, to making it better" and, in an apparent reference to the Los Angeles County Board of Supervisors, added, "We can overcome the tyrannies of the past, if we keep our eyes on the future." Seen are Councilmembers Bob Hill, Lesley Devine, Mayor Dennis Washburn, Edward Kreins (interim city manager), Karyn Foley, and Marvin Lopata.

Ballot Positions

PROPOSED INCORPORATIONS OF THE CITY OF CALABASAS

There are 13 candidates listed. Vote for no more than 5 of the 13 candidates.

DORIS A. LaVIOLETTE.......... ☐
Community Volunteer
MARVIN LOPATA.................... ☐
Real Estate Appraiser
MICHAEL FICHERA.............. ☐
Businessman/Attorney
KARYN FOLEY........................ ☐
Businesswoman
JACK SINCLAIR BETHEL...... ☐
Commercial Banker
DENNIS WASHBURN............. ☐
Marketing/Communications Executive
PETER L. EASON................... ☐
Banker
BOB HILL................................ ☐
Investment Banker
LESLEY LEVINE..................... ☐
Director, Conservation District
GARY S. KLEIN....................... ☐
City Planner
JEFFREY S. KURTZ............... ☐
Attorney
RONALD GOLD....................... ☐
Attorney, Managing Partner
BILL MELCHER...................... ☐
Attorney

CALABASAS CITYHOOD
COMMEMORATIVE BROCHURE COMMITTEE

Betty Noling, Marvin E. Lopata, Bob Hill, Tony Rotella, Mary Jane Rotella, Jenna Zinck, Madeline Williamson and Donna Cole.

The Candid

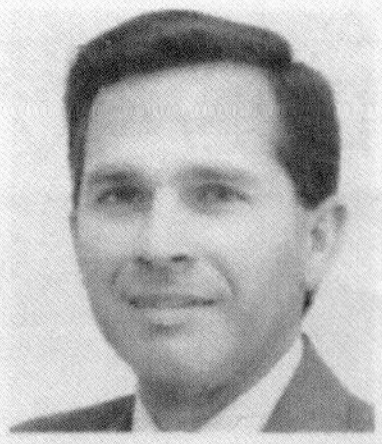

JACK SINCLAIR BETHEL
A residence of Calabasas, Jack is assistant vice president of Commercial Lending and Development at Union Bank. He is also president of the Las Virgenes Hill Homeowners Association; past president, Las Virgenes Park Executive Board; Calabasas Cityhood Committee member. Jack is committed to the development of responsible government while preserving the character and integrity of Calabasas. A graduate of USC, Jack is also Lieutenant Commander, Naval Reserves.

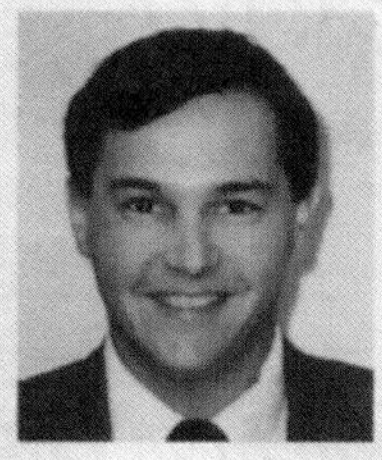

PETER L. EASON
A visible Cityhood Committee member, Eason is a project analyst at California Federal Bank, with eight years banking experience. Sponsored by the AQMD to attend USC's Environmental Management Institute, he earned a degree in Public Administration. Recycling, parkspace, historic preservation and maintaining capacity for sensible growth are on Eason's proposed agenda.

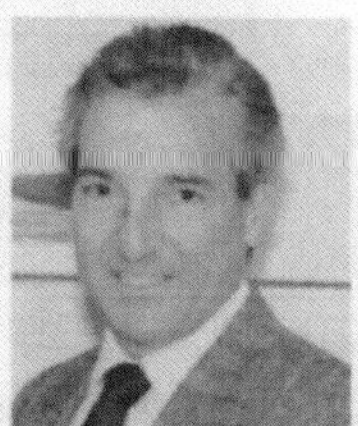

MICHAEL FICHERA, JR.
Michael has been a businessman in the Valley for 25 years and is also an attorney. He resides with his wife, Maureen, and two children in Calabasas Park Estates. He has been active in neighborhood affairs for three years, serving on the Architectural Committee, and is president of the Homeowners Association.

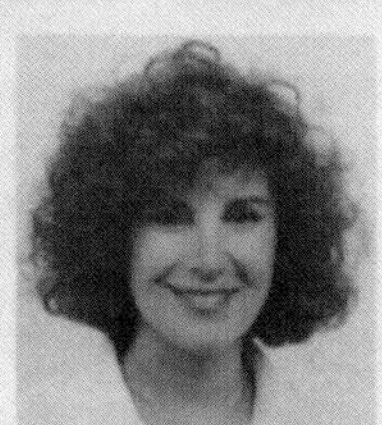

KARYN FOLEY
Since 1975, Karyn has been actively involved in local issues. She has worked on Calabasas Cityhood Committee both as director and secretary. A UCLA graduate, she is presently a real estate broker. Karyn is committed to the development of parks and recreation programs for children, youth and senior citizens.

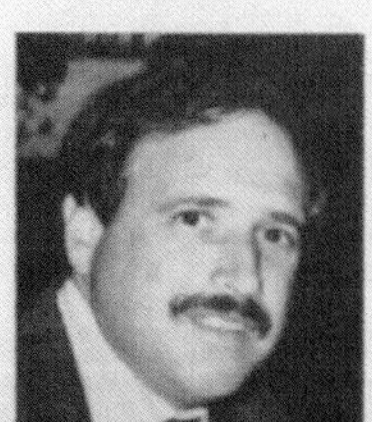

RON GOLD
A Calabasas attorney and resident, Ron is a proponent of strict growth controls, coupled with a concern for protecting the environment that makes Calabasas unique. Ron served as a Deputy Attorney General from 1972-1978. He established the Calabasas law firm, Murphy and Gold and has handled several cases on behalf of the community involving education and intergovernmental relations. He is married with two sons.

BILL MELCHER
(Bio and photo not available.)

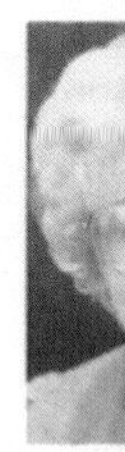

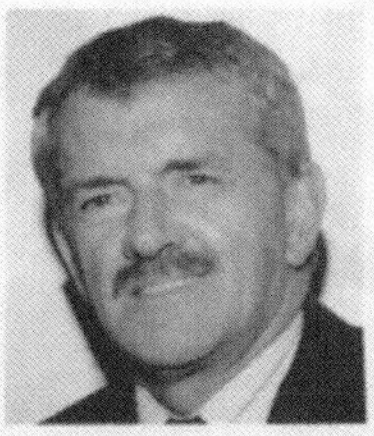

BOB HILL

Hill is president of Calabasas Cityhood Committee, past president of Calabasas Homeowners Association, and a 19-year resident of Calabasas. He favors using budgets to emphasize better quality of life, greater adherence to Santa Monica Mountains General Plan for development, and city cooperation to solve common infrastructure problems.

GARY KLEIN

Gary is a city planner with the City of Los Angeles. He resides in Calabasas Park with his wife and two children. A graduate of California State University, Northridge, Gary has 11 years of extensive city planning experience. He is a member of the board of Calabasas Park Homeowners Association and the Park Verdi Homeowners Association. He believes in a strong, workable general plan for the city of Calabasas. (Not pictured here.)

JEFFREY S. KURTZ

Kurtz has been a practicing family law and business attorney for 16 years. He is a graduate of UCLA and Southwestern University. His key concerns are responsible future planning and the establishment of recreation facilities. Kurtz has been an active director of the Calabasas Cityhood Committee since 1988. He is married with two children.

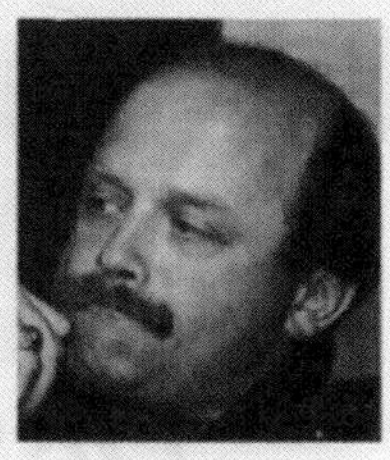

DORIS LaVIOLETTE

Doris is a community volunteer and has been a Calabasas resident for 25 years. She helped organize the Cityhood Committee and is executive vice president. She believes future development must be sensitive to the environment. Doris pledges to establish fiscal responsibility and sound planning, giving citizens a voice in local issues.

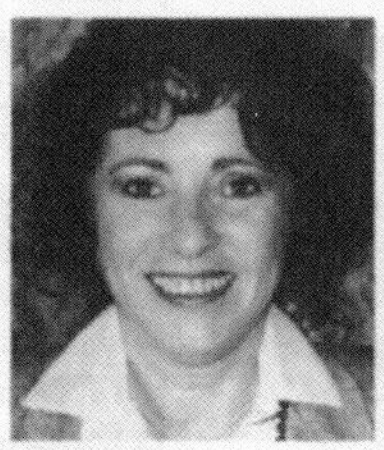

LESLEY LEVINE

Lesley is director of the Topanga-Las Virgenes Resource Conservation District; member, Cityhood Committee; former president, Mulwood Homeowners Association, and vice president, Las Virgenes Homeowners Federation. She is committed to retaining the small town atmosphere of Calabasas, introducing children's services and preventing gridlock. An independent businesswoman, Levine is a 16-year resident.

DENNIS WASHBURN

Dennis has devoted 20 years to preserving Calabasas -- as founding member and first vice president of the Cityhood Committee; president of the Topanga-Las Virgenes Resource Conservation District and the chair of its State Association Land/Urban Impact committee; Las Virgenes Homeowners Federation president; co-chair Santa Monica Mountains Parkland Assoc.; and member of the Old Town Calabasas Coalition. Dennis is a marketing/advertising executive.

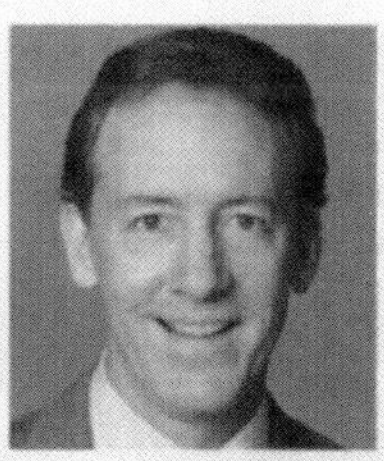

PATA

ood Com-
en at the
ment for
is a resi-
rving as
nd presi-
Iulwood
ation. He
lecision
es, while
especting
e among
systems.

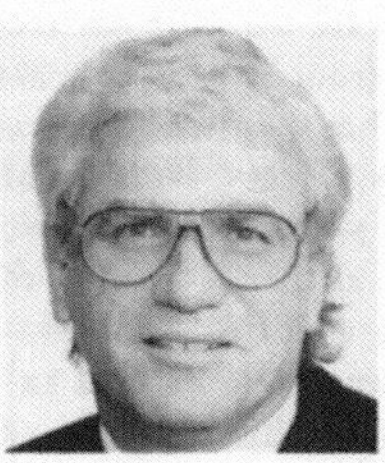

TYHOOD

The 13 candidates for city council are seen at left; the five who received the most votes were elected to the new council. Voter results for this important election were Dennis Washburn (2,840), Bob Hill (2,353), Marvin Lopata (2,048), Lesley Devine (1,910), Karyn Foley (1,716), Doris La Violette (1,655), Ronald Gold (1,540), Bill Melcher (1,244), Gary S. Klein (936), Michael Fichera Jr. (806), Peter L. Eason (705), Jack Sinclair Bethel (621), and Jeffrey S. Kurtz (568). Councilmembers serve staggered, four-year terms and are elected at large. Each year, the council chooses one of its members to act as mayor and preside over meetings. (Courtesy of Mayor James R. Bozajian.)

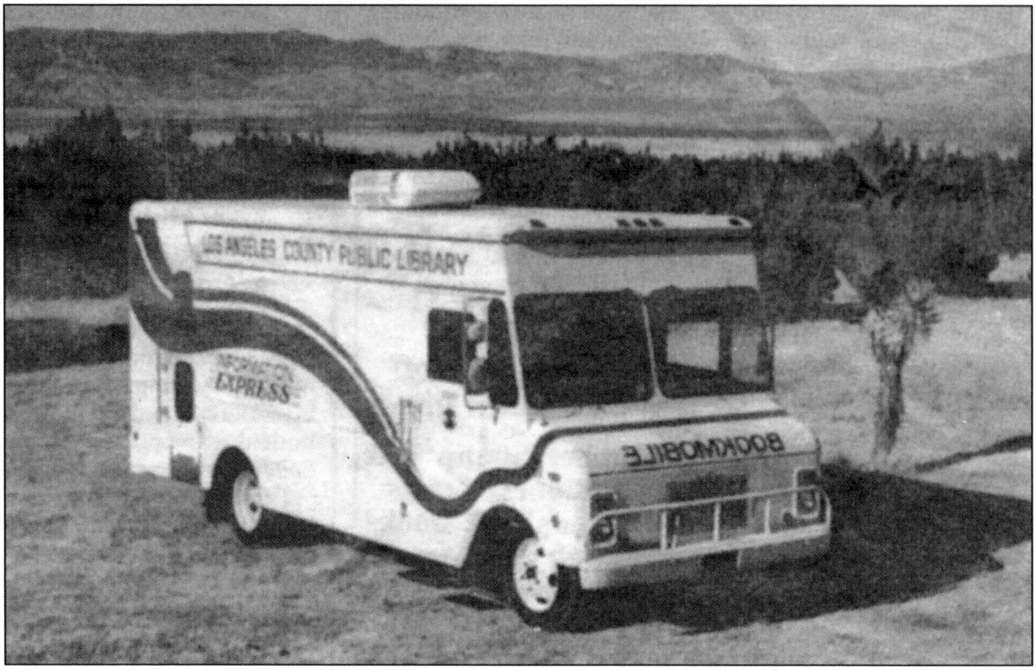

Originally, library service for the community of Calabasas was provided by the Los Angeles County Library System. On July 11, 1998, the library in Calabasas officially became the Calabasas Municipal Library. Partially funded by a state bond, a new library was built in 2008 at the Calabasas Civic Center next to city hall. Today, the library offers 70,000 items and provides ample work space, study rooms, and the Calabasas Historical Society Archival Collection. (Courtesy of the Calabasas Media Department.)

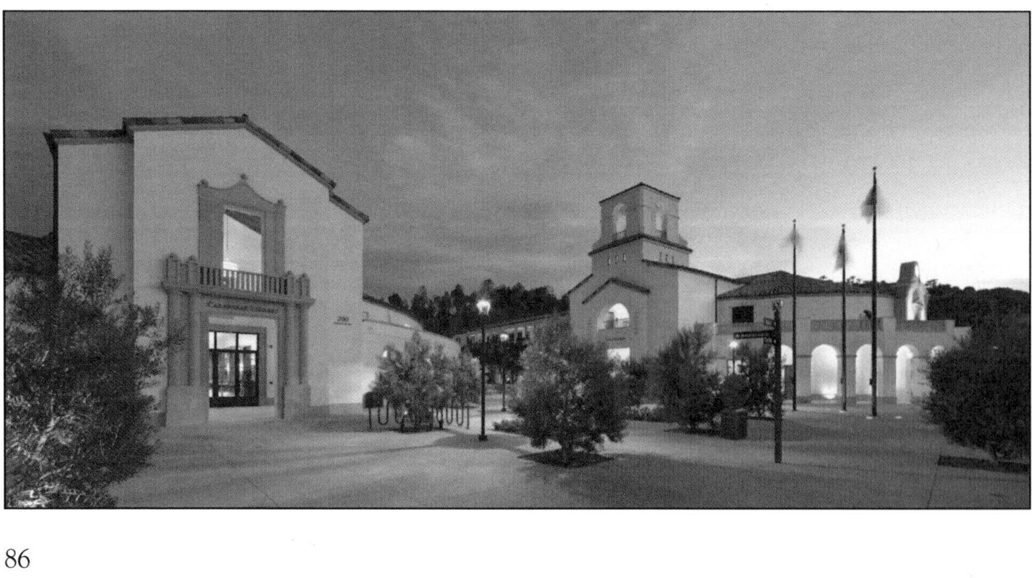

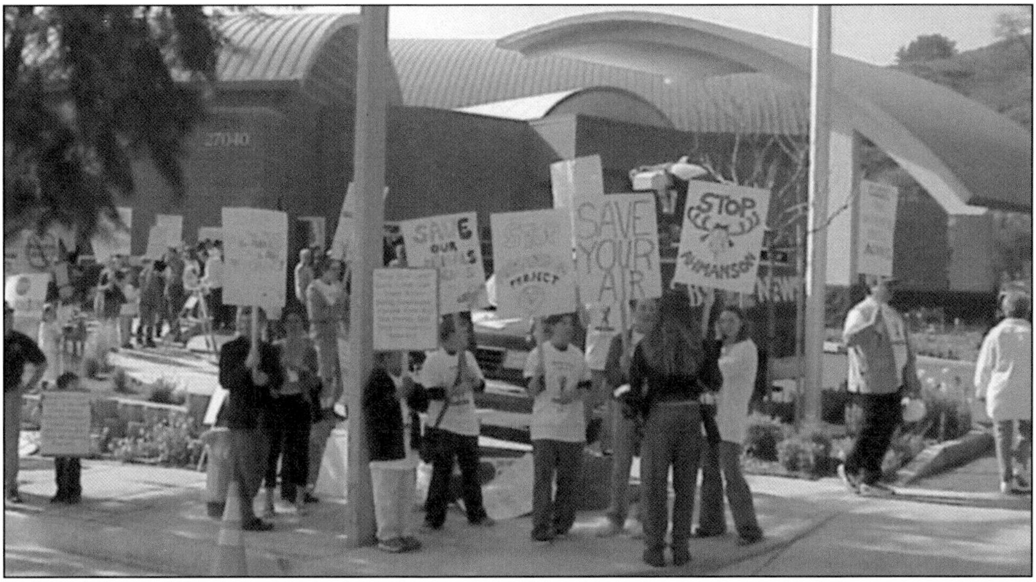

At nearly one year old, in March 1992 the newly formed Calabasas City Council took aim at the Ahmanson Ranch Development. They challenged the serious impact of gridlock traffic and commuter congestion, in addition to the environmental issues that would disrupt the quality of life. The 11-year protest spurred many rallies throughout the valley, like this one outside the Agoura Hills/Calabasas Community Center in 2000. (Courtesy of the Calabasas Media Department.)

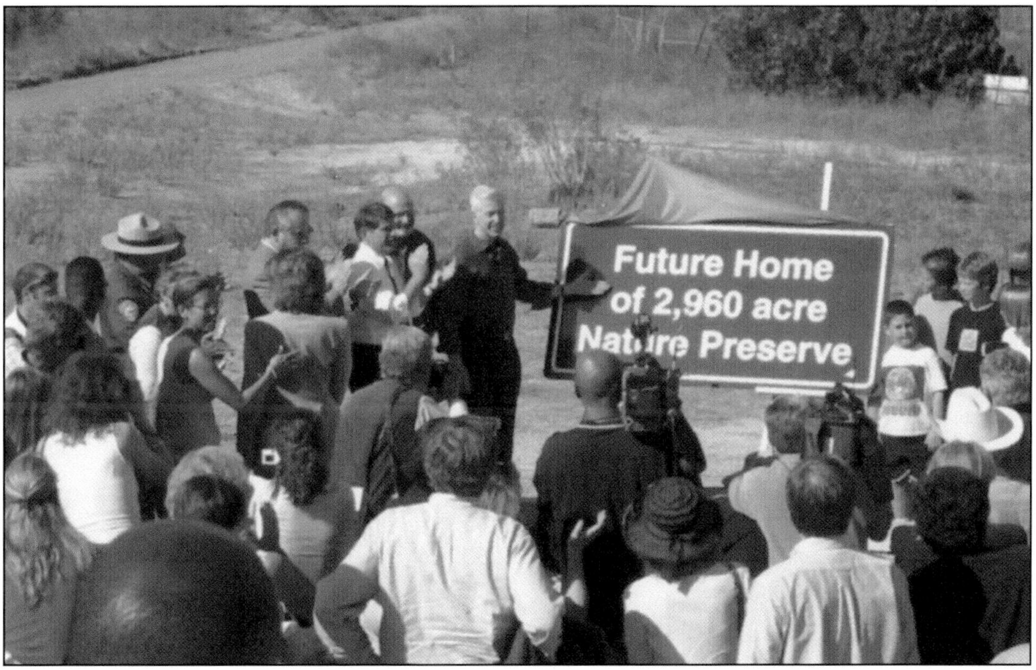

Here, a landmark sign is unveiled by Gov. Gray Davis with the support of Los Angeles County supervisor Zev Yaroslavsky, Ventura County supervisor Linda Parks, state assemblywomen Fran Pavley, actor Rob Reiner, and other community activists and residents. The year 2003 marked the end result of the battle to provide "The Future Home of 2,960 acre Nature Preserve" and avoid possible development. (Courtesy of the Calabasas Media Department.)

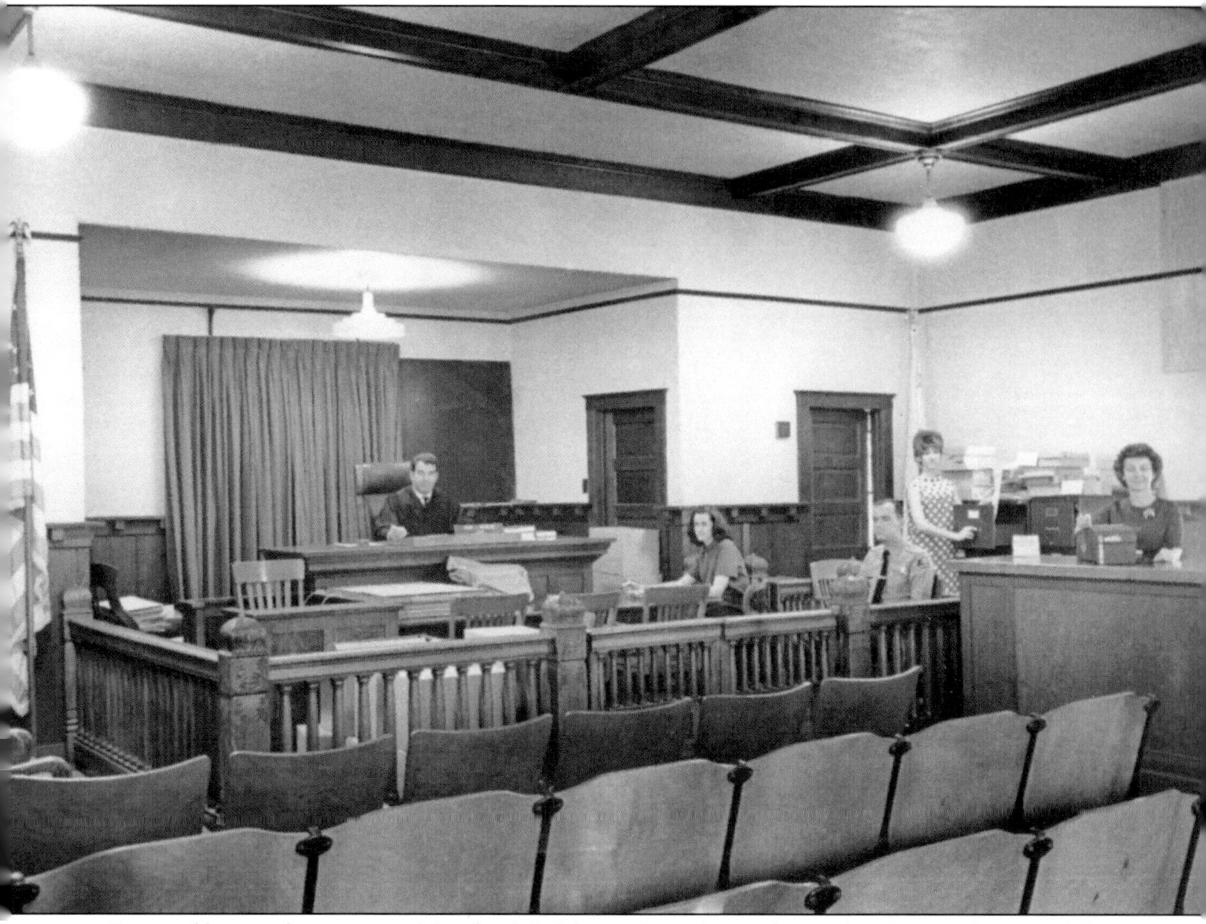

Pictured here is the interior of the third Calabasas Courthouse, located at 5030 Parkway Calabasas and opened on February 29, 1968. Since there were not any holding facilities, prisoners were kept on a bus parked in front of the courthouse while waiting to go on trial. Another quirk of the courtroom facilities was that staff was not able to use their typewriters nor flush toilets, as the walls were paper thin and the noise would disrupt proceedings. The court was upgraded on December 4, 1973, to a judicial district. Judge John Merrick presided over this one-room courtroom until 1992, and in September 2000, the courtroom closed its doors.

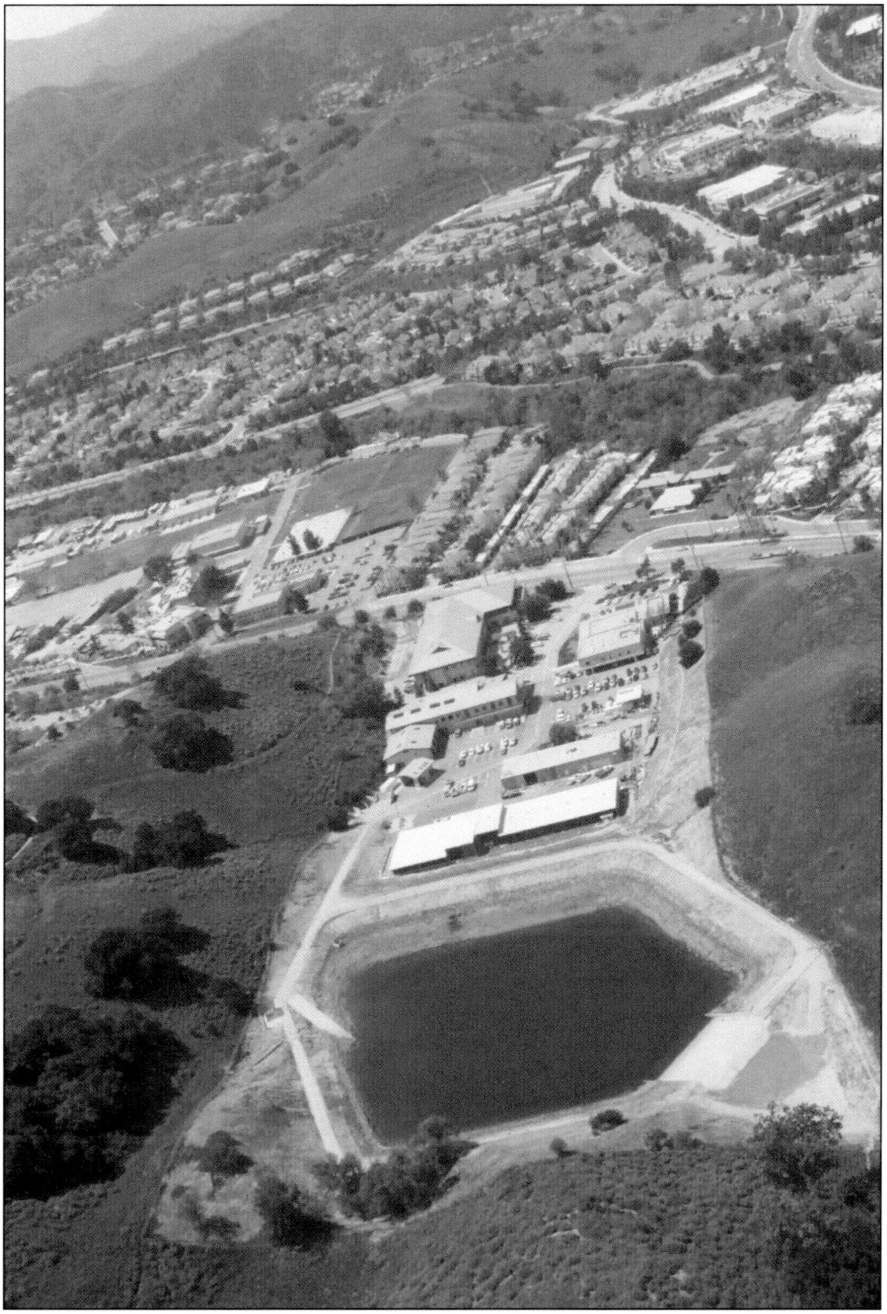

Las Virgenes Municipal Water District was a pioneering agency in using recycled water as a valued resource. In 1972, LVMWD worked to replace some of its imported potable water with recycled water from the Tapia Water Reclamation Facility to be used for irrigating golf courses, parks, school grounds, highway landscapes, and common areas of certain housing developments. Today, 20 percent of water served by LVMWD is tertiary-treated Title 22–compliant recycled water used for irrigation, reducing the region's dependence upon imported water. LVMWD's recycled water system consists of four tanks, five pumping stations, three reservoirs, and 66 miles of pipeline. (Courtesy of the Calabasas Media Department.)

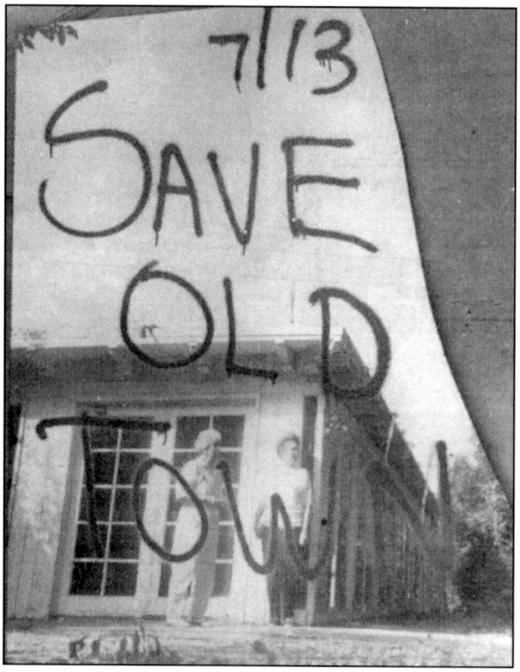

This is a handwritten plea to "Save Old Town" on a broken mirror found behind the Kramer Store in Old Town. This photograph was taken by the *Country Canyon Times* on October 4, 1990. The two people seen are Beverly Daic Tabor (left) and Sally Cooper Cawelti (right), descendants of Calabasas homestead families.

In 1998, after a renovation project was complete, there was a grand reopening and rededication ceremony of Old Town Calabasas. Improvements softened the beaten pathways by creating boardwalk and cobblestone pedestrian connections, replacing street lighting with gas lamp replicas, recreating hitching posts, adding beautifully planted medians and barrel flower pots, and dropping in signage that complemented the Western aesthetic. (Courtesy of the Calabasas Media Department.)

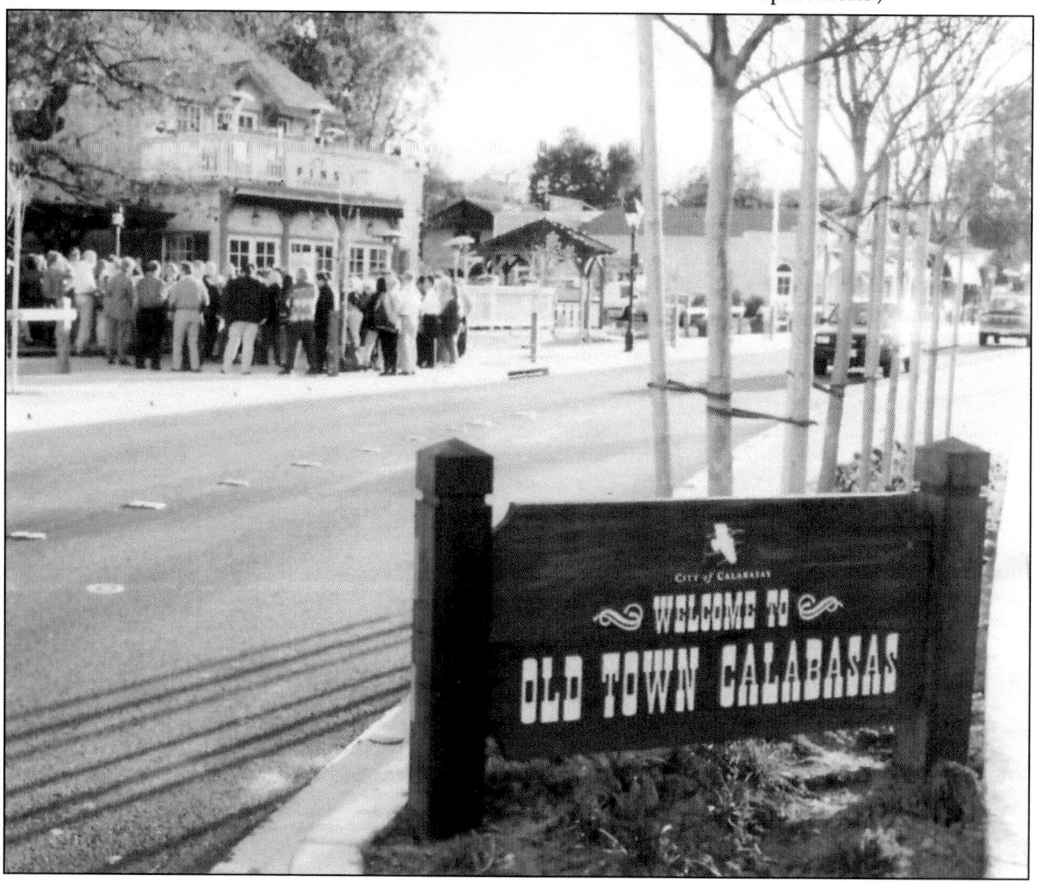

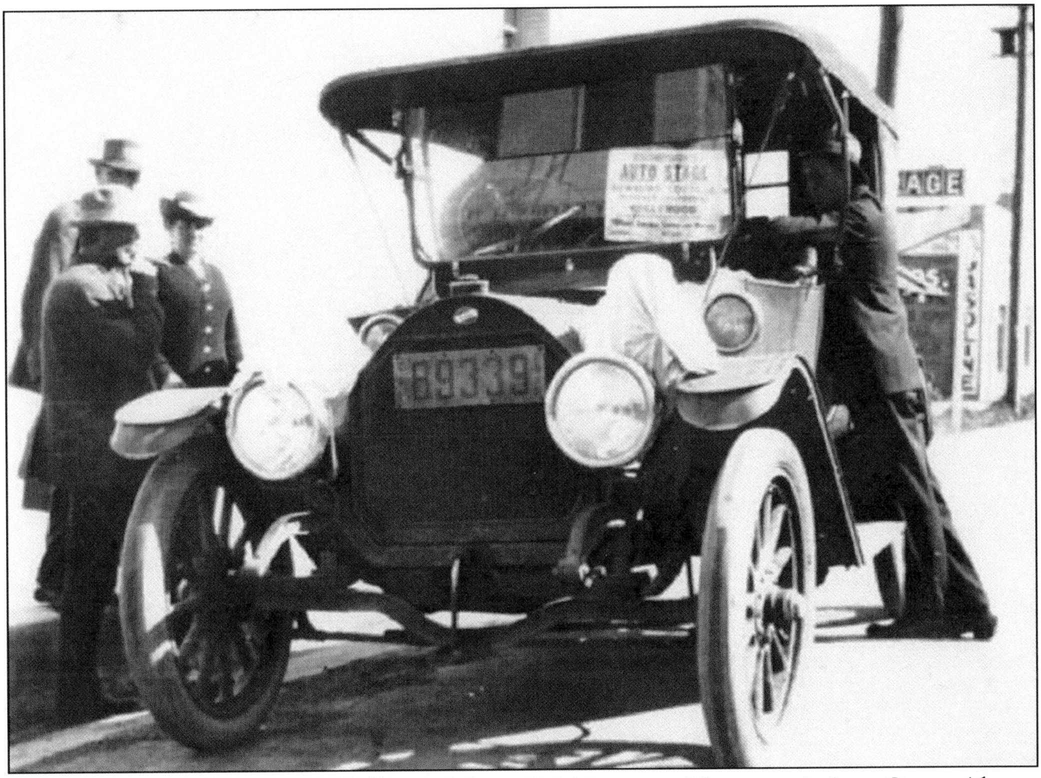

The first bus (taxi) service to Hollywood from Calabasas was Thompson's Auto Stage. Above, people from Calabasas leave for a shopping trip to Los Angeles. The taxi serviced Newbury Park, Cornell, Calabasas, and Hollywood, c. 1915. Today, the Calabasas Trolley is a convenient mode of transportation for city residents and visitors. The red bus runs on compressed natural gas (CNG) and performs a loop route in one direction throughout the city. Below, members of the Calabasas City Council, staff, family, and friends board the trolley to participate in the 2014 annual Hidden Hills Fiesta parade. (Below, courtesy of the Calabasas Media Department.)

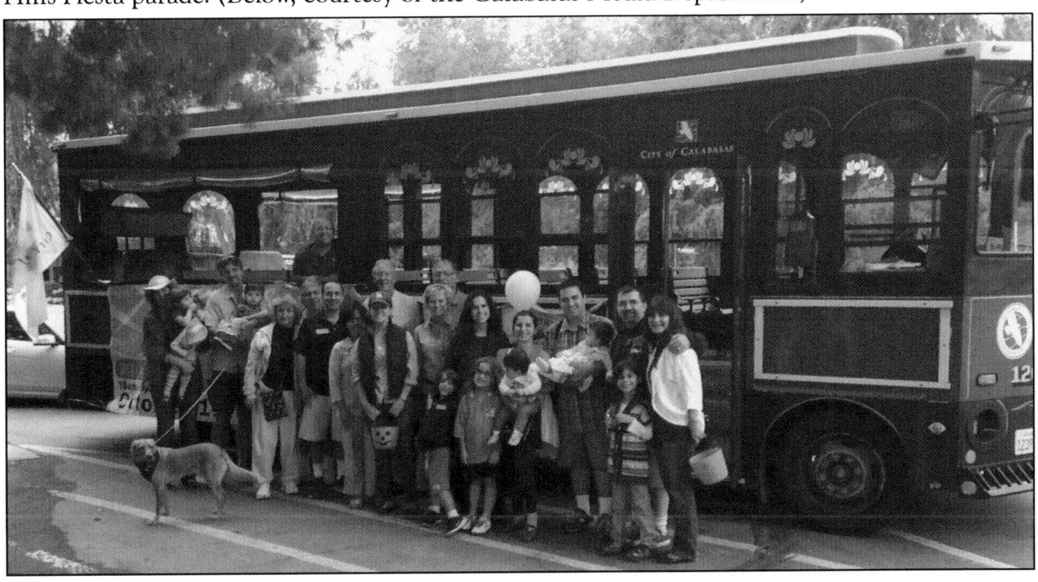

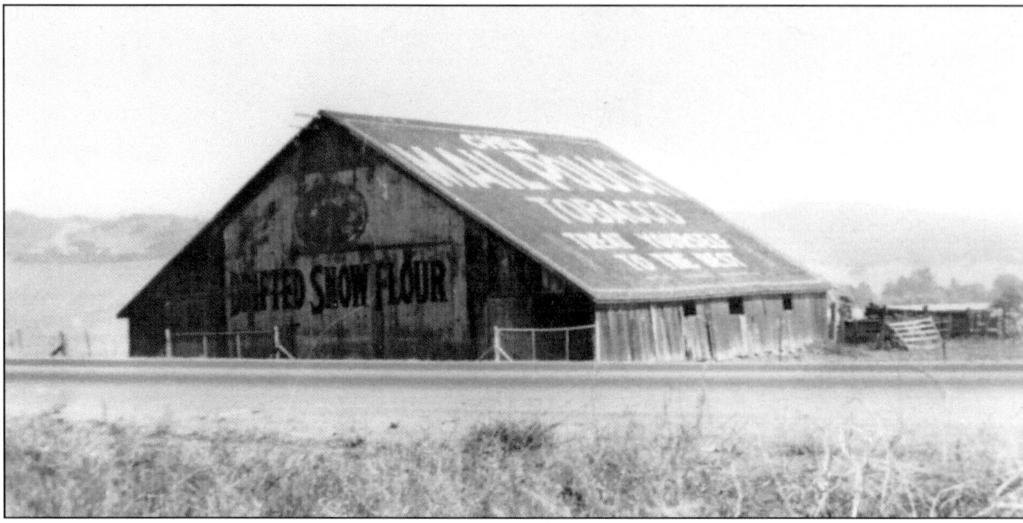

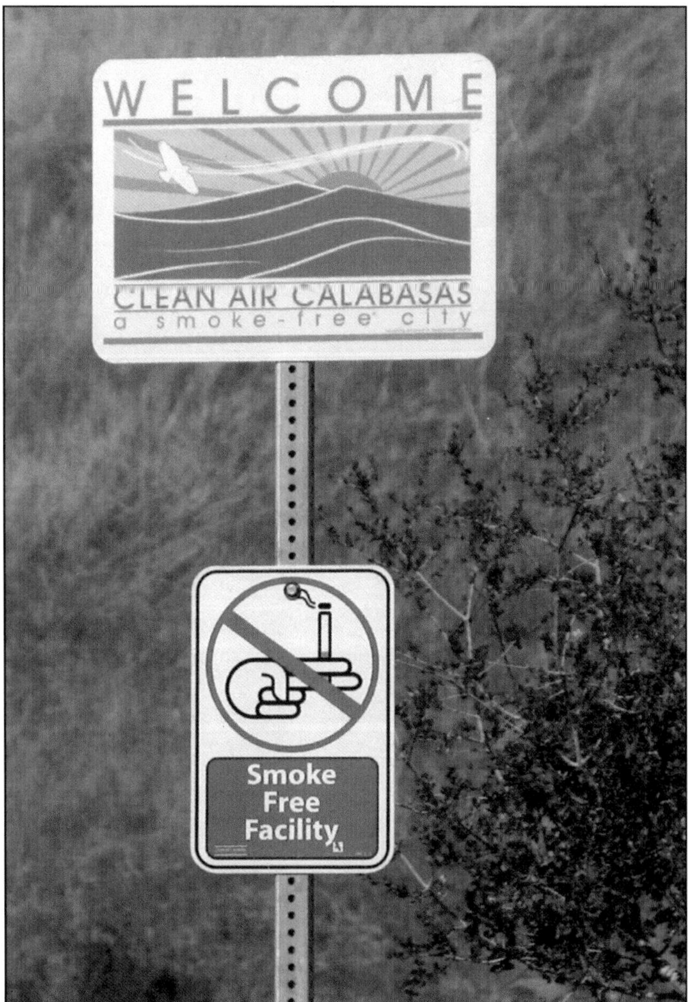

Above is the Daic Barn, located west of Las Virgenes Road, about 1910. The advertisement on the side of the barn is for "Drifted Snow Flour," and the one on the roof advises: "Chew Mail Pouch Tobacco—Treat Yourself to the Best." Almost 100 years later, Calabasas was a leader in adopting a no-smoking ordinance. On March 17, 2006, the Calabasas City Council unanimously adopted a comprehensive secondhand smoke control ordinance, which limited public exposure to secondhand smoke in public areas within the city. (Both, courtesy of the Calabasas Media Department.)

Seven

Decades of Growth

Although the Calabasas area has developed over the years, the spirit of the Wild West has not faded away.

Is history repeating itself when one reads about the "King of Calabasas" and his relationship with Major Horace Bell, who was known for telling self-declared stories with his tongue-in-cheek cynical style? It is true that the early Calabasas City Council used psychologists during a tumultuous period to resolve clashes while local newspapers criticized councilmembers for lacking maturity?

Even though legends paint a colorful portrait of early Calabasas residents burying treasure, dealing with bandits, and taking the law into their own hands, the truth about Old Town's Wild West image is more grounded. Archie Hanson purchased some Western movie sets from the old RKO studio and used them to dress up the exteriors of the buildings in Old Town in the 1950s. Although it is just a facade that has been embraced and romanticized, it is the community spirit that shines through—engaging and drawing interest to an area that once encompassed Hollywood's largest movie ranch and now is home to many well-known celebrities. Calabasas has layers, but once peeled back, it is more than a golden gourd of luxury homes and expensive cars.

Calabasas's continued preservation of land is akin to the early homesteaders ensuring that their land boundaries were not infringed upon. In 2005, Calabasas residents overwhelmingly approved Measure D, which requires a two-thirds majority vote to change zoning on any property in the city designated as open space. Nearly half of the city's acreage today is designated open space.

As recently as 1978, many supermarket pumpkins in Southern California came from Calabasas. Calabasas rancher Wilda Sampo leased 3,500 acres along Las Virgenes Road and planted 40 acres in pumpkins each year. At that time, the Sampo Ranch pumpkin patch was said to be the largest between San Diego and San Luis Obispo. Does this mean that there is some truth to the legend about the overturned rancher's wagon?

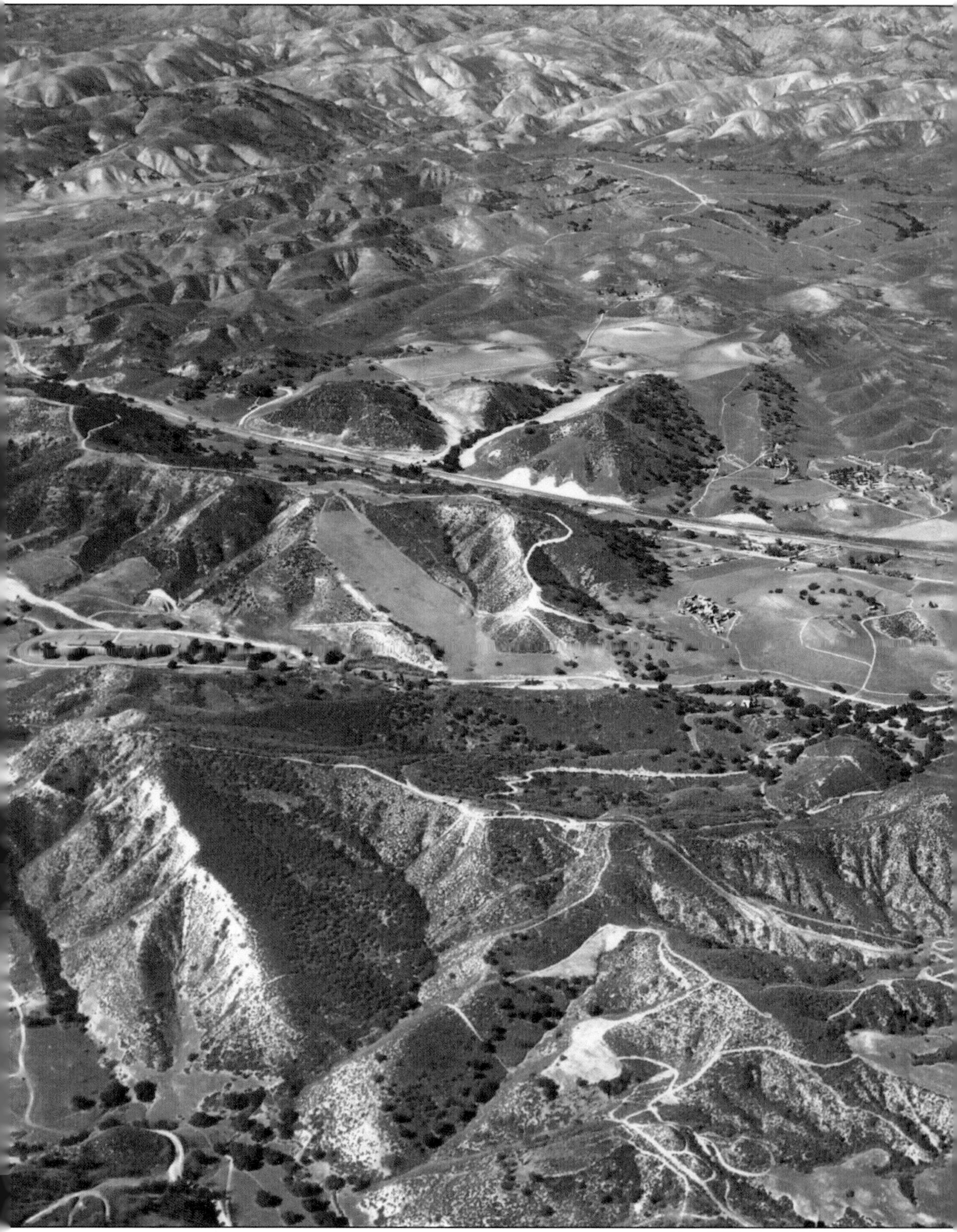

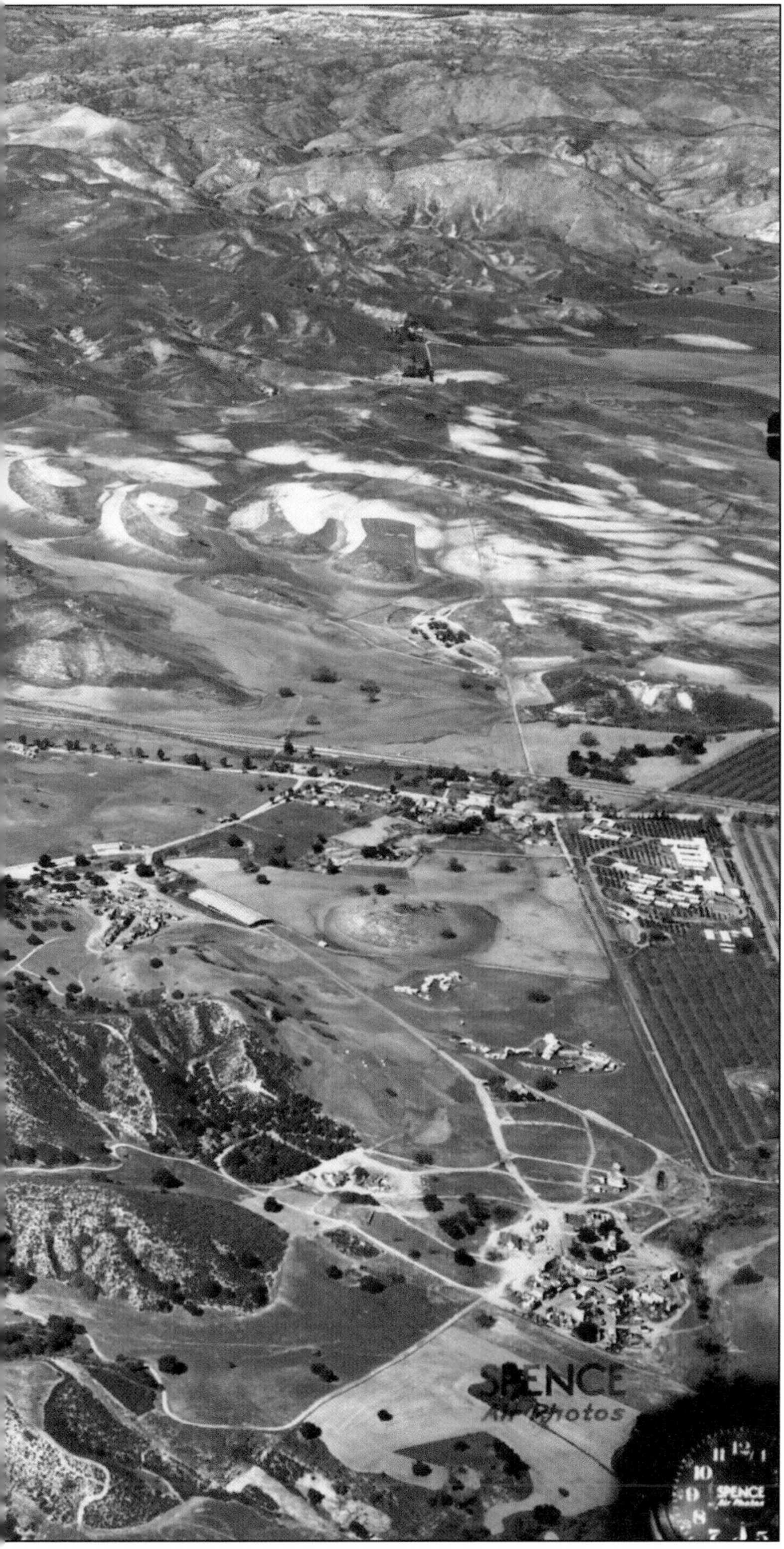

This is an aerial photograph of Calabasas, Hidden Hills, and Woodland Hills from 1950. The Motion Picture Relief Foundation can be seen at the far right just below the highway that runs through the center of the images. Old Town Calabasas is to the left of the facility with Hidden Hills across the highway, identified only by the twin oaks visible on the Long Valley dirt road. To the far left, below the highway and tucked in a shallow valley, is the Warner Ranch house and barn. (Courtesy of Bison Archives.)

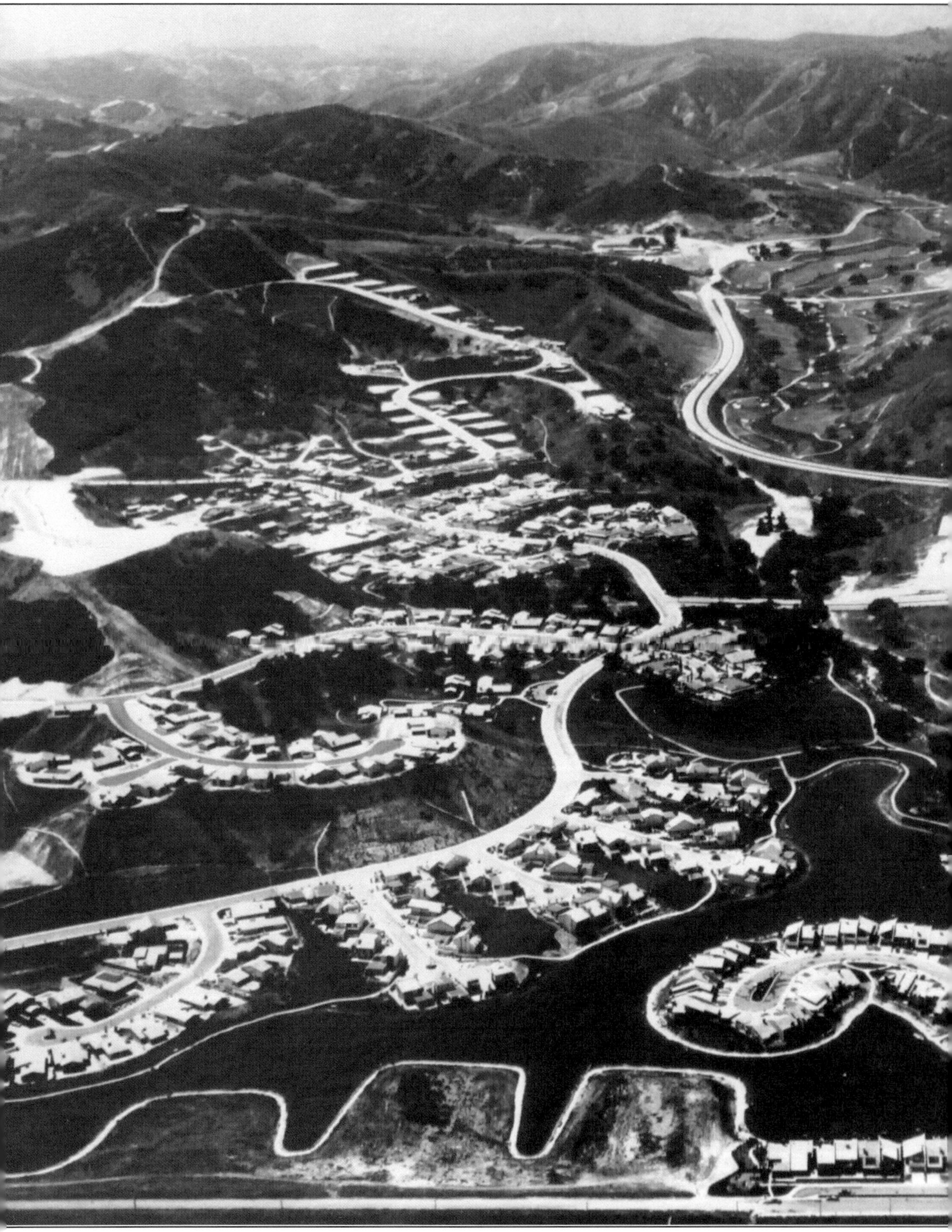

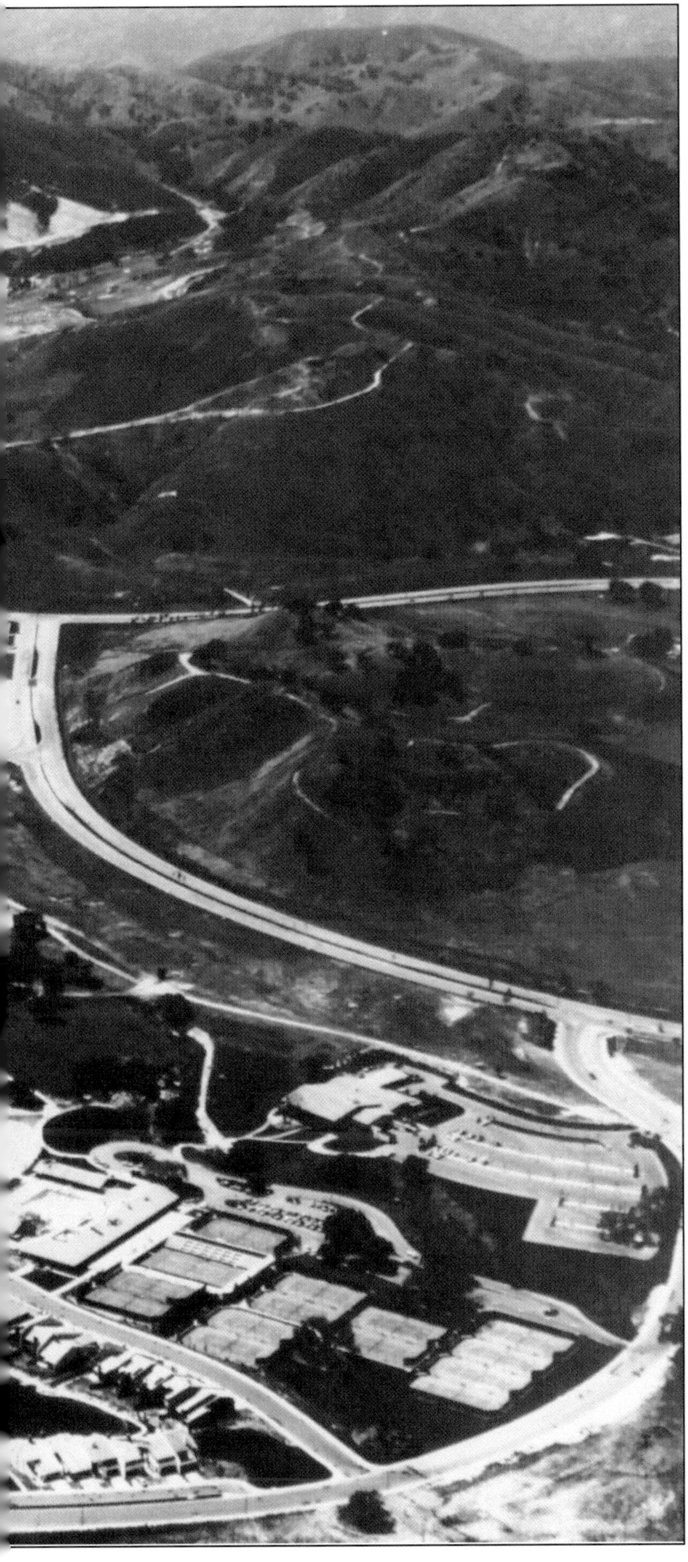

Associated Southern Investment Company, a subsidiary of the Edison Company, purchased Warner Ranch in 1959 and began an all-electric subdivision for 15,000 inhabitants. The plan was stifled for several years by a battle with environmentalists. Today, the community includes an 18-hole golf course, 21-acre lake, and several types of housing. Julian George designed the landscaping around the lake in 1968. Robert Trent Jones and his son laid out the golf course that same year. The surrounding homes (1974 and later) were designed by Dorman/Muselle Associates. This photograph is from about 1970 and was gifted to the historical society by the Smiths, a local Calabasas family.

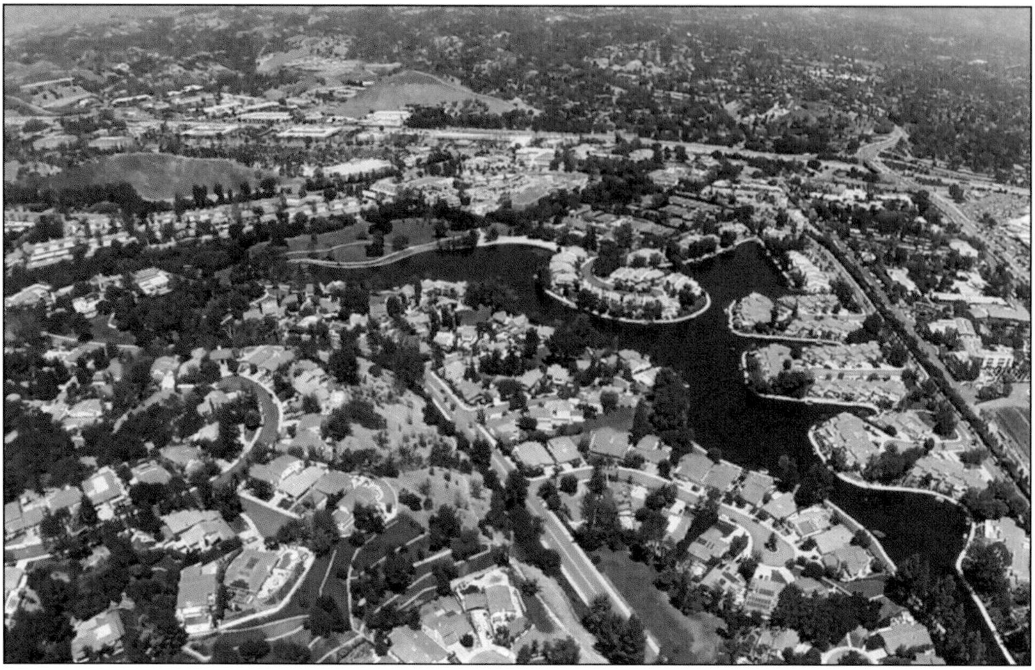

This is another aerial view of Calabasas, Hidden Hills, and Woodland Hills, fast-forwarded to 2015. (Courtesy of the Calabasas Media Department.)

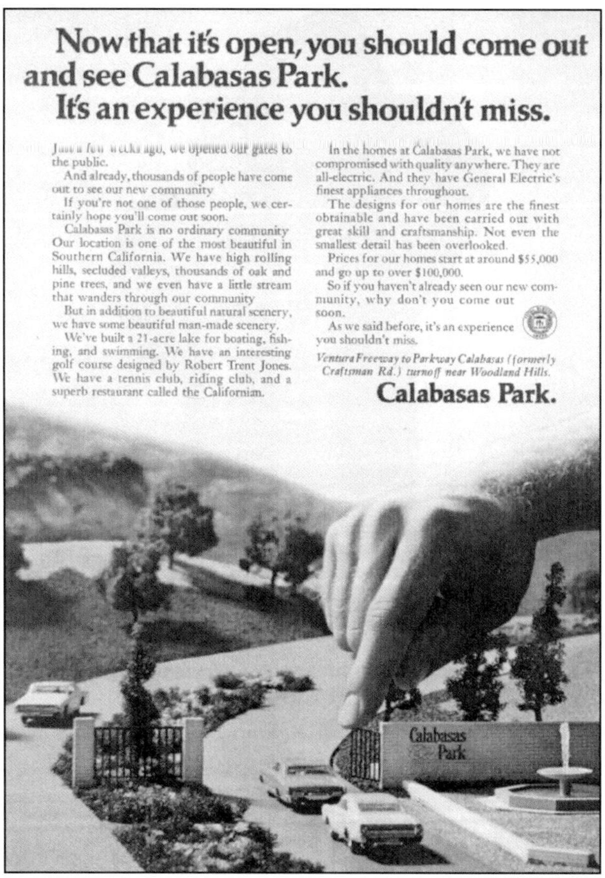

Calabasas Park, one of the first all-electric planned communities, launched its marketing campaign in 1968. This and other advertisements, boasting of beautiful natural scenery and many other amenities, were featured in *Life* magazine and *Los Angeles Times Home* magazine. The advertisement touts that Calabasas was designed using quality materials and General Electric's finest appliances. Home prices started around $55,000 to $100,000. (Courtesy of Mayor James Bozajian.)

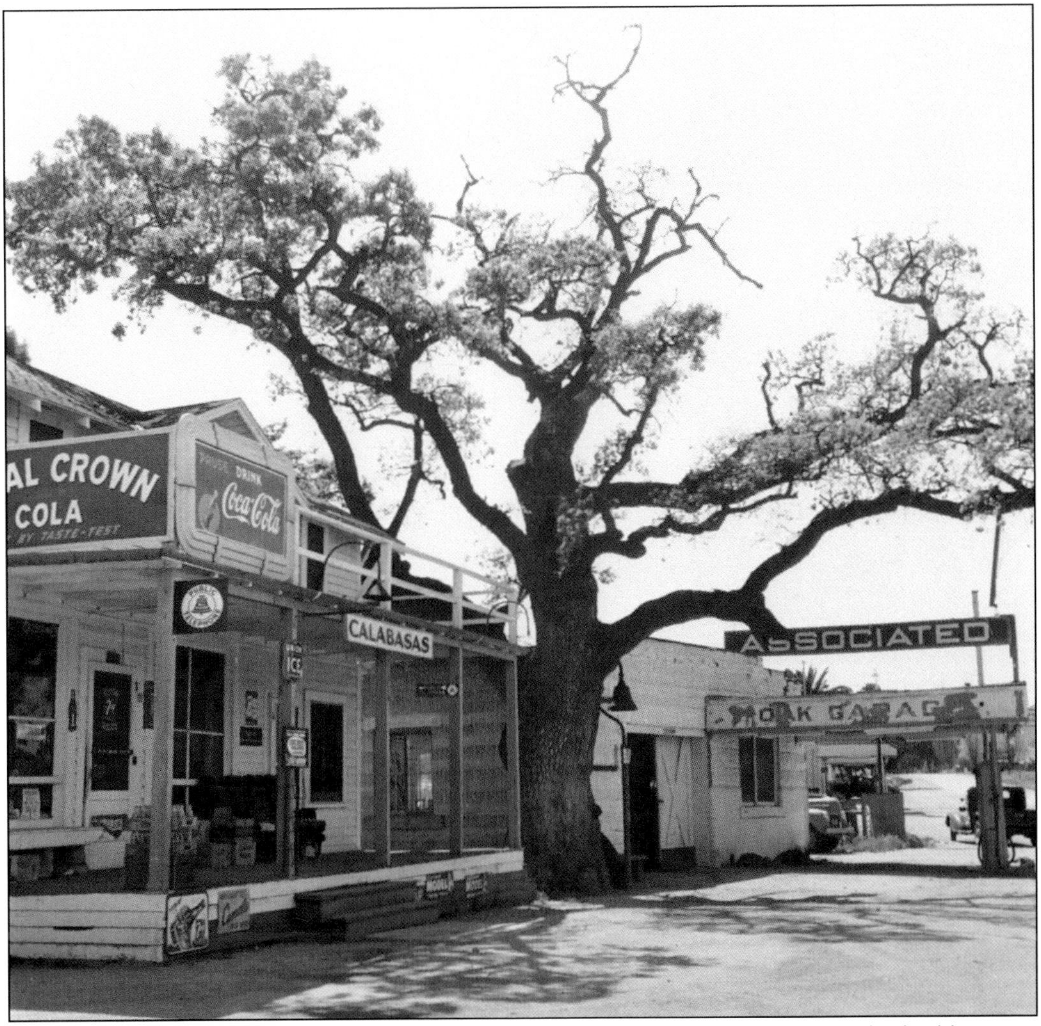

This is a view of the Kramer Store looking west in 1951. From 1969 to 1978, the building was leased by Helen Woodward as The Sundance Saloon. Some of the top country and country rock musicians in the nation appeared there, either on stage or at the bar. Some of the notorious artists were Rick Danko, Buddy Emmons, Woodwork, Albert Lee, and Dr. John. On Tuesday nights, a pickup group of musicians called the Sundance Band got together with members ranging from established celebrates to relative unknowns. (Courtesy of Bison Archives.)

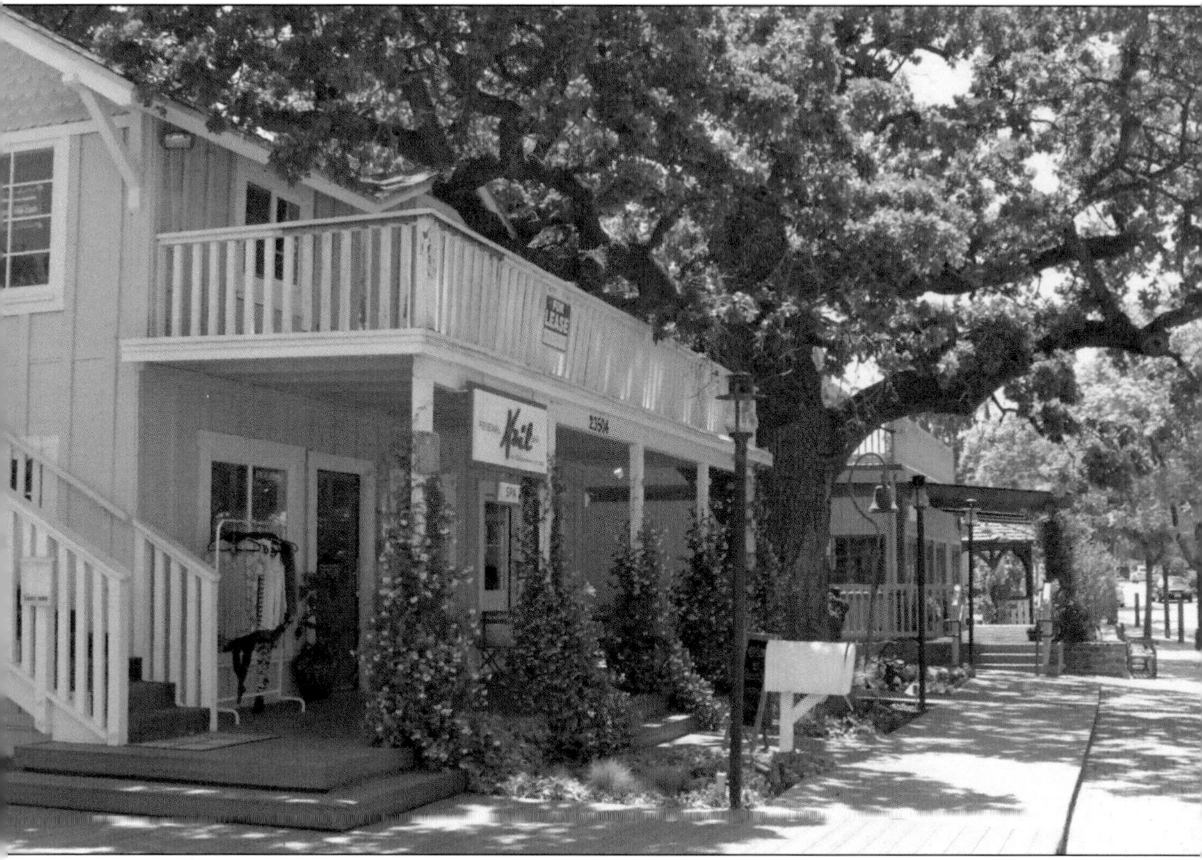

This is a recent photograph of the same location. (Photograph by Karlo Gorgin; courtesy of the Calabasas Media Department.)

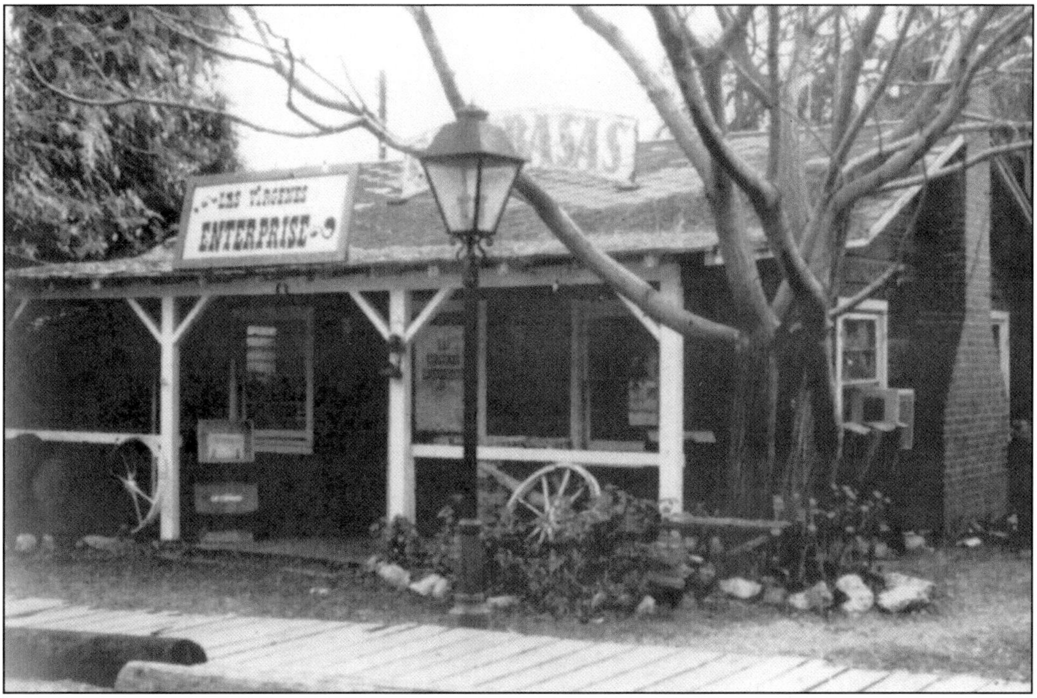

Pictured here around 1960 is the *Las Virgenes Enterprise* office on Calabasas Road. The Las Virgenes Municipal Water District was formed in 1958, a grassroots effort spearheaded by Hidden Hills residents, Elizabeth Hughes, and the Agoura Water Committee. Alice Stelle and Eleanor DeCarteret, both Hidden Hills residents, owned the *Enterprise* newspaper in Calabasas and were tasked with getting the word out to the voters to support the water bond.

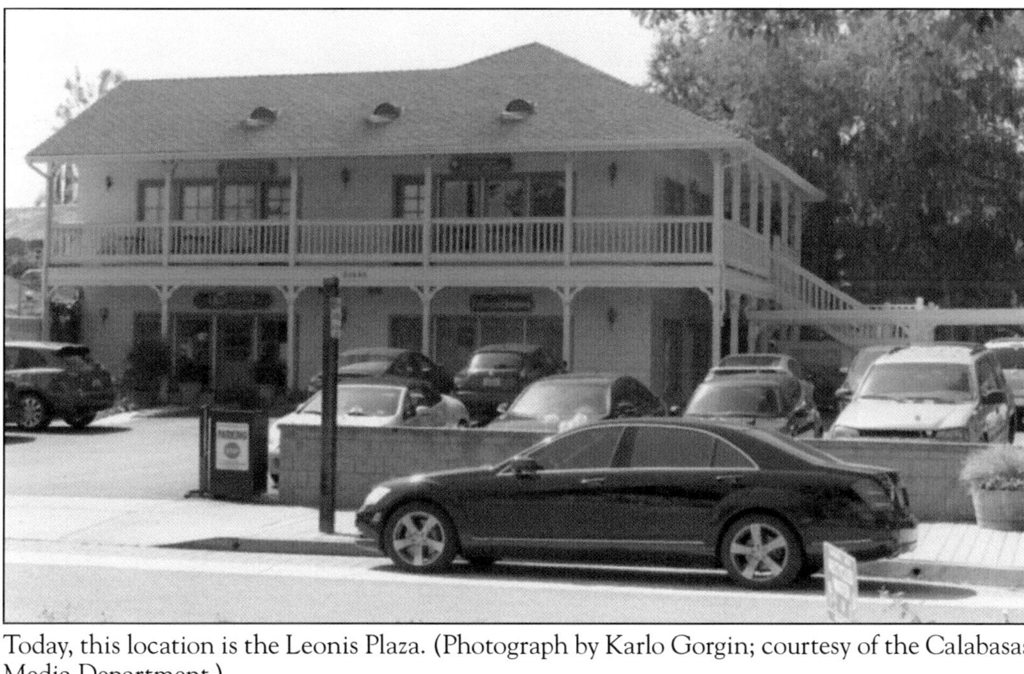

Today, this location is the Leonis Plaza. (Photograph by Karlo Gorgin; courtesy of the Calabasas Media Department.)

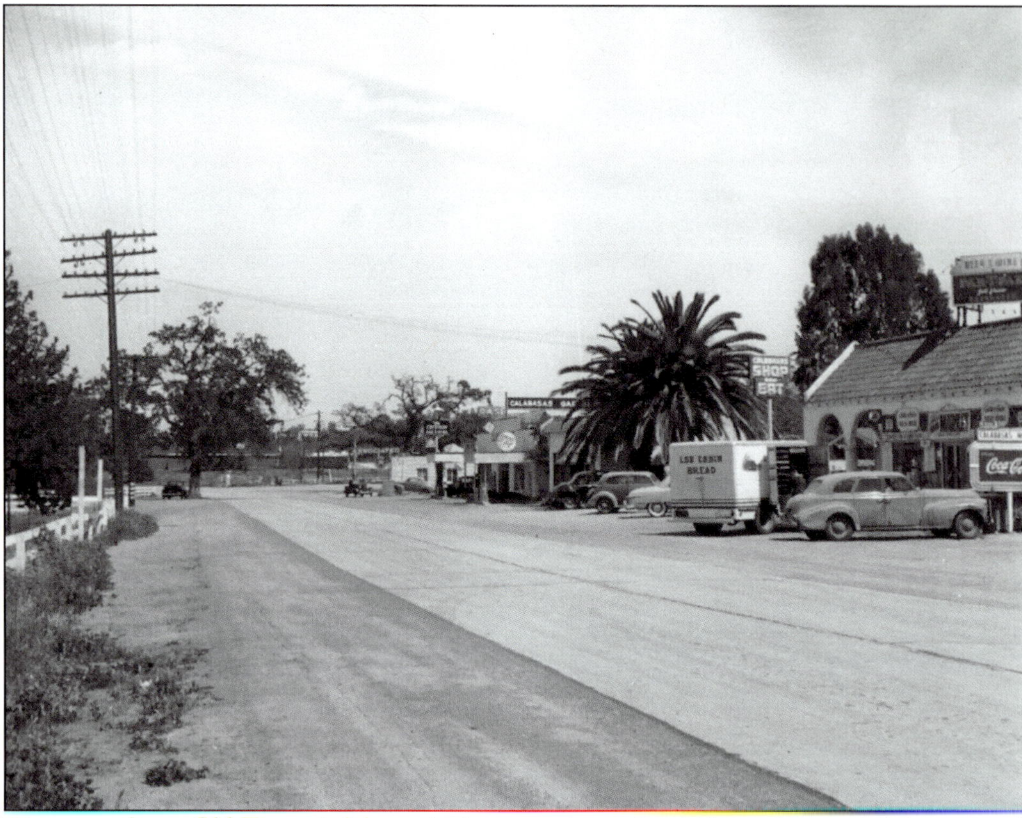

This view shows Old Town Calabasas looking south on the Old Road, now Calabasas Road, in 1951. Looking far south, coming north, is the Kramer Store, Wally's Rancho Store, the Oak Garage, the Calabasas Garage, and the Calabasas Market.

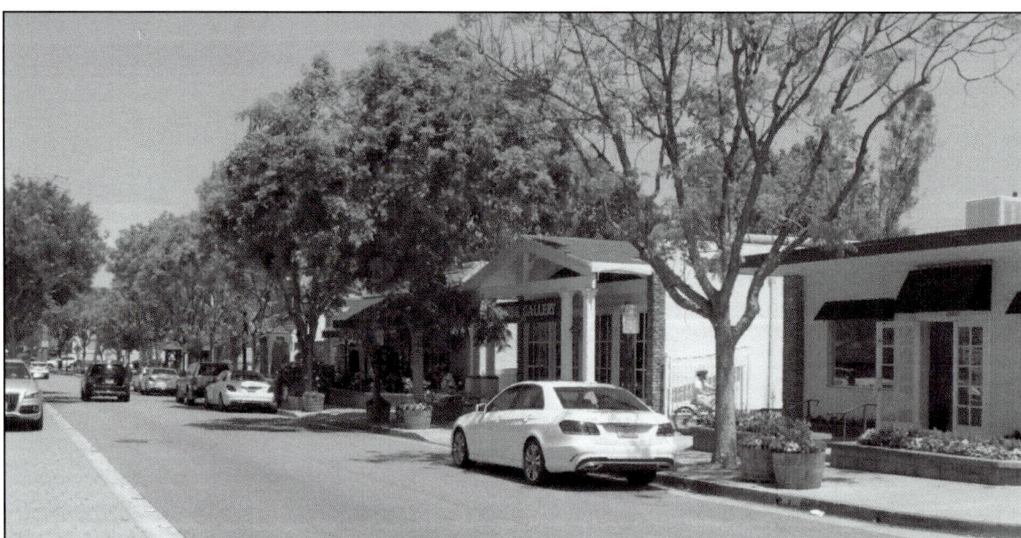

Here is Calabasas Road today looking southeast. (Photograph by Karlo Gorgin; courtesy of the Calabasas Media Department.)

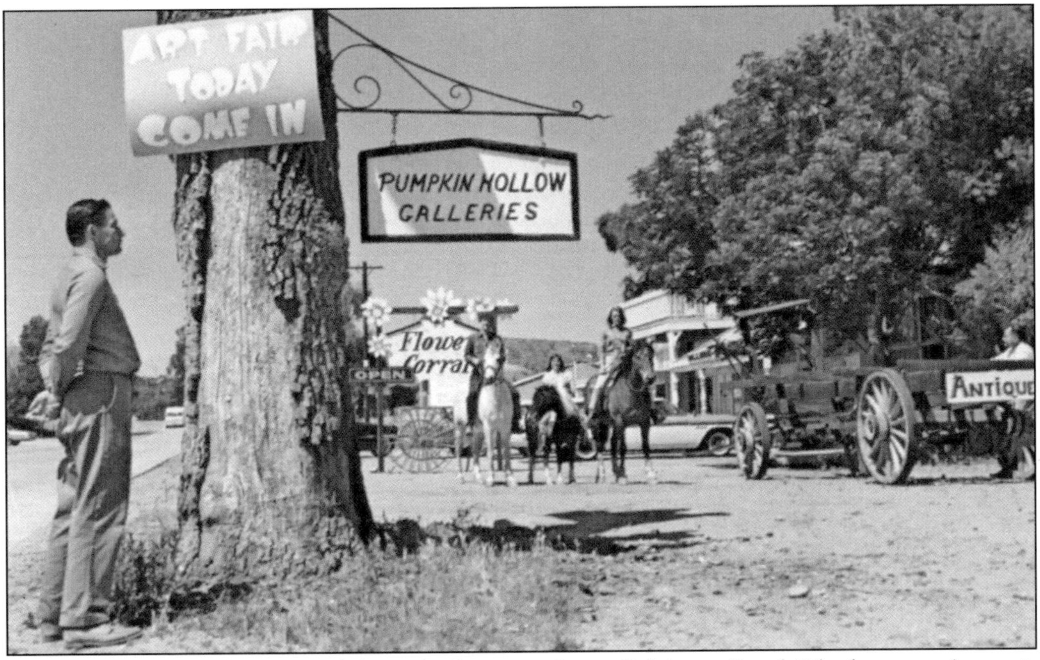

This view shows Old Town Calabasas looking north on Calabasas Road. The hangman's tree is seen used as a post for commercial shop signs that dotted the road advertising the local shops. Rustic wagons, dirt paths, and shoppers on horseback all set the stage for this 1964 *Last of the Old West* postcard scene produced by the Calabasas Chamber of Commerce. Today, although the hangman's tree is long gone, trees are abundant, and the Sagebrush Cantina has taken over the small shops' square footage. (Below, photograph by Karlo Gorgin; courtesy of the Calabasas Media Department.)

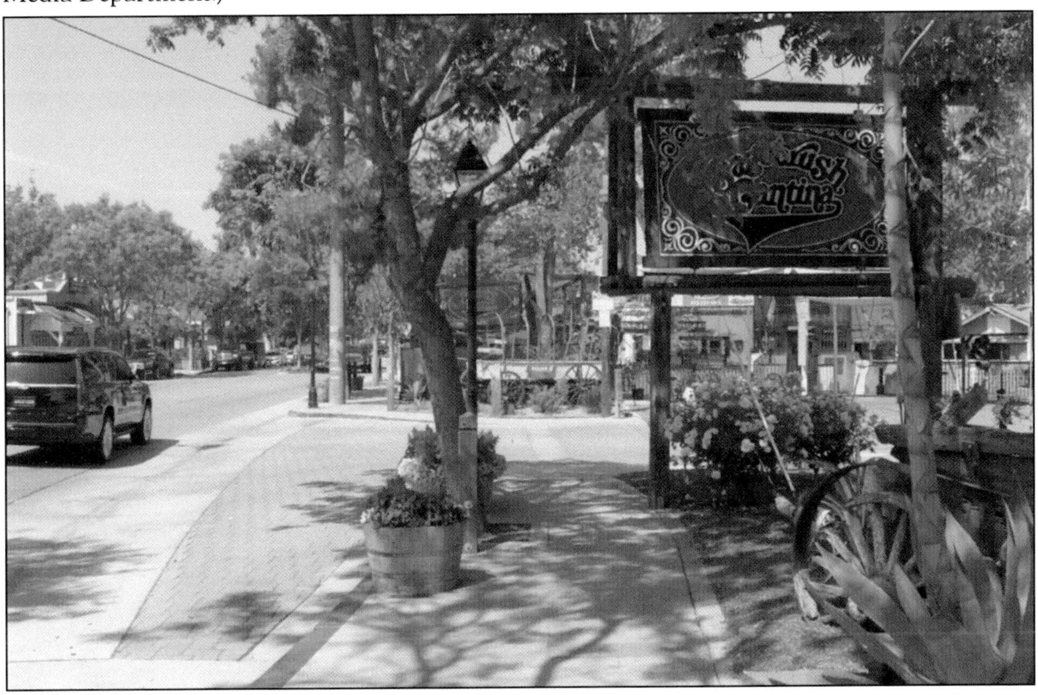

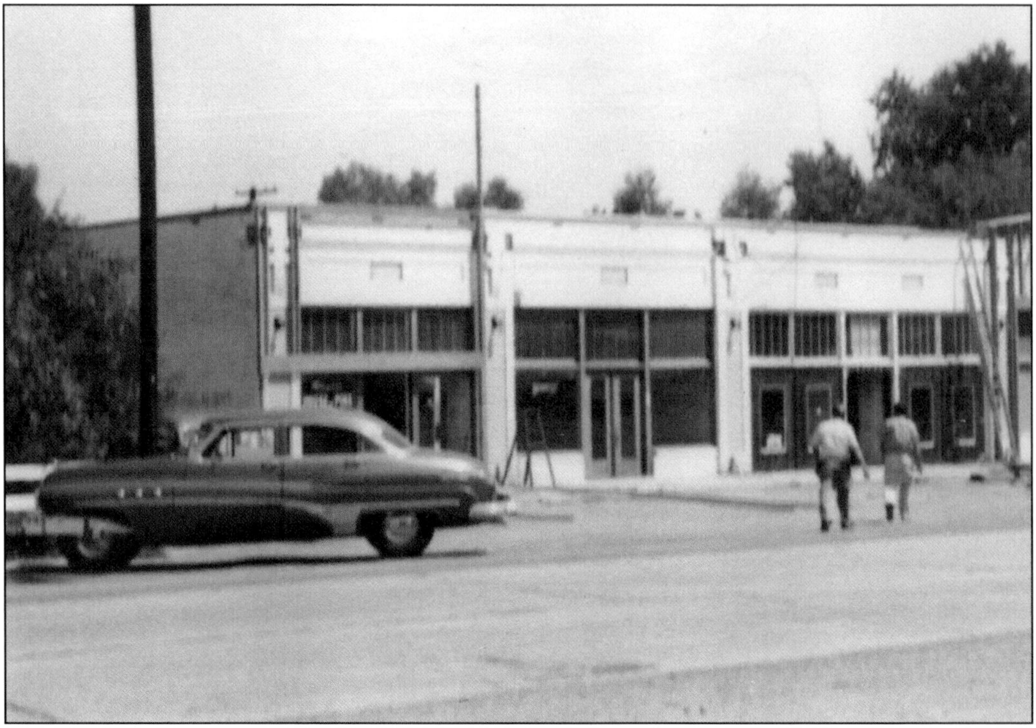

The photograph above shows a section of storefronts on Calabasas Road that were originally built by Lester Agoure Sr. in the early 1920s. This section of shops housed various businesses throughout the years, but a few favorites stick out: Howard Snow's Antiques and Things, Casa Medina (Mexican restaurant), a bakery, a flower shop, cheese factory, butcher shop, and the Sagebrush Cantina.

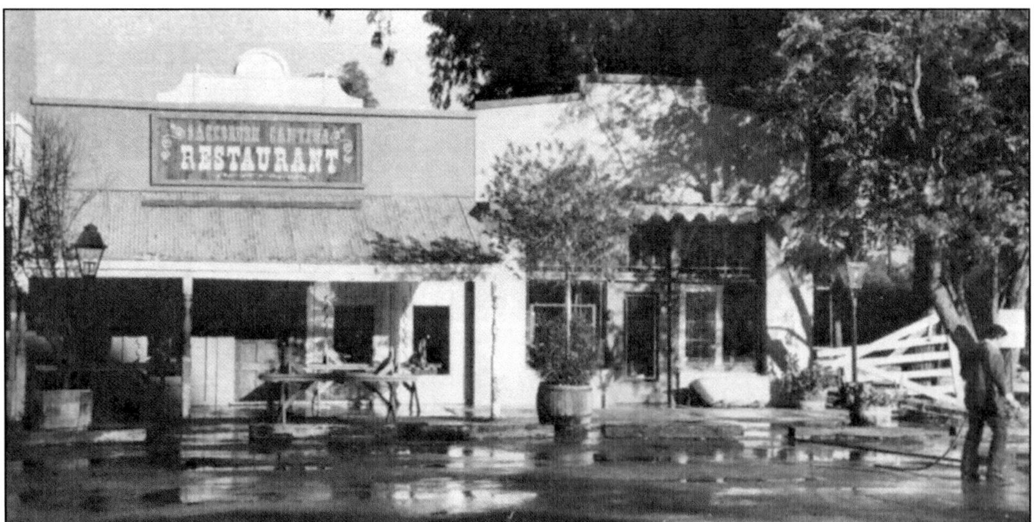

Bob McCord leased a space in the strip of storefronts and started his restaurant, the Sagebrush Cantina, using his settlement money received from a plane accident in Arizona.

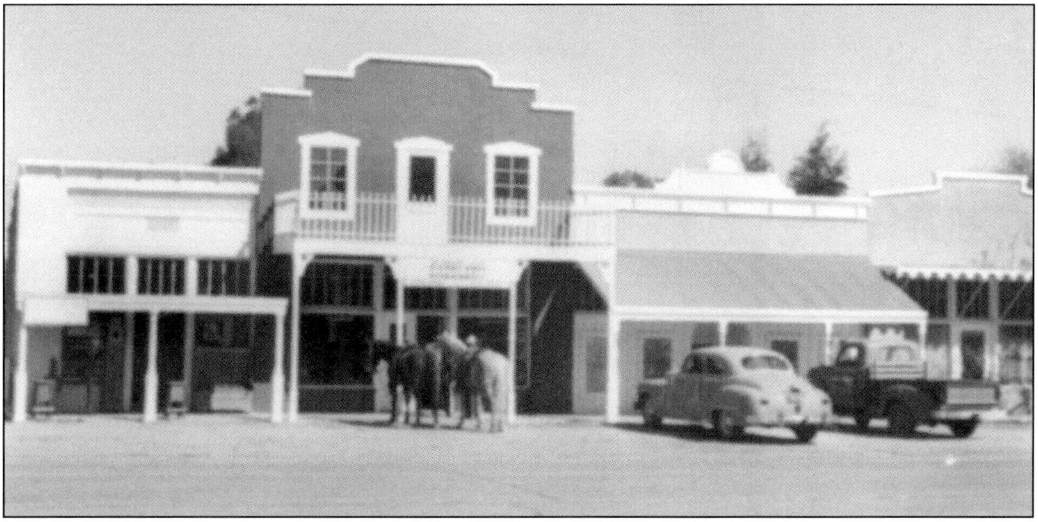

Pictured above are the Agoure buildings skinned with the Western set facade. Bob McCord leased a space and started his restaurant, the Sagebrush Cantina, using his settlement money received from a plane accident in Arizona. In 2000, McCord estimated that 5,000 customers per week walked the sawdust-covered floors of his facility, which occupied the entire block. As seen today, even though McCord passed away in 2008, this popular destination continues to be a successful restaurant and entertainment venue. (Below, photograph by Karlo Gorgin; courtesy of the Calabasas Media Department.)

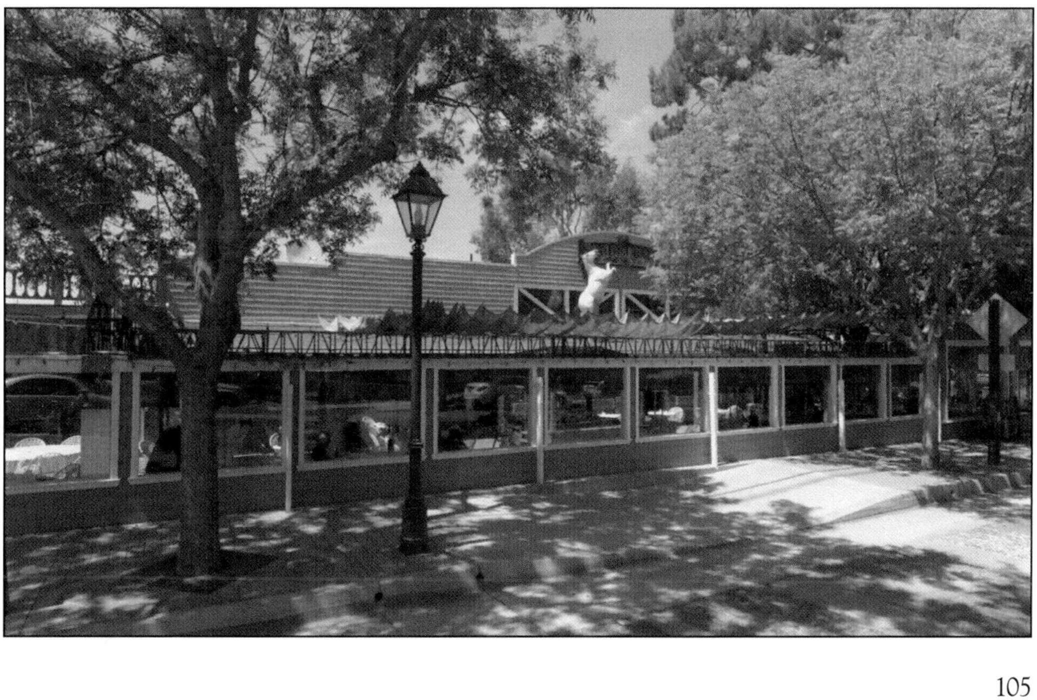

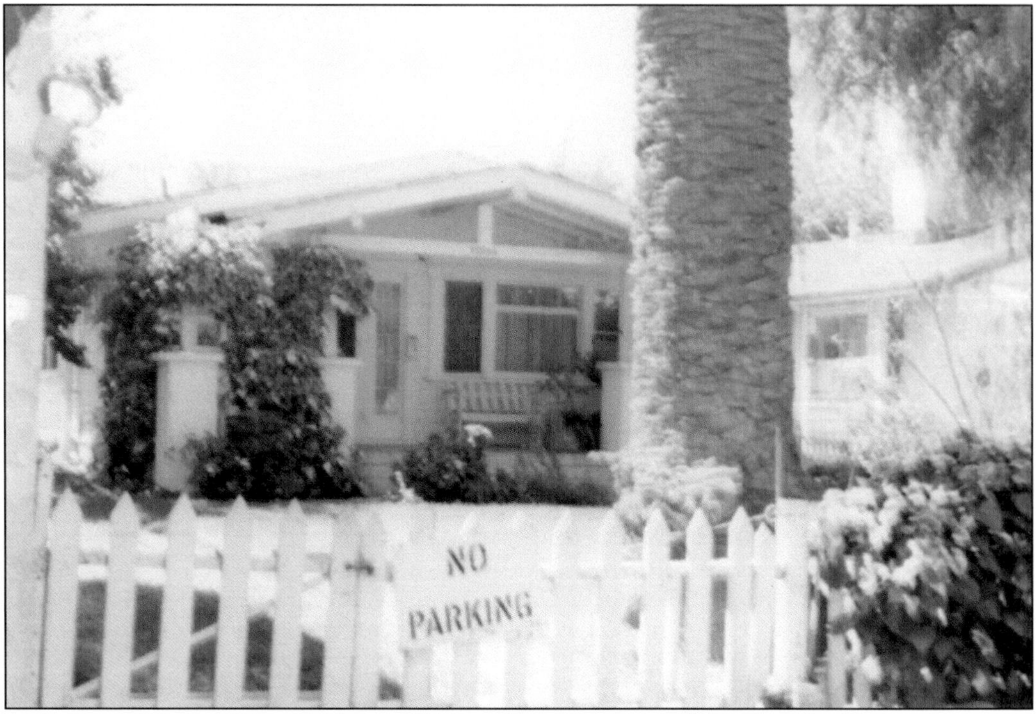

Originally, the Daics built several buildings in Old Town Calabasas. Pictured here is the residence of Theresa Thilmony, an early revered schoolteacher. In the 1970s, the house was relocated farther south on Calabasas Road and designated as a retail space. Old-timers would remember the upscale party supply boutique called A Touch of Class. Today, this location is the Wine Gallery at 23538 Calabasas Road. The back portion of the home is still intact. (Below, photograph by Karlo Gorgin; courtesy of the Calabasas Media Department.)

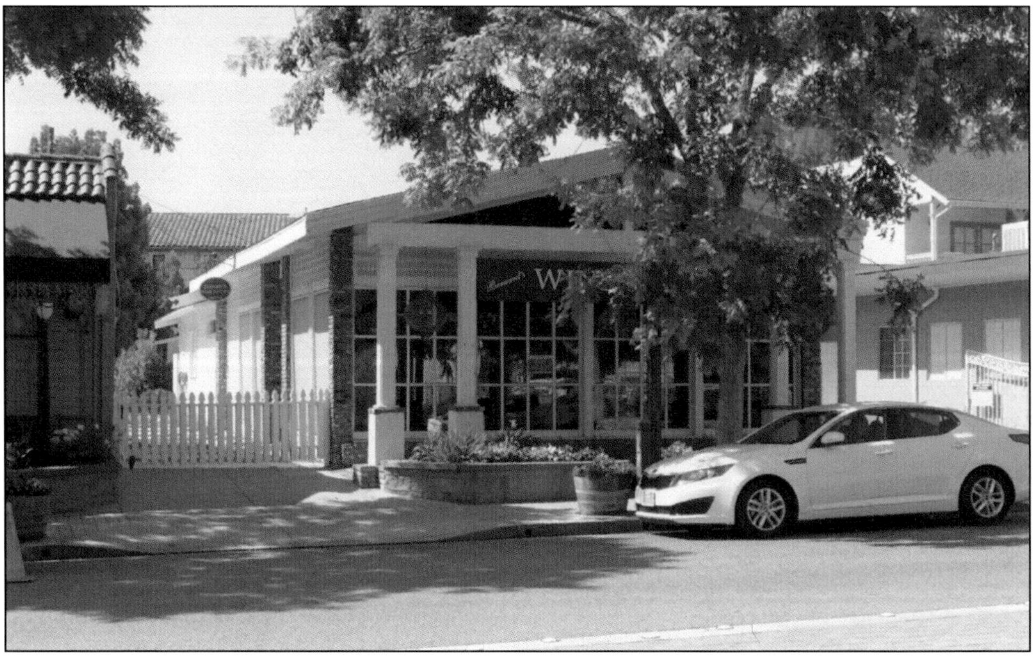

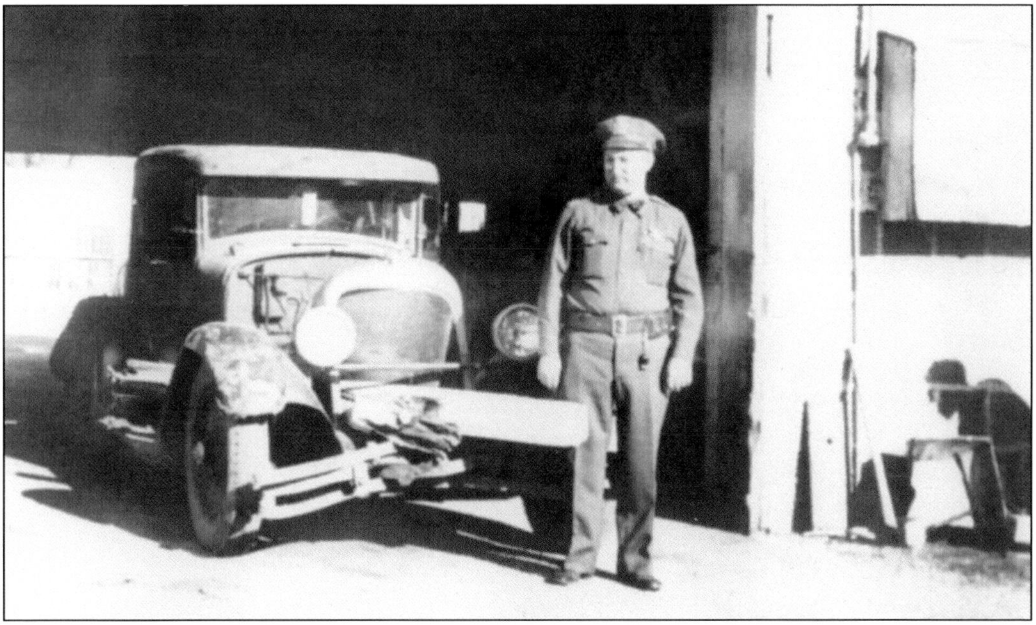

Walt Penland is seen standing outside the Daic Bros. Garage around 1920. He became a deputy constable in the township of Calabasas, receiving a promotion in status during 1935 when he transferred to the Malibu station.

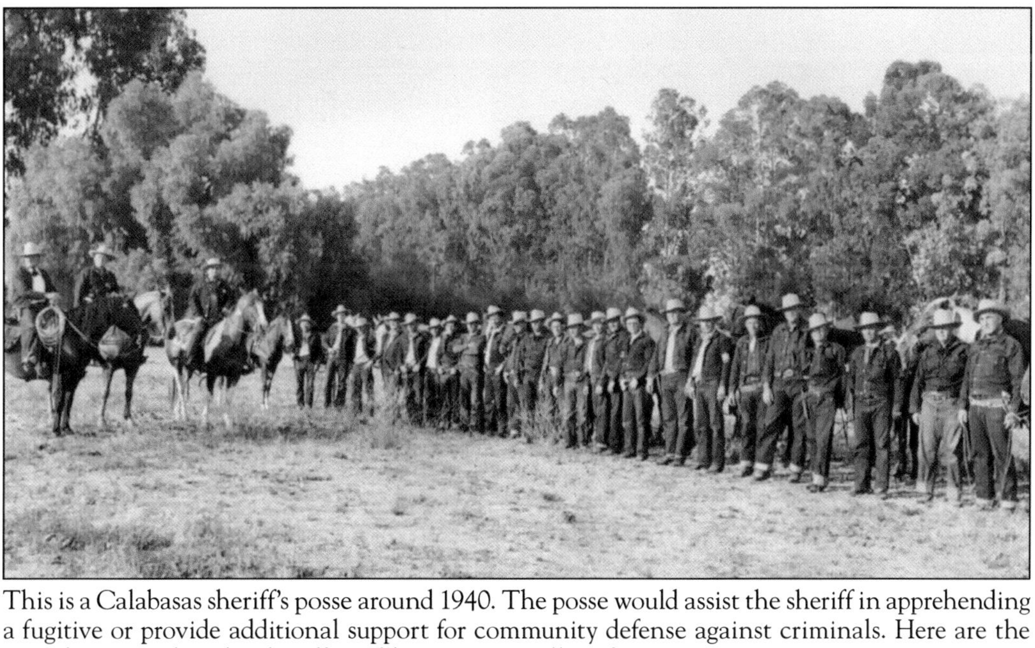

This is a Calabasas sheriff's posse around 1940. The posse would assist the sheriff in apprehending a fugitive or provide additional support for community defense against criminals. Here are the armed citizens that the sheriff would sometimes call on for assistance.

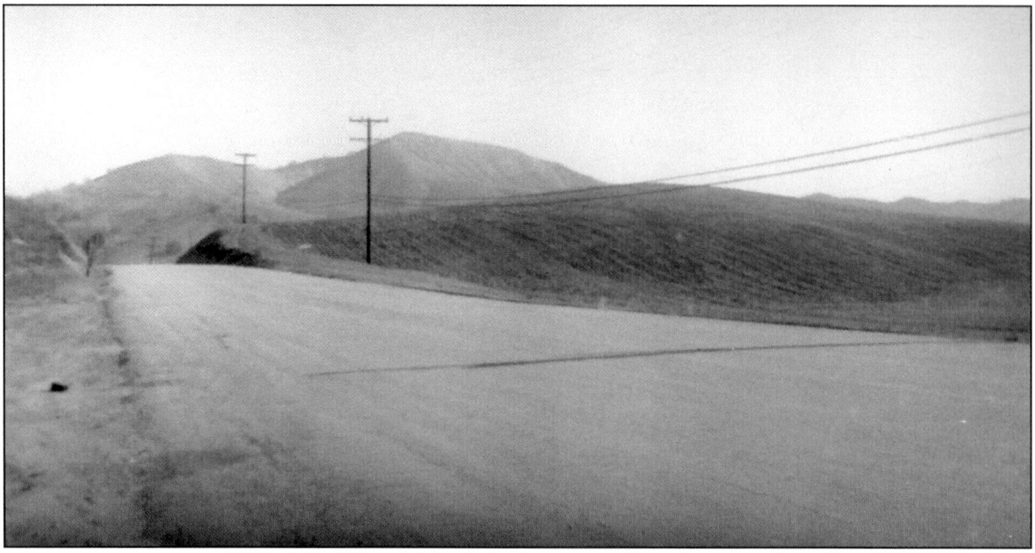

Ventura Road, facing southeast, is pictured here around 1940. Today, this road has developed into the 101 Freeway, a far cry from its origin as an Indian trade route, Juan de Anza's route, the El Camino Real, and the Ventura Highway.

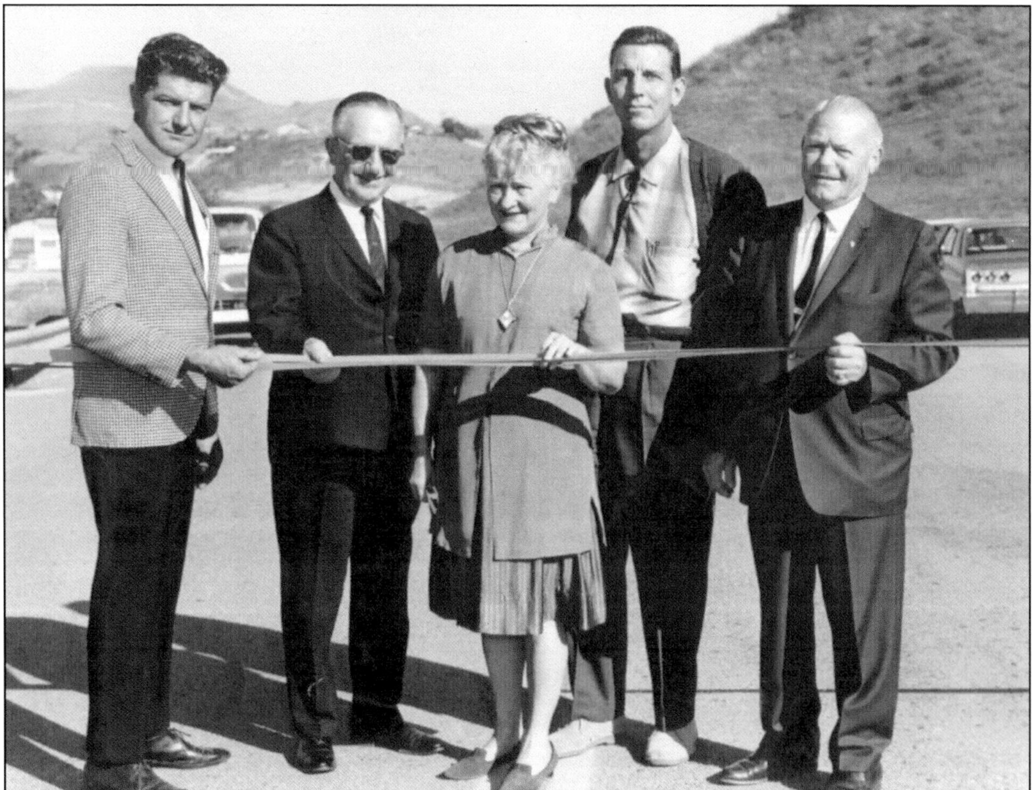

The Ventura Freeway (101) opened in 1967. Seen cutting the ribbon are the state engineers, a county supervisor's representative, the Calabasas Chamber of Commerce president, and a local historian.

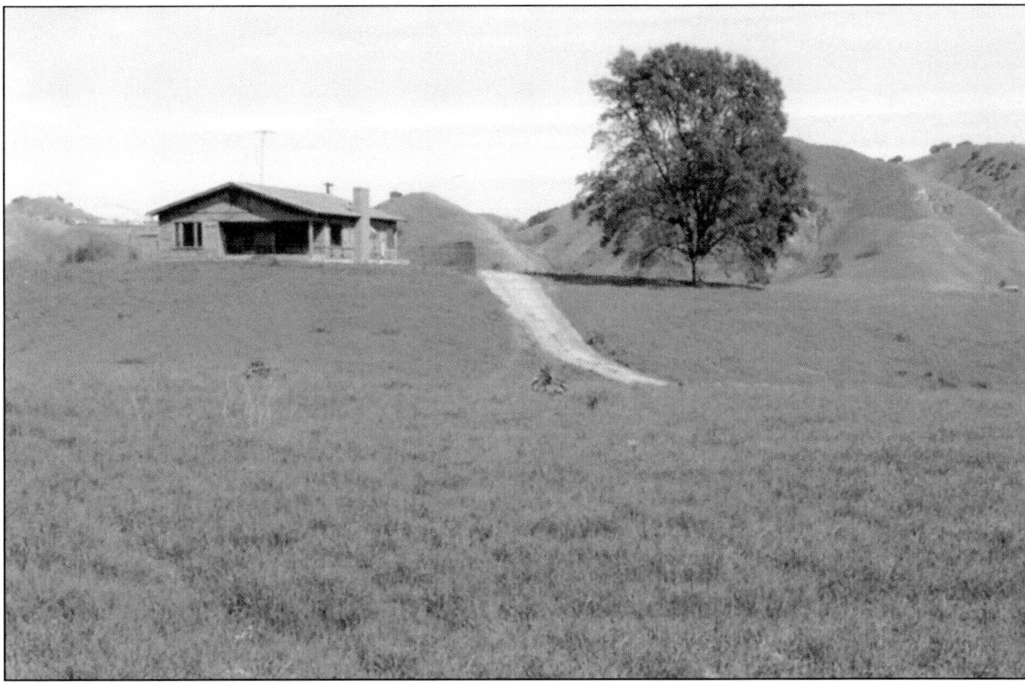

Pictured here in 1997 was the little brown house that once sat on the hill known as Maddy's. This wood home was built in 1912 by a scientist who had worked at the top secret Area 51 site in Nevada. Annalisa Maddy, his wife, stayed in the home after his death and according to the *Acorn*, "lived into her 100s . . . reportedly went blind and rolled out string between the rooms of the house to help her find her way around." (Courtesy of the Calabasas Media Department.)

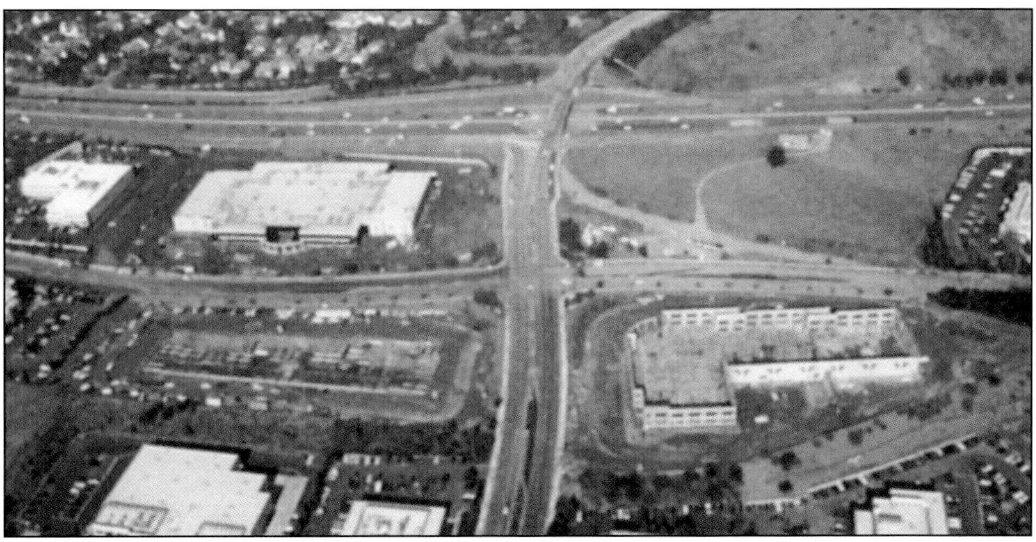

The 101 Freeway is in the top half of this photograph from 1997, with Lost Hills Road splitting the business developments on either side. On the right side of Lost Hills Road, at the intersection of the 101 Freeway, is Maddy's home. This undeveloped hilltop eventually became the Summit shopping center. When the center opened in 2007, there was an organic grocery store named Maddy's. (Courtesy of the Calabasas Media Department.)

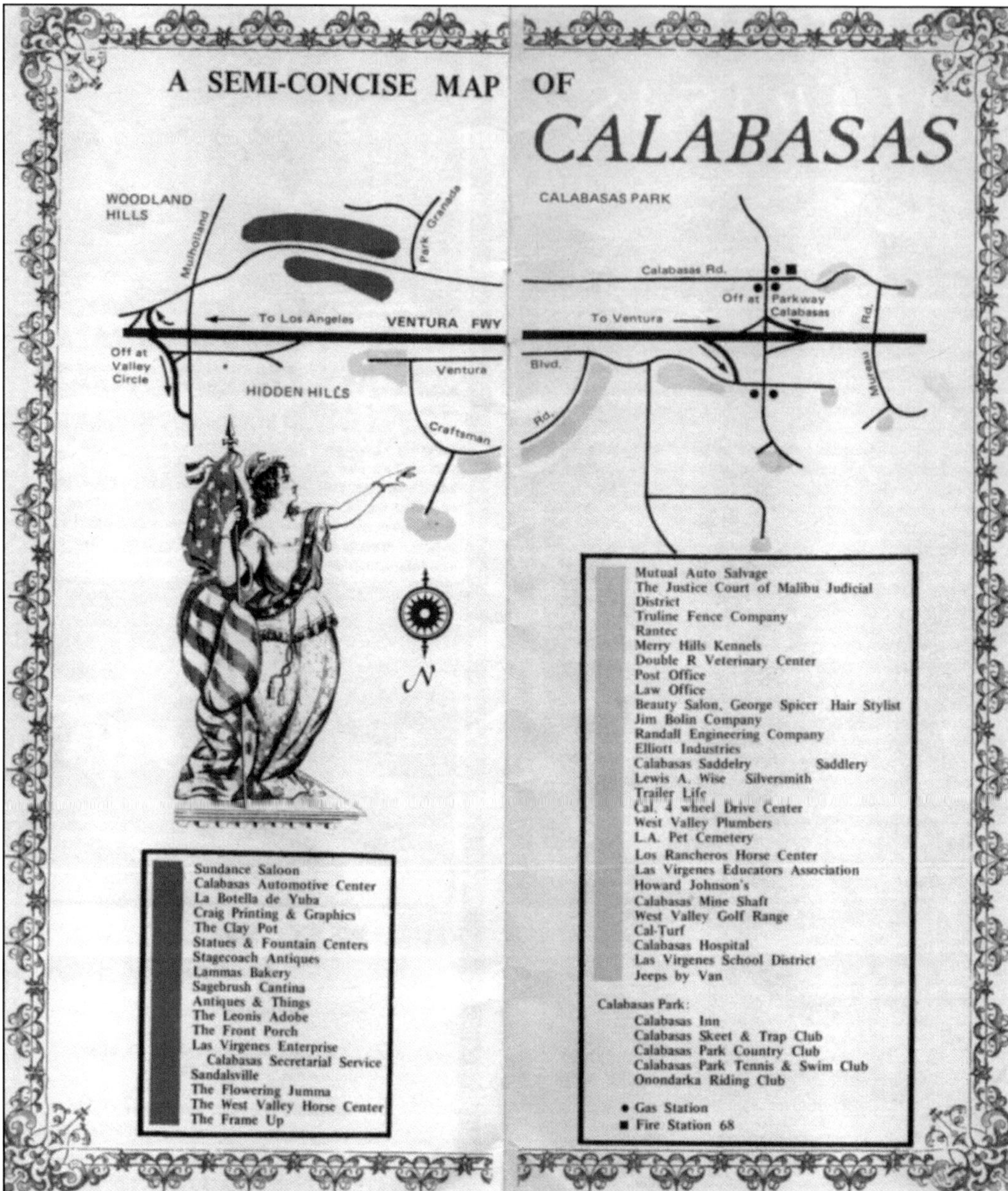

This is a business booklet that was produced by the Calabasas Chamber of Commerce in the early 1970s. The design featured the Old Town shops on a semi-concise map of Calabasas. The back cover of the booklet gave a brief history: "A great many of the settlers in Calabasas, were of the 'ol' school' who believed in settling on land, then keeping it for their children. This was one of the prime reasons why Calabasas did not 'break-open' to influence of progress until as late as the 1960s."

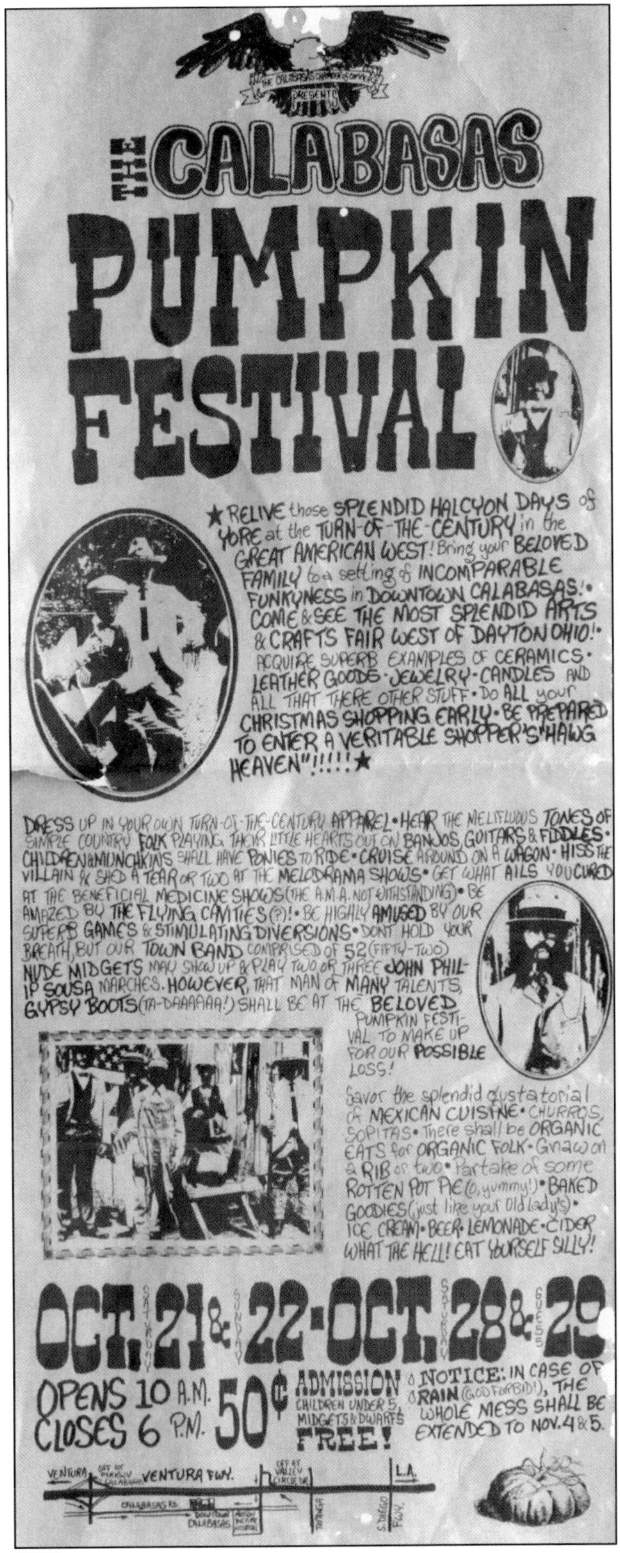

The Calabasas Pumpkin Festival has been celebrated for 44 years. Originally located in the dirt parking lot at the Leonis Adobe, it continued to grow, using Paramount Ranch as its venue. Later, the annual festival moved to Juan Bautista de Anza Park. This is the poster designed in 1972 for the second pumpkin festival celebration. Arlene Bernholtz, a longtime community activist, was a popular artisan who sold handmade macramé items at her booth named Knot-Inn. (Courtesy of Arlene Bernholtz.)

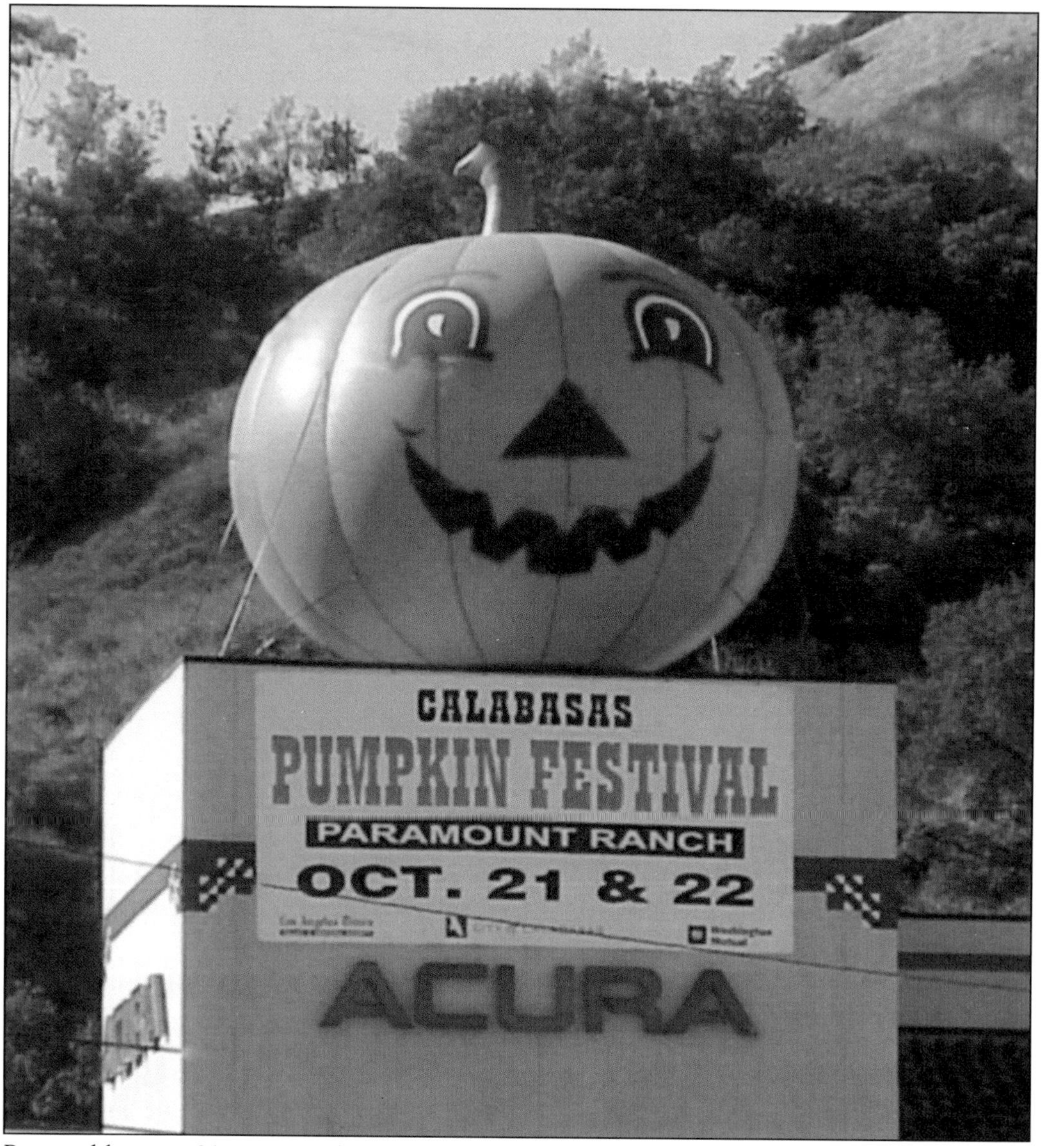

Pictured here in 2012 is "Punkie," a beloved icon giving passersby a big heads-up that the annual Calabasas Pumpkin Festival event is near. Punkie rests on top of a local dealership seen just off the 101 Freeway, where the Calabasas School once stood. (Courtesy of the Calabasas Media Department.)

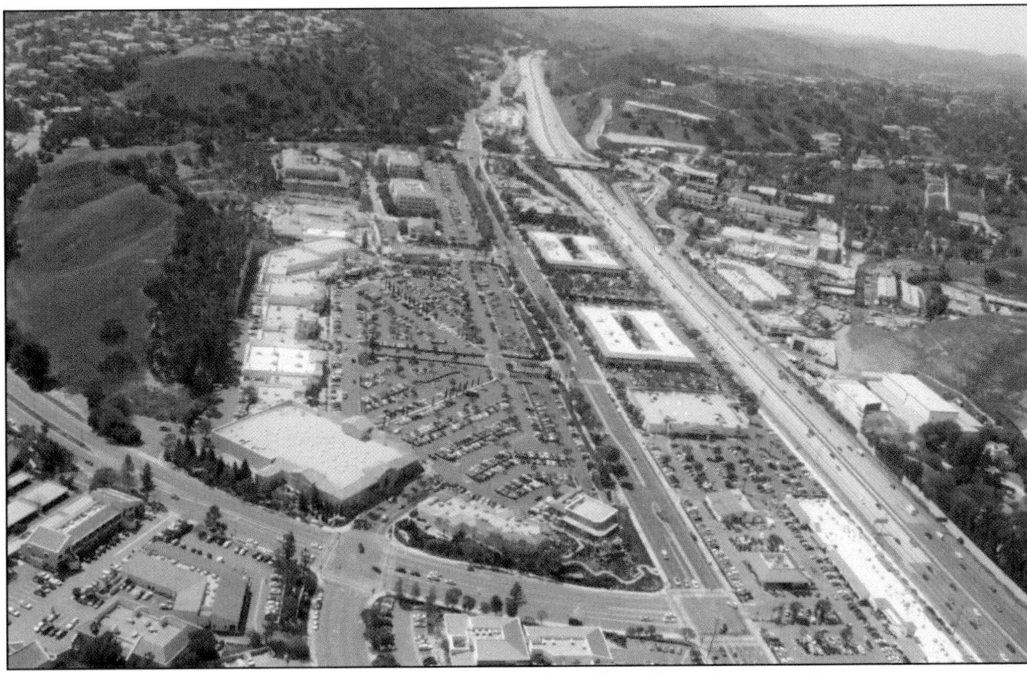

Pictured here is the Commons at Calabasas, a high-end outdoor shopping destination, just prior to opening in 1998. Rick Caruso, a graduate of Pepperdine University, is the founder of Caruso Affiliated, which developed, owns, and manages the Commons at Calabasas, one of his five shopping centers in Southern California. Caruso's design for the Commons at Calabasas was intended to emulate an Umbrian village to complement the community's dominant Mediterranean architectural style. (Courtesy of the Calabasas Media Department.)

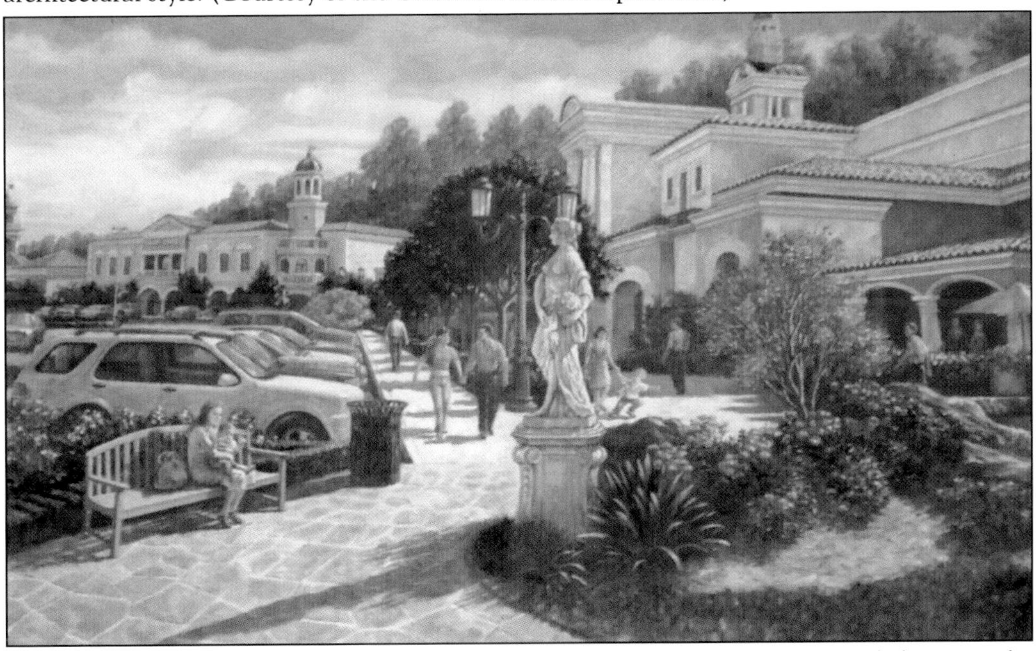

This is Carlos Lacamara's painting of the Commons at Calabasas, which currently hangs in the Calabasas Municipal Library located at 200 Civic Center Way.

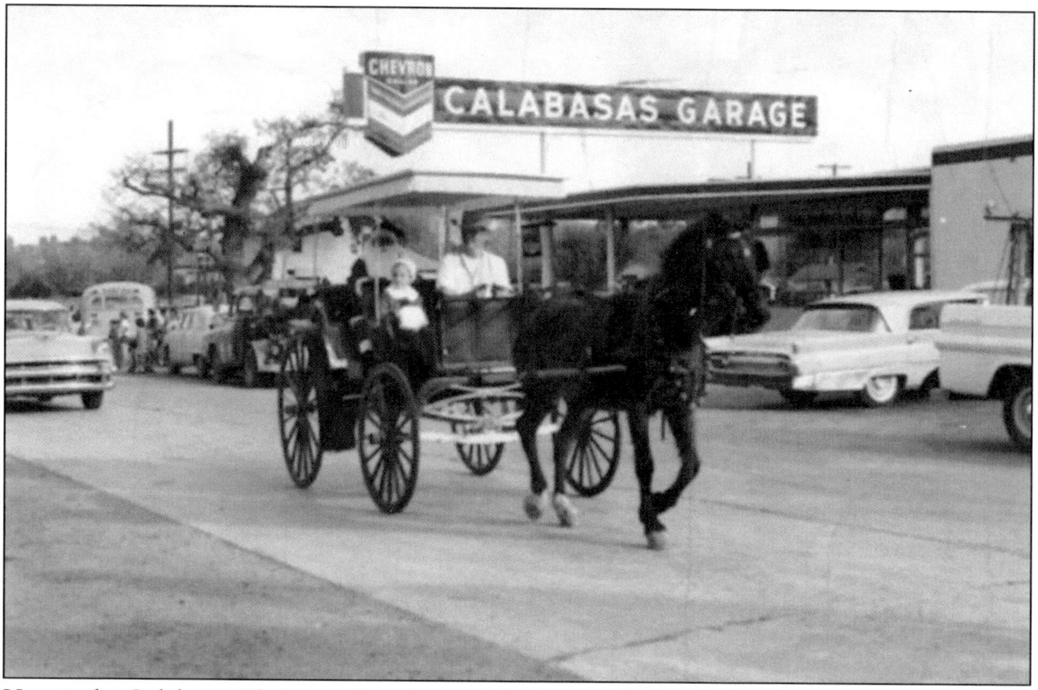

Here is the Calabasas Christmas Parade in 1960. Archie Hanson Jr. and daughter Lisa ride with Santa through Old Town Calabasas on Calabasas Road.

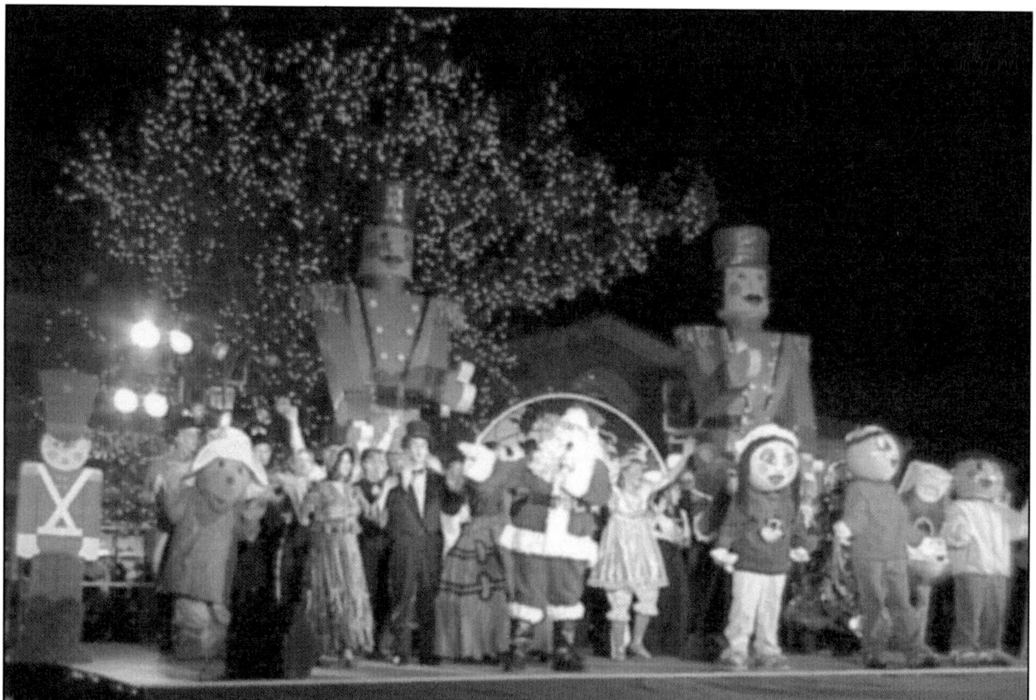

Pictured here are holiday festivities at the Commons at Calabasas in 2008. The elaborate production was produced by Caruso Affiliated for the grand celebration to kick off the 2008 holiday shopping season. (Courtesy of the Calabasas Media Department.)

A "second" Calabasas School was built in the fiscal school year of 1924–1925 on the site of a smaller first school. It was a one-teacher school until June 1948. In 1950, the building was sold to Charles Mureau, who repurposed the space into County Manor, a venue for private parties advertising "convenient paved parking," exclusive catering service with a spacious kitchen and latest equipment, and wiring for continual musical projection with a stage, surrounded by acres of beautiful landscaping. Mureau later leased the property to various specialty businesses. Today, the property stands vacant and the structure demolished, as the retaining wall was the only original architectural feature that had not been remodeled. (Below, photograph by Karlo Gorgin; courtesy of the Calabasas Media Department.)

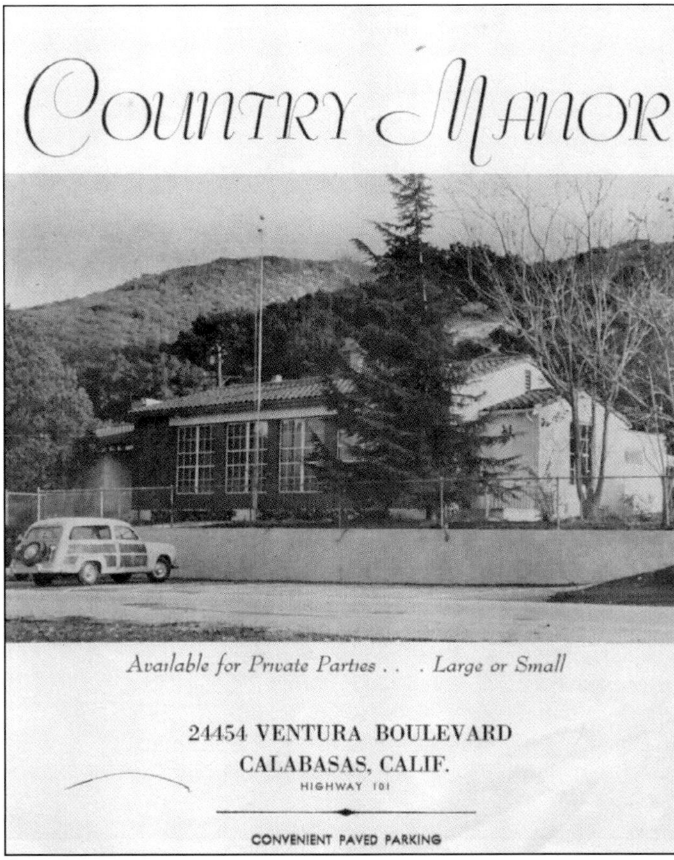

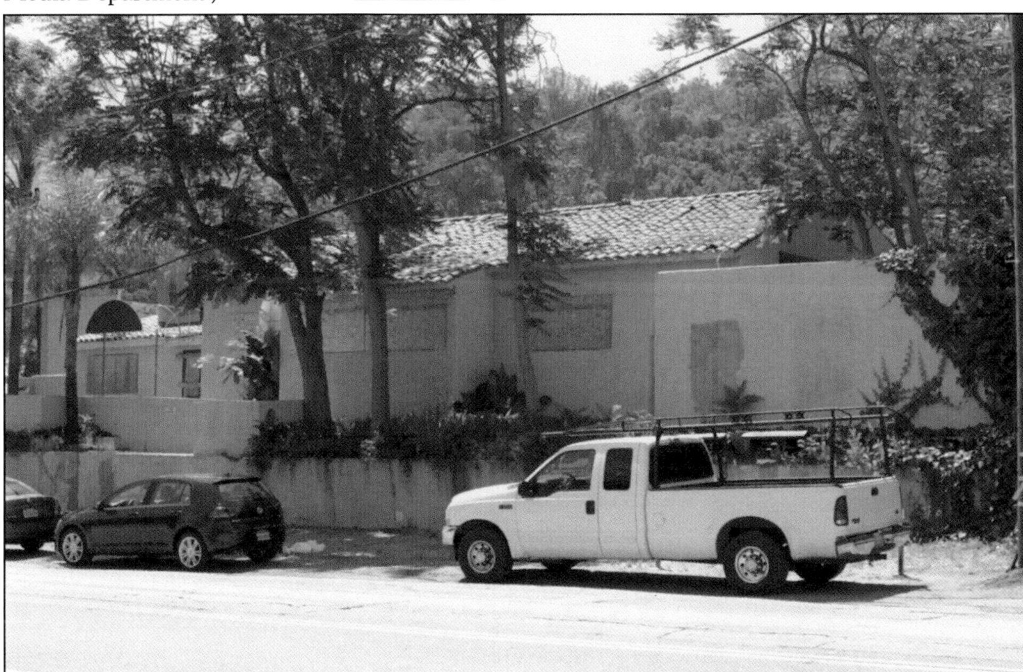

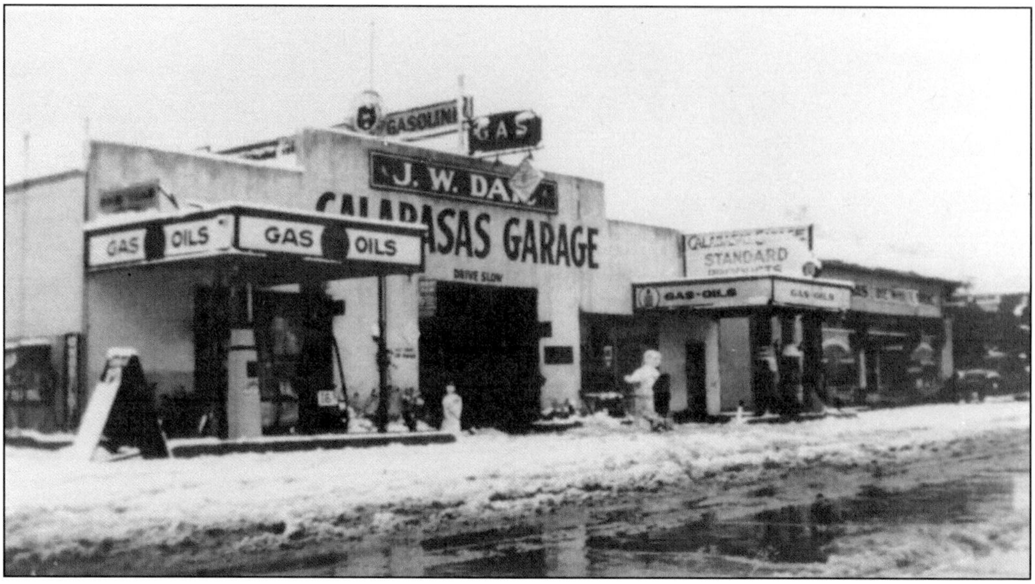

The Daic Garage, pictured here during an unusual snowfall in 1932, serviced the community until 1978. Other snowfalls were reported in 1915, 1957, and 1989.

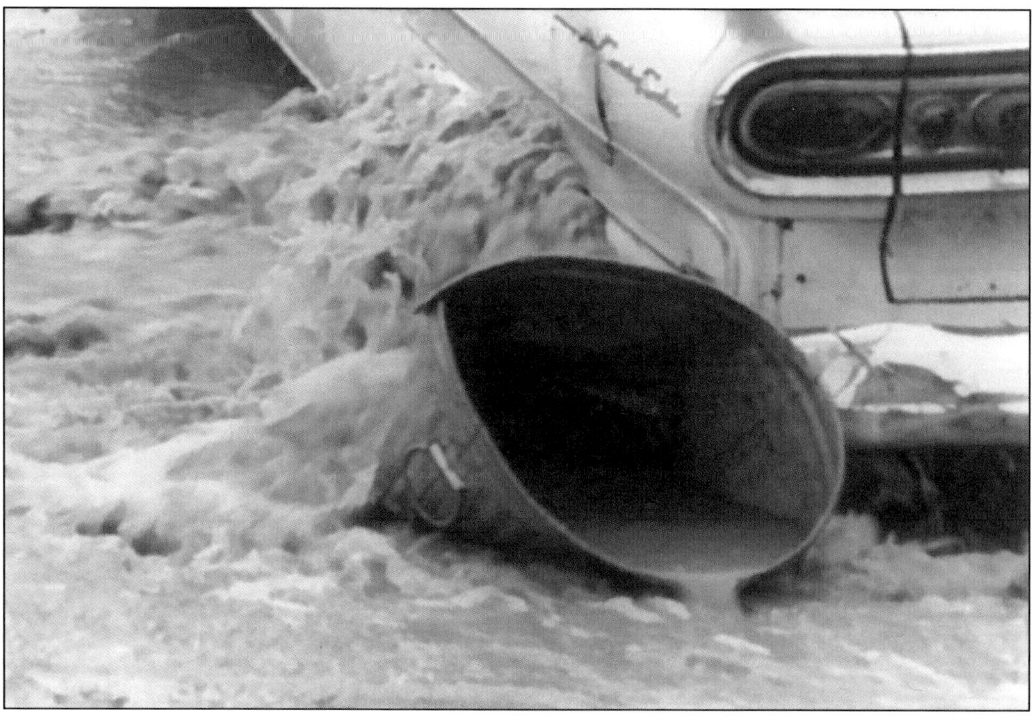
Pictured here are the rushing waters of a storm during 1980. The damage prompted an investigation of the surrounding areas' drainage infrastructure. (Courtesy of the City of Hidden Hills.)

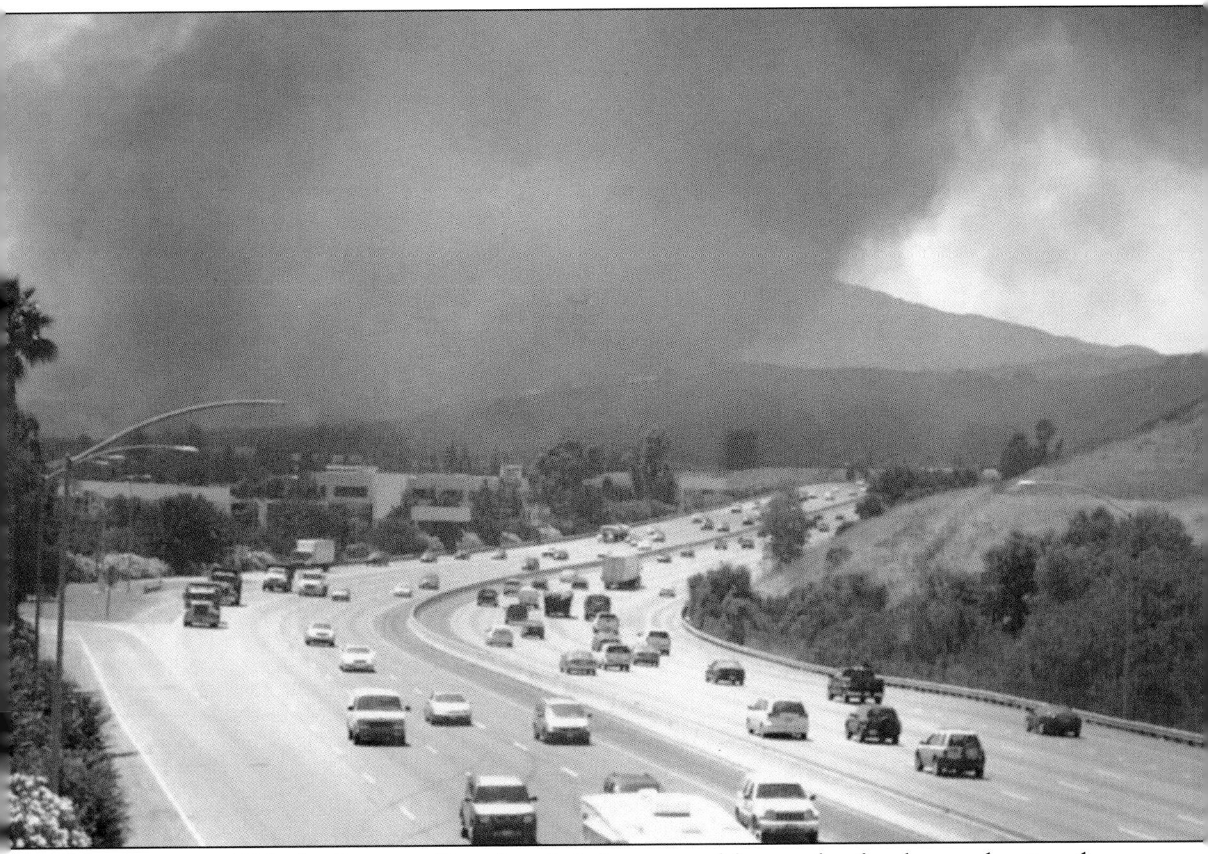

Beginning in 1925, the County of Los Angeles's forester and fire warden first began charting the history of local fires. A strong correlation between point of origin and the path a fire spreads to the coast, has been documented in Santa Ana wind-driven fires. Such fires often travel an identical route through the canyons despite varying wind conditions. During fires, experienced fire officers amass resources at certain island points in an effort to stop blazes before they hit the Las Virgenes, Lost Hills, Liberty, Kanan, Triunfo, and Topanga corridors. Significant blazes besieged Calabasas in 1943, 1970, 1993, 1996, 2008, and 2013. The largest of these fires was the 1970 Newhall fire that burned to Malibu, destroying over 435,000 acres. Pictured here was the Lost Hills fire that burned 60 acres in 2008. (Courtesy of the Calabasas Media Department.)

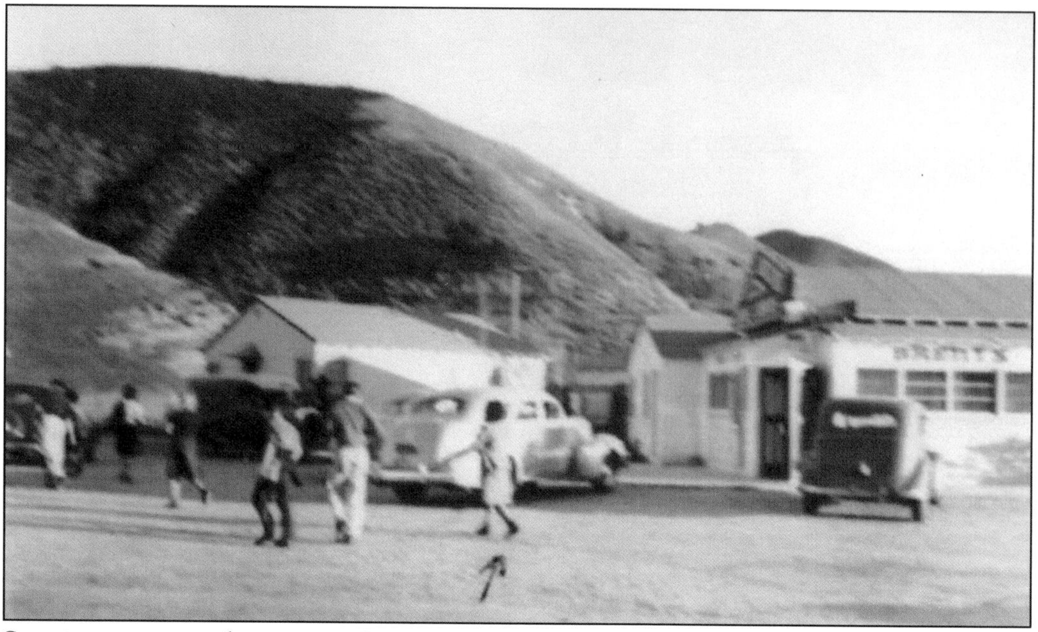

Seen is an area traveling west on Las Virgenes Canyon Road before Agoura Road called Brents Junction. A Mr. Brents, originally from Holland, purchased acres of a mountain range that became known as the Brents Mountain Crag, while he developed land farther down the road into a summer resort. Brents Junction appeared on old highway maps until 1947.

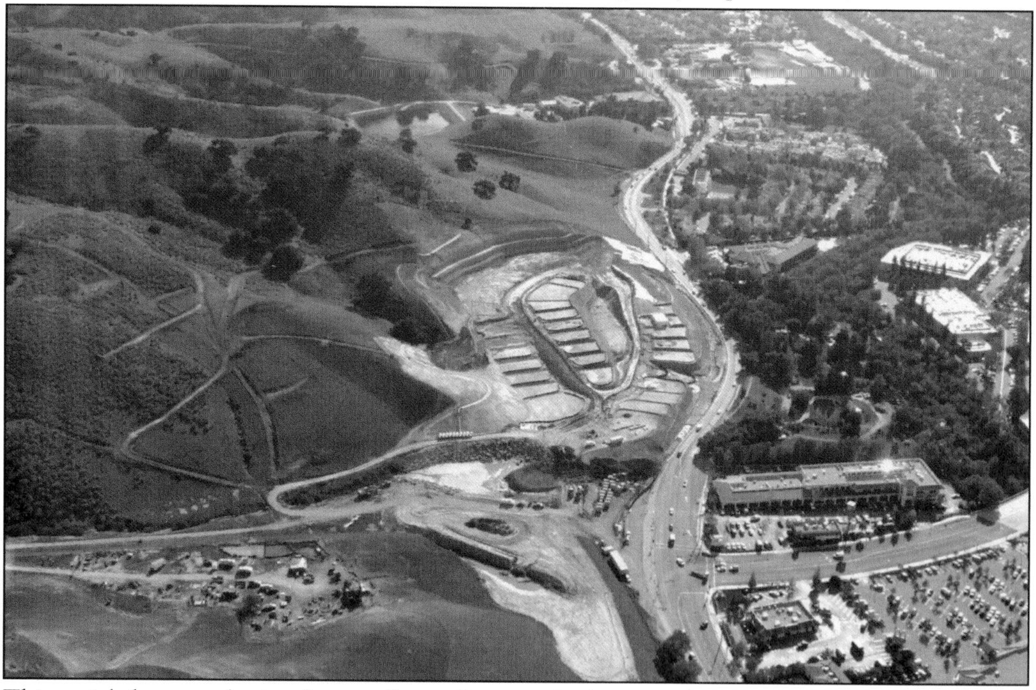

This aerial photograph view features Brents Junction looking south on Las Virgenes Canyon Road. The cross street is Agoura Road. Las Virgenes Municipal Water District is seen in the distance on the left. A.E. Wright Middle School is seen in the background to the right. (Courtesy of the Calabasas Media Department.)

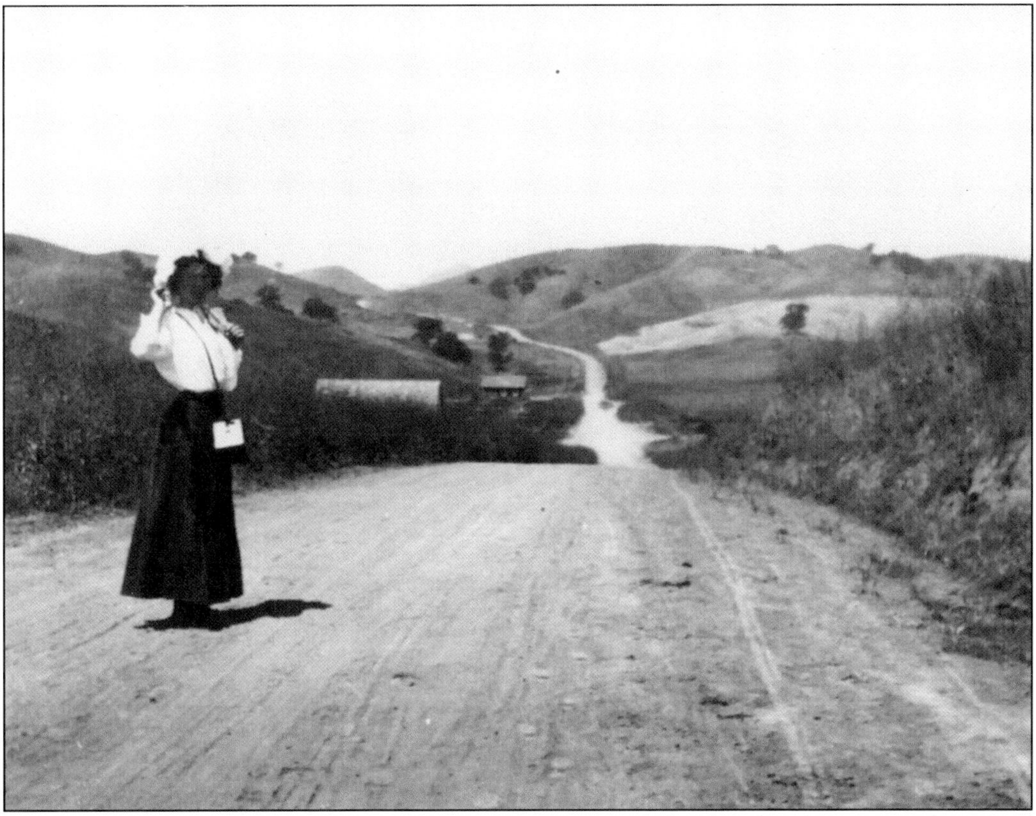

Looking northeast on Las Virgenes Road, Mary Daic is seen holding her bonnet on the side of the then dirt road, about 1900. Today, the hills have been carved to accommodate the expanded road, residential areas, and businesses. (Below, photograph by Karlo Gorgin; courtesy of the Calabasas Media Department.)

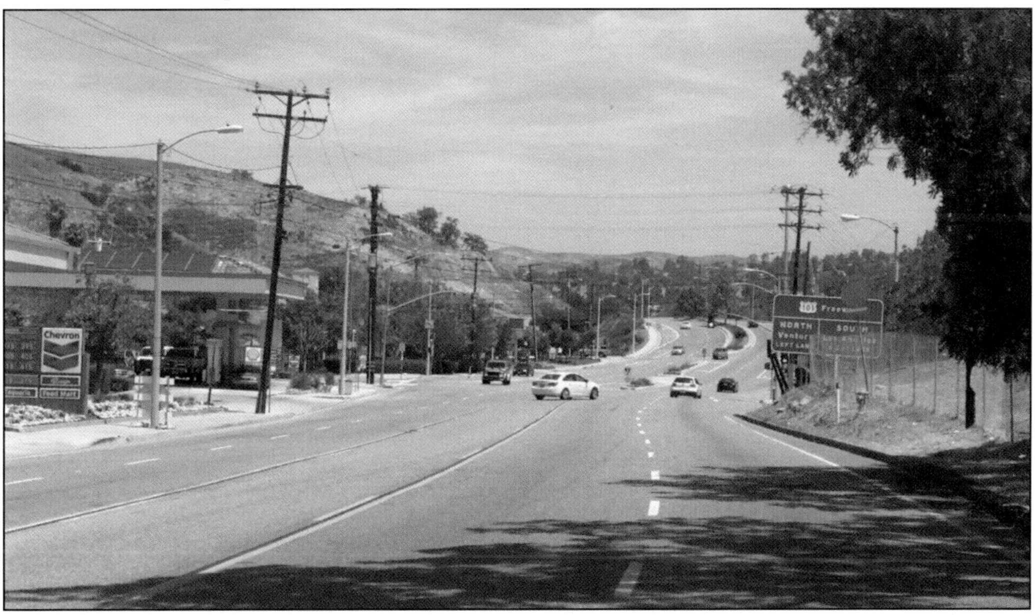

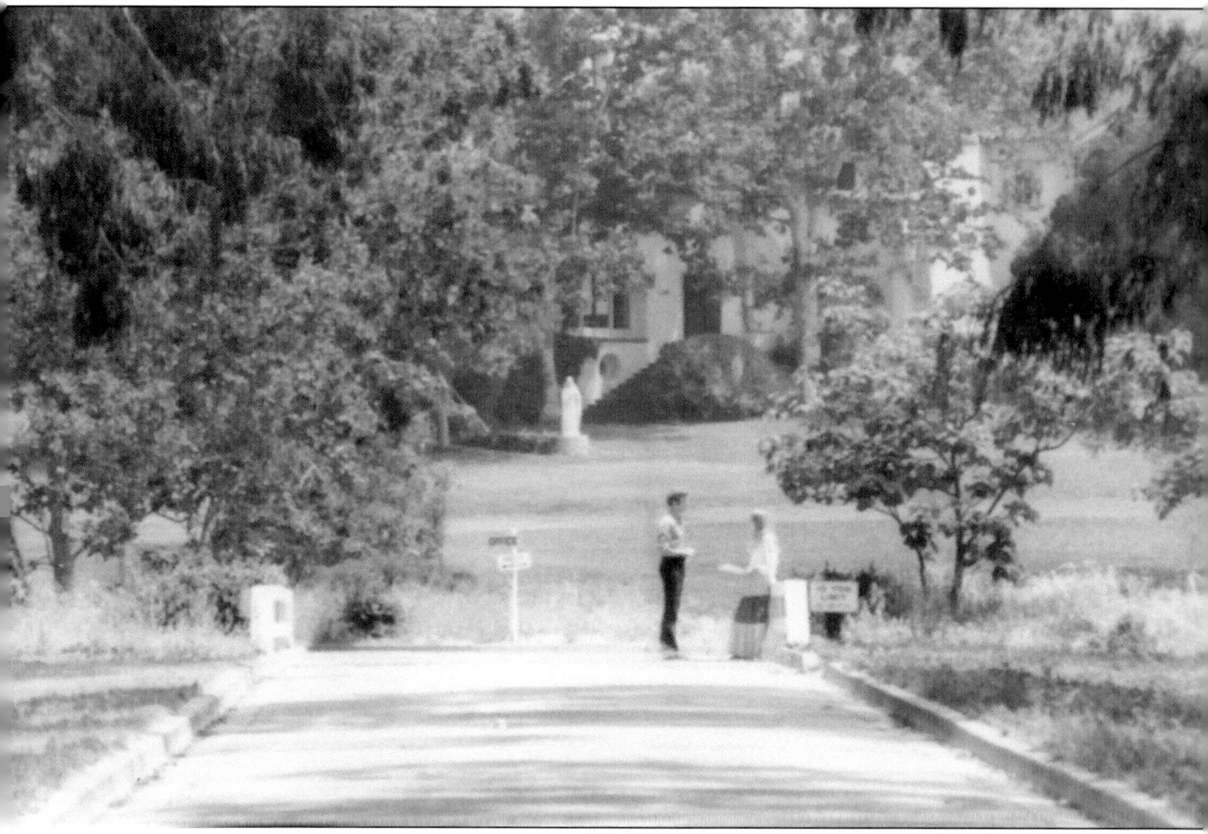

Razor baron King Camp Gillette bought this property in 1926 and built an estate designed by architect Wallace Neff. MGM movie director Clarence Brown (*Anna Karenina*, *National Velvet*) bought the property in 1930, following Gillette's death. In 1952, the director sold the ranch to the Claretian Order of the Catholic Church after which it became Claretville. From 1971 to 1975, a New Age minster, Elizabeth Clare Prophet, founded the Church Universal and Triumphant on the site. Soka University of America purchased the property in 1987, providing education and a home for the Juliana and John Gensley Botanical Native Plant Garden. Community outreach offered renowned speakers such as Rosa Parks, African American civil rights activist. In 2005, Soka University sold the 588-acre property to become part of the state parkland and host the Anthony C. Beilenson Interagency Visitor Center. (Courtesy of Bison Archives.)

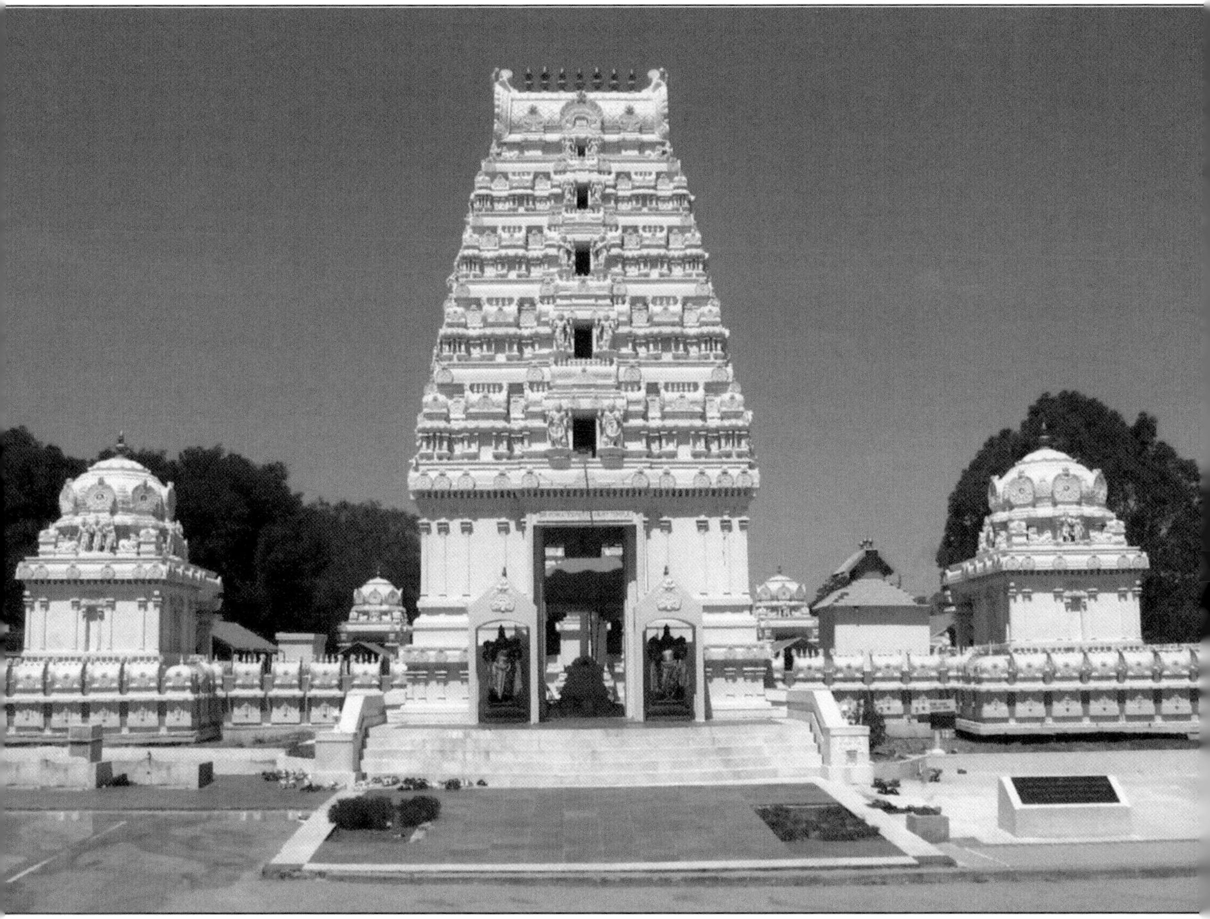

The Hindu temple, a temple of the Hindu god Venkateswara, was built in 1981 and is located off Las Virgenes Canyon Road. The temple is built in the traditional South Indian style and frequented by followers of Hinduism in Southern California. The Hindu Society of Southern California was incorporated in the state of California as a nonprofit religious organization in August 1977. (Photograph by Arvin Petros; courtesy of the Calabasas Media Department.)

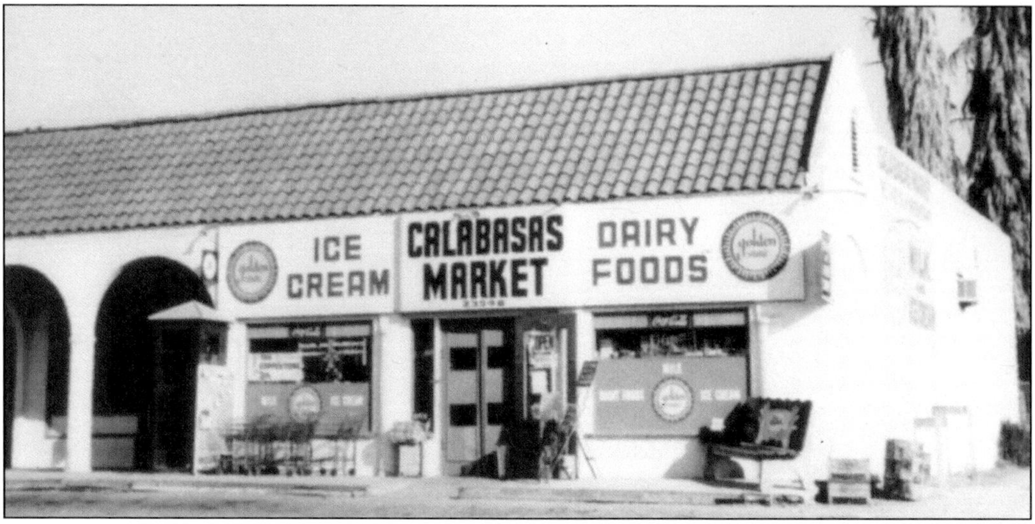

This location was once on the south side of Calabasas Road. It was then a market owned and operated for many years by Larry and Ada Beymer. The building later housed two artisan shops: the Clay Pot and a goldsmith jewelry store. The location was replaced by Leonis Plaza in the late 1980s.

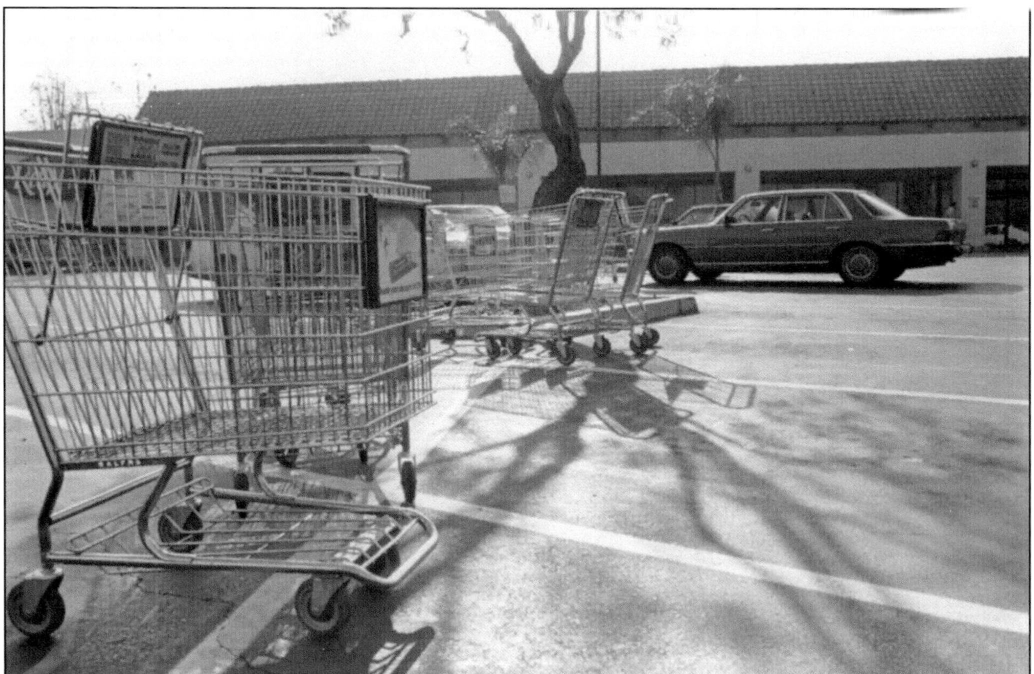
Here is the parking lot of the Ralphs market that was once located in what is known today as the Courtyard at the Commons, prior to moving to the Commons at Calabasas in 2008.

The Calabasas Junction shopping center has emerged from the 1920s into the present day. The building's charm lends itself to a cluster of quaint shops offering unique items. The location is next to Calabasas Creek, the headwaters of the Los Angeles River.

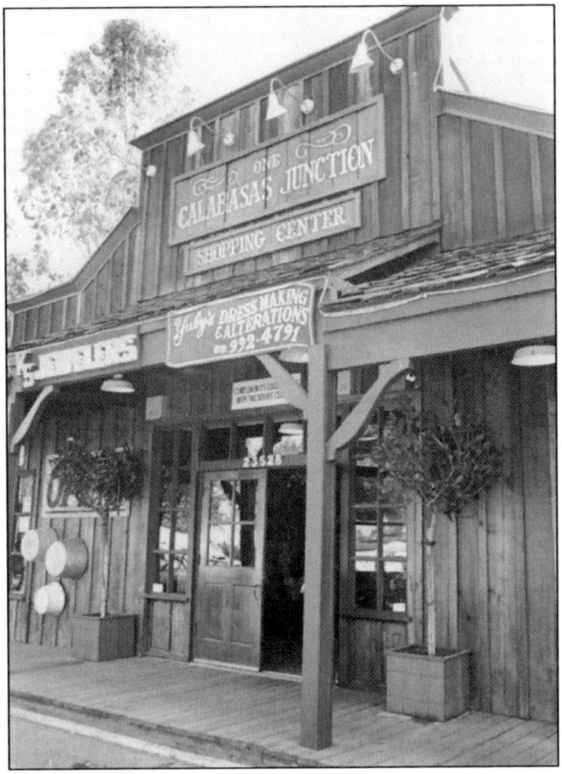

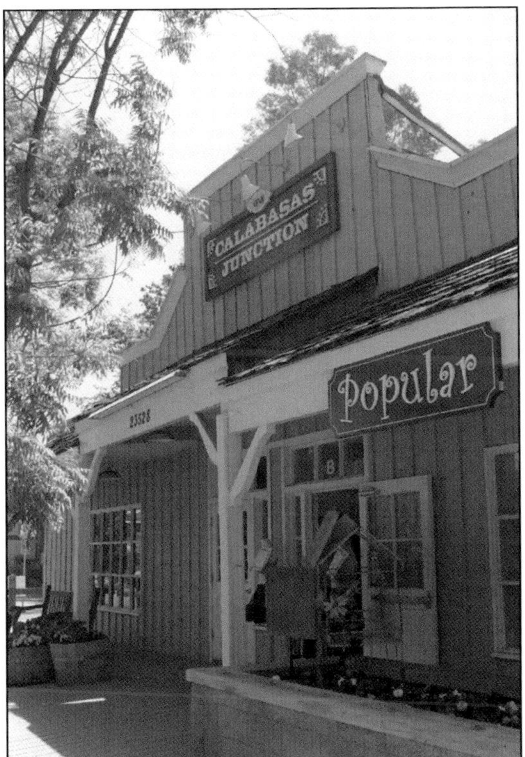

The Western storefront is still intact today, resembling the original facade erected in the 1950s. (Photograph by Karlo Gorgin; courtesy of the Calabasas Media Department.)

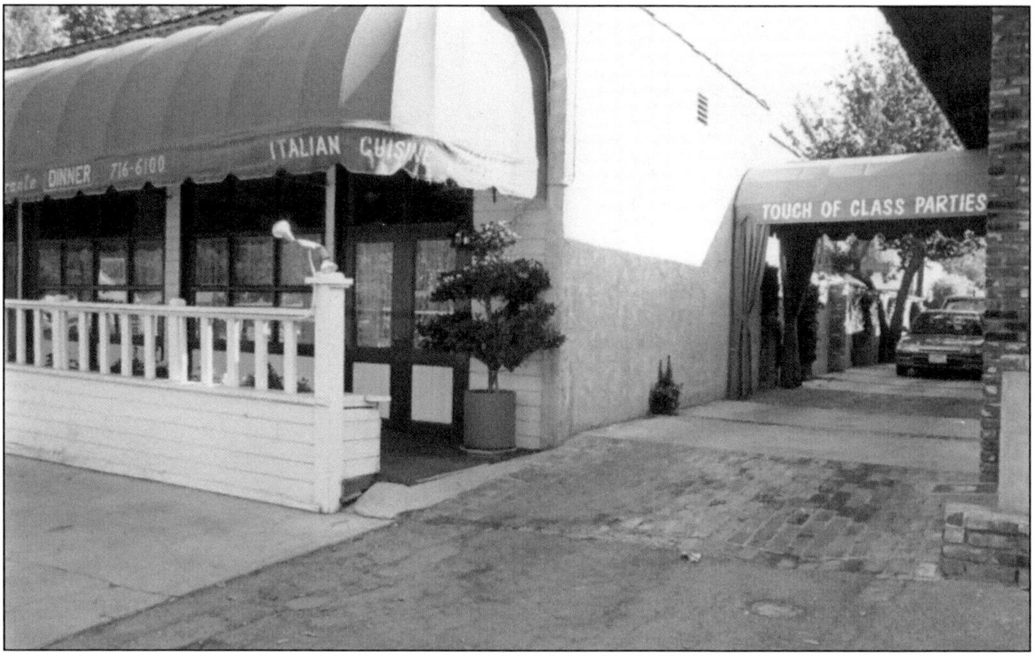

Those who know about Old Town Calabasas will remember an Italian restaurant on the south side of Calabasas Road. The *Los Angeles Times* described Gaetano's in 1993 as "an airy, high-ceilinged restaurant with a quiet atmosphere, tiled floors and ficus trees, styled after a country Italian restaurant. Its menu was northern Italian cuisine. Prices range from dinner pasta for $9.95 to chopped veal for $22.95." Gaetano's served many personalities, and the bar scene often produced outrageous stories worth repeating. Today, this location is another eating establishment called The Six. (Below, photograph by Karlo Gorgin; courtesy of the Calabasas Media Department.)

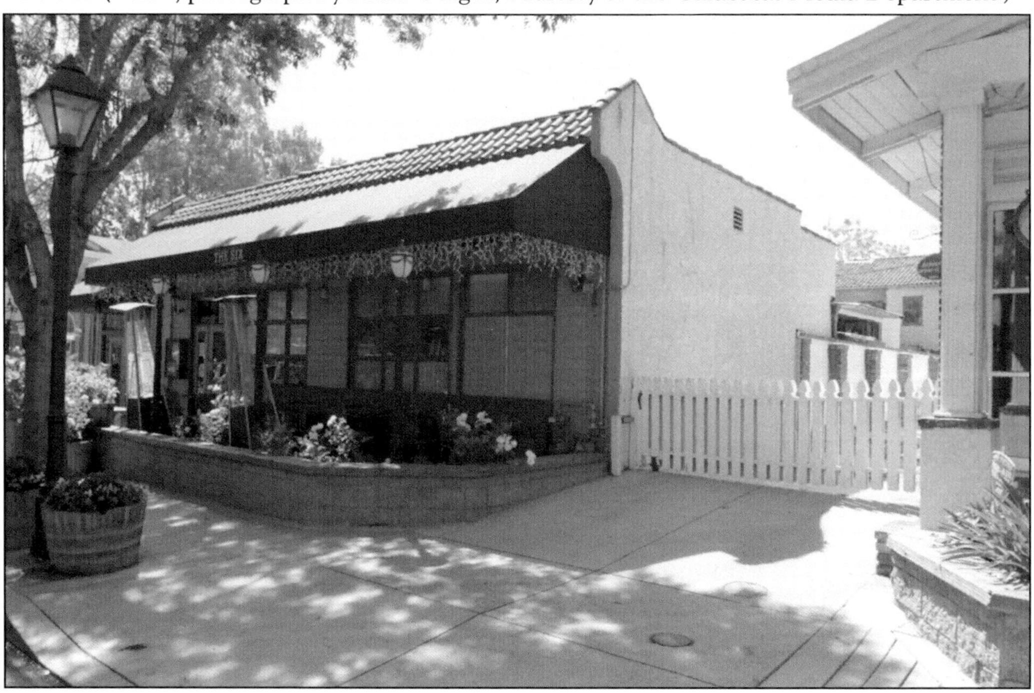

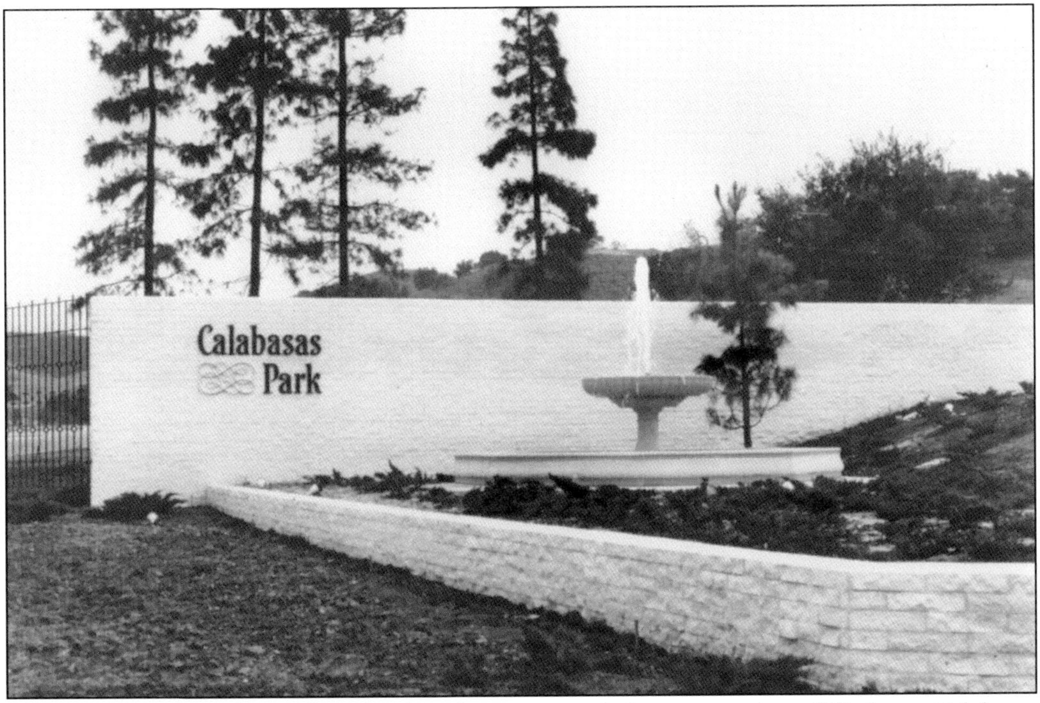

When Calabasas Park was first developed, one entered the community off Parkway Calabasas through large faux gates. The land marker statement visually created a grand entrance to this development that featured many modern amenities. Seen is the right side of the entrance which featured a water fountain, about 1970. Today, a partial gate and fountain remain among the foliage. Westridge, now a subdivision located in the Calabasas Park, is a deed-restricted community with a Homeowners Association (HOA) Board of Directors and fees that pay for amenities. (Below, courtesy of Cimberly Castellon.)

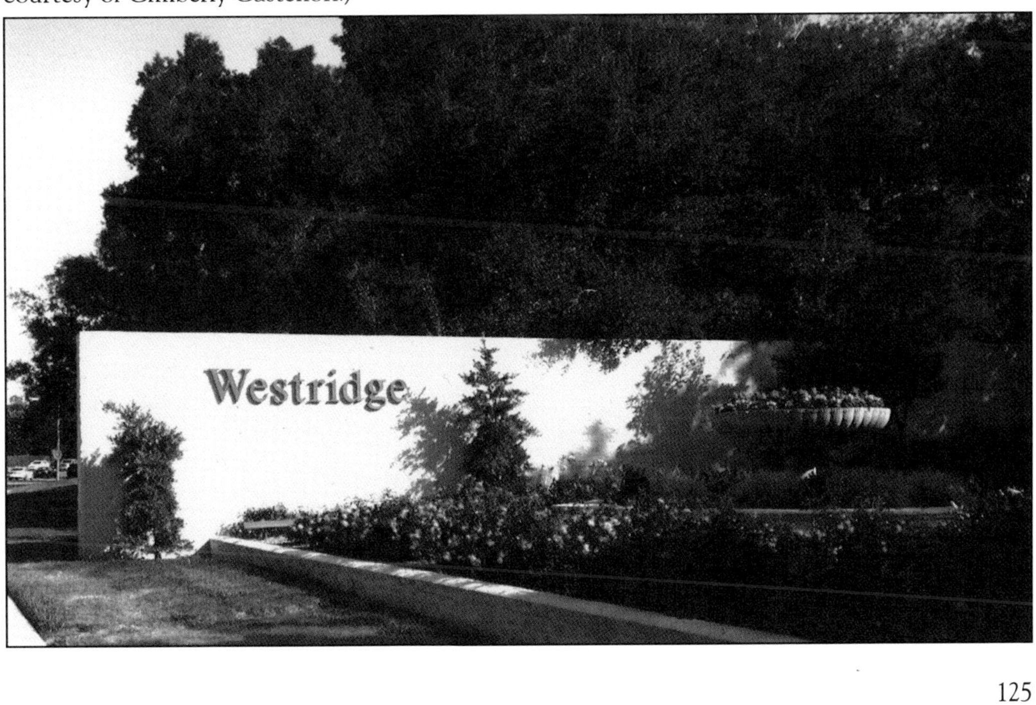

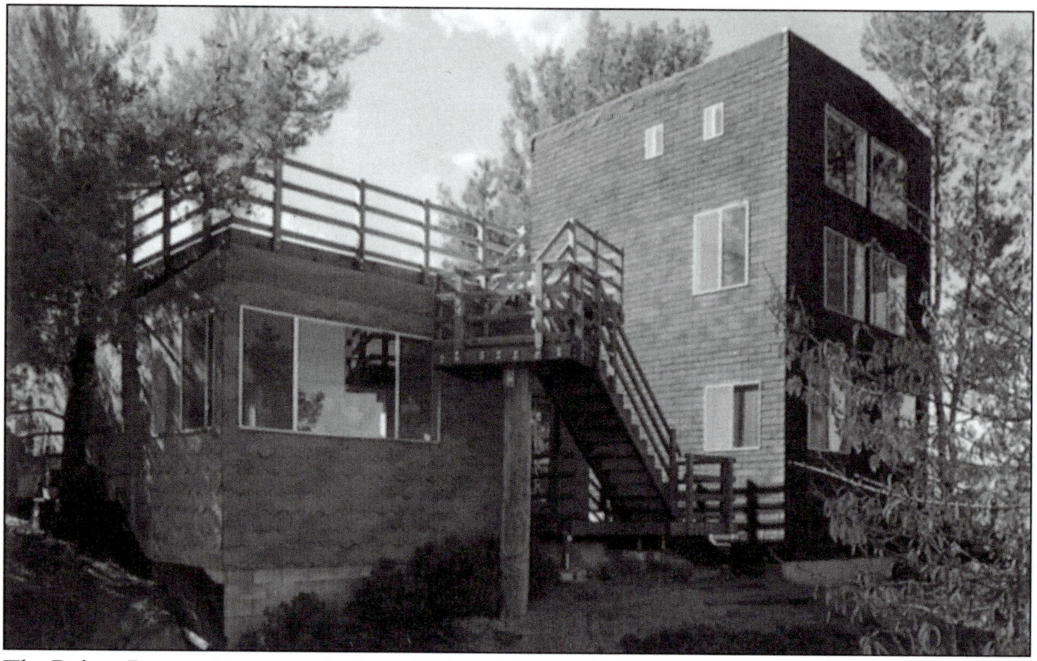

The Robert Benson House was built in 1981 and designed by architect Frank Gehry. The whimsical structure with connecting bridges is the "deconstructivism" style of architecture influenced in part by the Bensons' children, who reportedly made the suggestion that they wanted to "live in a castle with secret passageways." The Robert Benson House has been registered as Calabasas Historical Landmark No. 2. (Courtesy of the Calabasas Media Department.)

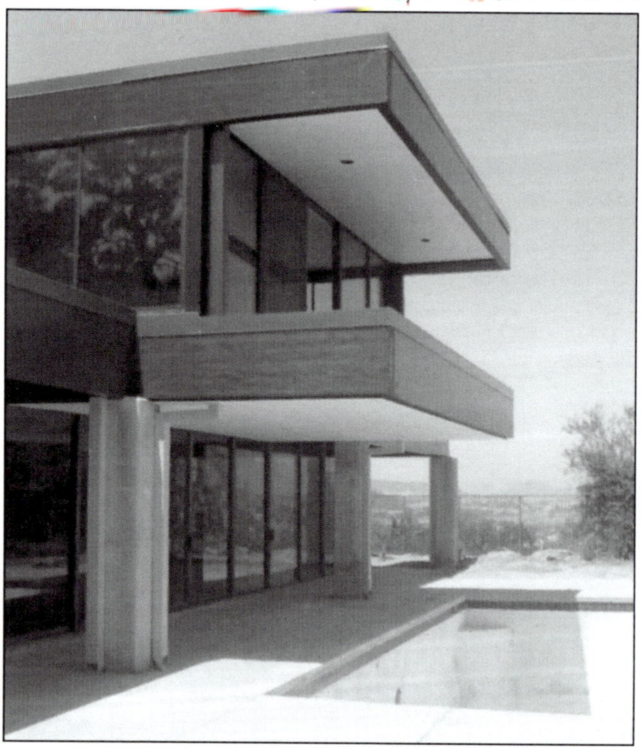

The Arthur Rouse home was built in 1973 and designed by architect Jerrold Lomax, a renowned modern architect referred to as one of the "Los Angeles 12." The house features many long uninterrupted glass windows (using glu-lam beams) to take advantage of the spectacular views. The residence is an excellent example of the International/Modern style of architecture and the Mid-century Moderne period of design and registered as Calabasas Historical Landmark No. 3. (Courtesy of the Calabasas Media Department.)

It Takes a Village

The City of Calabasas is home to many talented individuals who are actively vested in their community.

Special recognition must go to our contributing editors: Arlene Bernholtz, a longtime area resident, charter member of the Calabasas Historical Society, and longtime community volunteer; Mayor James R. Bozajian, whose suburb knowledge and passion of the city's history, in addition to his astute attention to detail, went well beyond; Bob Burris, public information officer, who guaranteed the substance was syntactically right and that Warner Bros. motion picture stills were incorporated in the book; Michelle Covello, the fact-correcting curator at the Leonis Adobe; and Deborah Steller, media operations supervisor and masterful department pioneer who motivated the group to incorporate it all. I admire this "team" of willing contributors who partnered with me composing the Calabasas book to celebrate the city's 25th incorporation birthday in April 2016.

Since incorporation on July 3, 1979, the Calabasas Historical Society (CHS) has been dedicated to promoting and preserving the historical interest of Calabasas and its surrounding environs through education, programs, and the exchange of ideas and information with other organizations.

The society maintains the Calabasas Historical Society Collection, containing important photographs, books, artifacts, and documents from two former archives: the Kathleen Beachy Memorial Library and the Ruth Loring Collection of Southern California History at the Calabasas Library. In 2014, the CHS merged with the Las Virgenes Historical Society, creating the Calabasas-Las Virgenes Historical Society and broadening its outreach and access of historical archival information.

The Calabasas-Las Virgenes Historical Society (CLVHS) is the connection to the city's past. The CLVHS relies on both financial and volunteer support and is a 501(c)3 nonprofit organization. To become a member or find out more about the CLVHS, visit www.calabasashistoricalsociety.org or mail an inquiry to PO Box 8067, Calabasas, California, 91372.

For additional information about Calabasas and city programming please contact:

City of Calabasas
100 Civic Center Way
Calabasas, California 91302
(818) 224-1600
www.cityofcalabasas.com

Calabasas-Las Virgene Historical Society
P.O. Box 8067
Calabasas, California 91372
www.calabasashistoricalsociety.org

Calabasas Chamber of Commerce
23564 Calabasas Road, #101
Calabasas, California 91302
(818) 222-5680
www.calabasaschamber.com